MAB

Margaret Virginia Foster Brehaus

New years 1983

Marquette

THE PRYTANEION

THE PRYTANEION

Its Function and Architectural Form

STEPHEN G. MILLER

UNIVERSITY OF CALIFORNIA PRESS
BERKELEY · LOS ANGELES · LONDON

Publication of this book has been aided by a grant from the Hetty Goldman Fund of the
ARCHAEOLOGICAL INSTITUTE OF AMERICA

University of California Press
Berkeley and Los Angeles, California
University of California Press, Ltd.
London, England

ISBN 0-520-03316-7
Library of Congress Catalog Card Number: 76-24590
Printed in the United States of America

CONTENTS

LIST OF ILLUSTRATIONS

PLATES

FIGURES IN TEXT

ABBREVIATIONS

AAA *Athens Annals of Archaeology*

AAW *Anzeiger der Akademie der Wissenschaften, Wien, Phil-hist. Klasse*

Agora III R. E. Wycherley, *The Athenian Agora III: Testimonia* (Princeton 1957).

Agora XIV H. A. Thompson and R. E. Wycherley, *The Athenian Agora XIV: The Agora of Athens* (Princeton 1972).

AJA *American Journal of Archaeology*

Annuario *Annuario della Scuola Archeologica di Atene*

AJPh *American Journal of Philology*

Ath. Mitt. *Mitteilungen des deutschen archäologischen Instituts, Athenische Abteilung*

BCH *Bulletin de correspondance hellénique*

BSA *Annual of the British School at Athens*

CIG *Corpus Inscriptionum Graecarum*

CP *Classical Philology*

Dessau H. Dessau, *Inscriptiones Latinae Selectae* (Berlin 1892)

Ditt^{3} W. Dittenberger, *Sylloge Inscriptionum Graecarum*^{3} (Leipzig 1915)

EAA *Enciclopedia dell'arte antica, classica e orientale*

Ephesus III J. Keil, *Forschungen in Ephesos* III (Vienna 1923)

FD E. Bourguet, *Fouilles de Delphes III: Epigraphie* (Paris 1909–1952)
HSCP *Harvard Studies in Classical Philology*
ICr *Inscriptiones Creticae*
ID *Inscriptions de Délos* (Paris 1926–1937)
IG *Inscriptiones Graecae*
IGRom *Inscriptiones Graecae ad res Romanas pertinentes*
IVM O. Kern, *Die Inschriften von Magnesia am Maeander* (Berlin 1900)
IVP F. Hiller von Gaertringen, *Inschriften von Priene* (Berlin 1906)
IVPerg M. Fraenkel, *Die Inschriften von Pergamon* (Berlin 1895)
Jahreshefte *Jahreshefte des oesterreichischen archaeologischen Instituts in Wien*
JdI *Jahrbuch des k. deutschen archäologischen Instituts*
JHS *Journal of Hellenic Studies*
JPh *Journal of Philology*
Keil J. Keil, "Kulte im Prytaneion von Ephesos," *Anatolian Studies Presented to William H. Buckler* (Manchester 1939) 119–128
Kerameikos W. Peek, *Kerameikos* III (Berlin 1941)
Lindos II C. Blinkenberg, *Lindos* II, *Inscriptions* (Berlin 1941)
McDonald W. A. McDonald, *The Political Meeting Places of the Greeks* (Baltimore 1943)
MélRome *Mélanges d'archéologie et d'histoire de l'École française de Rome*
Michel C. Michel, *Recueil d'Inscriptions Grecques* (Brussels 1900)
Miller S. G. Miller, "The Prytaneion at Olympia," *Ath. Mitt.* 86 (1971) 79–107
OGIS W. Dittenberger, *Orientis Graeci Inscriptiones Selectae* (Leipzig 1903)
RHR *Revue de l'histoire des religions*
SEG *Supplementum Epigraphicum Graecum*
SGDI H. Collitz, *et al.*, *Sammlung der griechischen Dialekt-Inschriften* (Göttingen 1884)
Sokolowski, F. Sokolowski, *Lois sacrées des cités grecques,*

Lois sacrées	Suppl. (Paris 1962)
Tosi	G. Tosi, "Contributo allo studio dei pritanei," *Arte Antica e Moderna* 33 (1966) 10–20, 151–172

PREFACE

SEVERAL years ago I was obliged to consider the validity of the identification of a building at Morgantina as a prytaneion (see chapter five, pp. 115–117). Toward this end I searched for a study of the prytaneion as a type, which would go beyond the brief statements encountered in the general handbooks on ancient architecture. There was, I soon discovered, only one general study of the prytaneion in this century (Tosi, *Arte Antica e Moderne* 1966) and that study had not the benefit of an examination of the remains at the various sites, nor was its scope as exhaustive as might have been desired. Recourse to *Pauly-Wissowa* was futile: no article on the prytaneion had appeared there. Moreover, those studies from the previous century (Hagemann, *De Prytaneo*; Michel, "Prytaneum," *Daremberg-Saglio*; Frazer, *JPh* 1885) had been written before the excavation of any remains which might have been included in a study of the building as an architectural form. More recent studies (most notably Charbonneaux, *BCH* 1925) were of great importance in disproving the older theory of the circular form of the prytaneion, but made no attempt at a positive definition of a generic building plan. Rather, the all too frequently unsubstantiated identifications of various buildings as prytaneia by their excavators were accepted and found their way into handbooks as typical representatives of this architectural genre.

It soon appeared that enough material existed to justify an attempt at a positive definition of the type. My studies were aided greatly by the generosity of W. A. McDonald, who, after I had expressed to him my interest in the subject, sent me a large body of material which he had collected earlier. This material included, most significantly, records made by him of architectural details which in several cases had disappeared between his visits to the sites in the early 1950s and 1967 when I first saw the remains of the various buildings.

The whole of this study has been read, in one form or another, by W. R. Connor, E. B. Harrison, T. L. Shear, Jr., E. Sjöqvist, R. S. Stroud, H. A. Thompson, E. Vanderpool, and the members of the Committee on Monographs of the Archaeological Institute of America. I gratefully acknowledge the helpful criticisms and suggestions of all these people. With regard to more specific problems, I have benefited from discussions with P. Ducrey, S. Glass, F. Gschnitzer, A. Mallwitz, J. Travlos, and C. K. Williams. Princeton University, the Fulbright Foundation in Greece, the Agora Excavations of the American School of Classical Studies in Athens, and the Institute for Advanced Study have provided the funds necessary for study and for observation at the sites in Greece, Turkey, and Sicily.

The Archaeological Institute of America has assisted with this publication and I would thank Professor C. Roebuck, then Chairman of the Committee on Monographs, for his careful editing of the manuscript in 1973. My gratitude goes also to the University of California Press and its Director, August Frugé, for undertaking to publish this study, and to Stephen Hart for his help with editorial problems. My largest single debt is, as always, to the patient assistance of my wife. With such help, errors and omissions can only be those of the author.

S. G. M.
Berkeley
October 1976

INTRODUCTION

WITHIN the realm of Greek civic architecture, the prytaneion is pre-eminent both for its ubiquity and for its obscurity. One cannot read far in the literature of antiquity without encountering mention of this building, but a vision of the architectural form of the prytaneion rarely, if ever, springs to mind when one reads or hears the word. Perhaps the best known of ancient references is the mention of the prytaneion by Plato in the *Apology* (A 62), but this is only one of numerous examples in the literature of Greece from Classical to late Roman times.[1] The principal cause of the obscurity surrounding the architectural form of the prytaneion is that, to date, only three securely identified prytaneia have been excavated. This situation provides very little in the way of parallel material for the identification of suspected prytaneia, and such parallels are necessary where other indications of identification are lacking.

The problem is to establish a set of criteria for identification

1 See Appendix A, under Athens in particular, for some idea of the attention paid to the prytaneion by ancient authors. References in the text of the discussion to ancient sources which are quoted in Appendix A appear in parentheses with the letter A and the number assigned to each source in the Appendix. For example, (A 62) in the text above refers to the sixty-second entry in Appendix A.

of prytaneia. In cases where a building is discovered with clear objective evidence as, for example, an inscription relevant to the prytaneion, such criteria are unnecessary. In fact, such a discovery would strengthen, and perhaps modify, these criteria. In the majority of cases, however, such evidence is lacking and other means of identification must be applied.

A handicap in establishing such criteria is the relatively small corpus of securely identified prytaneia. The three recognized examples do not, by themselves, supply sufficient evidence to allow a definition of the prytaneion type. A different body of evidence can, however, help. I refer to literary and epigraphic mentions of the prytaneion. These *testimonia*, gathered in Appendix A, not only mention specific elements of the prytaneion, but also describe many of the functions which the building had to perform. Thus one can assume in the building certain architectural elements which were demanded by its use.

The approach will be to derive from the *testimonia* as clear a picture as possible of the prytaneion. What elements are absolutely essential to its plan? What elements are possible but not necessary features of any prytaneion? Having derived these characteristics from the sources, we will next set them against the three securely identified prytaneia in order to define more closely the type. The end result of this synthesis should be a set of criteria for a generic prytaneion including typical location, quality of construction, general plan, and a group of elements which are characteristic of this plan, as well as other elements which may be present, but are not essential.

It is not to be expected, of course, that there was a single plan which was invariable and immutable. Rather, we shall attempt to define those features which are so characteristic of a prytaneion as to allow the identification of a building as a prytaneion. Another type of building, the stoa, will serve as an illustration of what is intended. In the Athenian Agora are four buildings, all stoas, which exhibit individual peculiarities, but which also have common features justifying their common name. The Royal Stoa, the Stoa of Zeus, the Middle Stoa, and the Stoa of Attalos,[2] although highly individualistic, have in common a rectilinear and rectangular general plan, a location

2 *Agora* XIV, 83–90, 96–103, 66–68, 103–107, respectively.

on a plateia or open area, and a columnar façade. They may or may not also have projecting wings, interior columns, small "shop" rooms, a completely columnar exterior on all four sides, an upper storey, and so forth.

The definition of a similar set of common essential characteristics and possible additional features for the prytaneion is the goal of this study.

CHAPTER I

The Function of the Prytaneion

BEFORE attention can be devoted to the architectural form of the prytaneion, the first task must be to define the purposes for which the building was used.

Dining

The Diners

Epigraphical notices concerning diners are plentiful, since to invite someone into the prytaneion for entertainment at the expense of the city was one of the highest honors paid by a Greek city to an individual. Consequently, there developed a formulaic quality to the expression of the invitation to the prytaneion. The words *καλέσαι δὲ αὐτοὺς ἐπὶ ξένια εἰς τὸ πρυτανεῖον εἰς αὔριον* are typical of one part of the honors paid to foreign ambassadors and proxenoi by a sovereign Greek state (e.g., A 122, 123, 126, 127).[1] There were three classes of entertainment offered in the prytaneion, all having a meal as a

1 For these formulaic invitations to the prytaneion see W. A. McDonald, "A Linguistic Examination of an Epigraphical Formula," *AJA* 59 (1955) 151–155. More work remains to be done regarding the linguistic characteristics of these formulae. It is to be hoped that the material assembled in Appendix A will be of assistance in further examination.

common feature, but differing according to the nature of the honoree and the length of time involved. These classes were *ξένια*, *δεῖπνον*, and *σίτησις*.

The first two of these had in common, in addition to the element of dining, a temporal quality, in that they both involved invitations for one meal only. This is shown not only by the implications of the *εἰς αὔριον* phrase, but also by the constant use of the aorist with both Deipnon and Xenia, while the present or imperfect is used with Sitesis. At Athens (elsewhere the evidence is too fragmentary) the obvious difference between Xenia and Deipnon was that the former was granted to foreigners, while Deipnon was reserved for citizens. This difference is most succinctly shown by several inscriptions from the fourth century B.C. in which ambassadors from other states are invited to Xenia in the prytaneion at Athens, while Athenian envoys to those same states are invited to Deipnon, likewise in the Athenian prytaneion (A 86, 88, 95, 96).[2]

There are, however, exceptions to this distinction between Xenia and Deipnon in Athens. Larfeld[3] noted that the distinction seemed to be breaking down by about 340 B.C., but there are exceptions even earlier. If one accepts an arbitrary date of 340 B.C. (for Larfeld's contention is generally correct), there are sixty-five earlier examples (listed in Appendix A) which follow the practice of Xenia for foreigners and Deipnon for citizens. Of these, we have already noted those which carry both awards in the same text. The others are too numerous to list here, although one might note that Aeschines (A 115) complies with the rule by using the formula *καλέσαι ἐπὶ δεῖπνον εἰς τὸ πρυτανεῖον* when describing the honors awarded his embassy on its return from Macedonia.

But what of the exceptions? The first of these (A 58) is equivocal since one set of people, clearly new citizens, are invited to Deipnon while another set are invited to Xenia. The latter set, however, does not clearly have citizenship status, and

2 Also see (A 118) where Arybbas, the exiled king of Molossia, is invited to Deipnon in the prytaneion since he is a citizen of Athens; his company is to receive Xenia. In the decree honoring Sthorys of Thasos (A 65) the *probouleuma* grants him Xenia while the decree of the Demos, which has awarded citizenship to Sthorys, changes the grant to Deipnon.

3 W. Larfeld, *Handbuch der griechischen Epigraphik* II (Leipzig 1902) 881.

their honors were received two years later than the first group. This decree could, then, be held to support the normal distinction regarding the type of recipient of the two honors.

Four other exceptions from before 340 B.C. remain (A 67, 81, 84, 97), and all of these involve the grant of Deipnon to non-citizens of Athens. It should be noted immediately that, while all of these have the restored phrase *καλέσαι ἐπὶ δεῖπνον εἰς τὸ πρυτανεῖον*, not one has the *ἐπὶ δεῖπνον* actually preserved on the stone. One of these texts (A 97) honors both Athenian ambassadors and those from allied Euboean cities with Deipnon in the prytaneion. One should have expected, by analogy to other such decrees (A 86, 88, 95, 96), that the grants be Deipnon and Xenia respectively. Could this be a mechanical error in the recording or inscribing of this decree, or a deliberate compression of the text for some purpose with regard to the stone?

For the remaining three abnormal decrees, *ἐπὶ δεῖπνον* cannot be replaced with another restoration without doing violence to the *stoichedon* of the inscriptions. I know of no way to restore these decrees to make them agree with the usual Xenia-Deipnon distinction, but it is fair to remember that they are not actually preserved as abnormalities on the stone. Moreover, a large percentage (95.7%) of the texts does conform and shows that the normal distinction is valid at least to the mid-fourth century B.C. After that time, the exceptions (e.g., A 156, 183) do increase, but they only reach a maximum of about 18 percent of the total.

The distinction made between Xenia and Deipnon calls to mind, by its very existence, that there is implicit another distinction of a qualitative nature between the two types of entertainment. Precisely what this difference entailed is not clear, although Deipnon would appear to have been the "higher" honor, either because of a better menu, or because of some religious ceremony closed to non-citizens.[4]

As a basis for defining these categories of diners, we have relied upon Athens where we have the largest and most coherent body of *testimonia* on the subject. Elsewhere, the entertainment offered to foreigners in the prytaneion might be

4 Note that, as part of their requirements for entrance into citizenship, the ephebes had to sacrifice at the common hearth in the prytaneion (A 195–202). Citizenship must have been prerequisite to certain rites at this hearth.

called Xenismos rather than Xenia (A 1, 269, 430),[5] but this difference in terminology does not necessarily imply a difference in meaning. Xenia could also be offered at places other than the prytaneion. In a Thracian town, for example, an honoree was invited to Xenia in the temple of Apollo.[6]

The third category of entertainment in the prytaneion, Sitesis, like Deipnon, was reserved initially for citizens, at least in Athens, although later it was conferred upon foreign benefactors. There is one case (A 322) where Sitesis replaced Xenia as one of the inter-city diplomatic awards. In the Classical and early Hellenistic periods, the difference between Sitesis and Deipnon was that the former honor allowed the honoree to dine in the prytaneion every day for a period of time limited by his office or his life. It was conferred for the lifetime of a man who had performed some great service to his city, and to victors at the four Panhellenic centers (A 26, 62, 153, 215, 216). Often Sitesis was granted to the oldest descendant of a deceased and previously unhonored benefactor of a city for the lifetime of the descendant. After his death the honor was inherited by the next oldest descendant of the original benefactor. The formula *εἶναι δὲ αὐτῶι καὶ σίτησιν ἐν πρυτανείωι καὶ ἐκγόνων ἀεὶ τῶι πρεσβυτάτωι*, with slight variations depending on whether or not *αὐτός* was still alive, was used to honor such men as the descendants of Harmodios and Aristogeiton (A 26, 70, 150), Lykourgos (A 158, 159), Demosthenes (A 172–174), Demochares (A 173, 177), and Hippokrates (A 218) among many others.

Other individuals who had Sitesis in the prytaneion were those who held a public office which carried this honor with it. A scholiast of Thucydides (A 242) hints at this in his definition of the prytaneion: "the prytaneion is a large building where

5 In one text (A 1), both Xenismos and Xenia are used in such a way that the former is clearly the meal itself and the latter must refer to gifts, but in another text (A 337) Xenion must refer to the gift, and Xenia to the meal. In yet another case (A 433) Xenia is the word applied to both types of award. A substantive difference in the nature of entertainment in the prytaneion may be implicit in the different terms, but equally implicit is the element of hospitality extended to foreigners. Precise correspondence of terminology from one state to another is no more to be expected than precise correspondence of menu from one prytaneion to another.

6 *Michel* 328; cf. *SEG* XVIII, 290.

Siteseis were given to those engaged in politics." More specific information in this context would be given by the fragmentary *IG* I², 77 (A 26) if we could understand its full original meaning. Certainly some politico-religious offices were to carry Sitesis with them according to the provisions of this decree: this much is clear both from the fragmentary text of the inscription and from Aristophanes taken together with his scholiast (A 41, 250, 252). One might hypothesize that Kleon (A 35, 38, 39, 40, 245, 249) and Iphikrates (A 107) had received Sitesis in the prytaneion because of their status as strategoi. It is equally possible, however, that they had received this honor because of some particular deed performed for and recognized by the city in a special decree.[7] Some officials had Deipnon rather than Sitesis in the prytaneion, but these were the games directors whose invitations were restricted to the month of Hekatombaion when they were concerned with arrangements for the Panathenaia (A 147). It is interesting to note that the preposterousness of the demand by Socrates for entertainment in the prytaneion as his "punishment" is heightened by his use of the words *σίτησις* and *σιτεῖσθαι*, for they implied, as has been seen, a lifetime of public sustenance (A 62).[8]

The public office most obviously connected with Sitesis in the prytaneion was, of course, that of the prytaneis. Unfortunately for the present discussion, the Athenian prytaneis had their meals in the tholos, not in the prytaneion, and *testimonia* concerning prytaneis in the prytaneion are accordingly rare. Yet it is certain that the prytaneion was the place where the prytaneis met and ate at cities other than Athens, and perhaps even in Athens, too, during the Archaic period.[9] Not only

7 Schöll, "Die Speisung im Prytaneion zu Athen," *Hermes* 6 (1872) 40, believes that the honor of Sitesis automatically belonged to a strategos, but his opinion is based, in part, upon his interpretation of the very fragmentary end of *IG* I², 77. Aeschines (A 141) mentions the strategoi and those who had received Sitesis as two types of men who were, or should have been, respectable citizens. One might argue that these two types were therefore different and that a strategos did not receive Sitesis *ex officio*, but it is also possible that the mention of strategoi called to Aeschines' mind all those honored with Sitesis. He certainly implies elsewhere (A 119) that Sitesis did belong to strategoi, or at least to successful ones.

8 The same ironical device is used by Lucian (A 464).

9 See chapter three for a discussion of the Athenian situation.

does the obvious linguistic connection between the two words suggest such a relationship, but more specific evidence exists in the form of a list of prytaneis for one month from Sinope which was dedicated to Hestia Prytaneia,[10] and we hear that at least one prytanis was in the prytaneion at Rhodes while the ekklesia was meeting in the theater of that city (A 419). In fact, the same scholiast of Thucydides (A 242) mentioned above defines the prytaneion in terms of the prytaneis: "the prytaneion . . . it was so called since there sat the prytaneis who managed all the affairs (of state)."

One other category of state diners needs to be mentioned. These are the *ἀείσιτοι*, who have sometimes been regarded as regular diners in the prytaneion. In technical terminology, the word *ἀείσιτος* refers to political functionaries such as the Secretary of the Boule and the Demos or the Herald of the Boule and the Demos who, at Athens, dined in the tholos together with the prytaneis.[11] Elsewhere, when the tholos and the prytaneion divided between themselves the normal functions of a single prytaneion, these aeisitoi will have dined in the prytaneion with the prytaneis.[12]

Just as political constitutions varied from city to city, so the titles of officials varied too. Hampered by inadequate knowledge of the governments of these other places, one can only speculate as to whether or not the Athenian prytaneis corresponded to, for example, the *συναρχίαι* of Cyrene (A 273) or the *κόσμοι* of

10 *AJA* 9 (1905) 313.

11 The *ἀεί* part of their title means not "forever," but "for the term of their office" as Dow has shown in his study "The Prytaneis," *Hesperia* Suppl. I (1937) 22–24. In a more general way an *ἀείσιτος* could be an "eater-forever" in reference to a distinguished man, or the descendant of such a man, who had received Sitesis in the prytaneion because of some service to the state. This is, for example, the meaning of the word in Pollux (A 466). See also Schöll, *op. cit.* (note 7) 51–52, who anticipates the views of Dow.

12 It is, of course, not possible to compose an exhaustive list of the officials who were aeisitoi at various sites, but relatively complete catalogues are preserved, from different periods, for the Athenian tholos: see Dow, *loc. cit.*; K. Clinton, "The Sacred Officials of the Eleusinian Mysteries," *Trans. Am. Philos. Soc.* 64 (1974) 121–124; B. D. Meritt and J. S. Traill, *Agora* XV: *Inscriptions, The Athenian Councillors* (Princeton 1974) 7–8, 18–20. Note also the lists from Ephesos (*Keil* 119–122), at Olympia (*Miller* 82), and at, probably, Rhegium (*IG* XIV, 617); for the last, cf. Ch. Picard, "Le relief inscrit de Lowther Castle et les cultes de prytanées en Grèce," *RHR* 129 (1945) 31–46.

Crete (A 346) whom we hear of as having meals in the prytaneion at their own cities. If such cities have a building known as a prytaneion, but not an office known as prytanis; and if, as will be maintained below, the name of the building prytaneion derives from the name of the office prytanis, then an interesting conclusion is forthcoming: the prytaneion was imported to those cities later than the establishment of terminology for their officials corresponding to the prytaneis at Athens and elsewhere. If, on the other hand, a city did not have prytaneis and did not import the prytaneion, then one might hear of buildings which appear to be fulfilling the function of the prytaneion, but which are called by other names. Some buildings of this sort are to be recognized, for example, in the ἱεροθυτεῖον at Lindos[13] and at Karpathos,[14] the δαμιοργεῖον at Knidos,[15] and the ἀρχηγέτειον at Cassandria.[16] Men honored with Sitesis or Xenia were invited into all these buildings in language much like that used repeatedly for the more usual invitations to the prytaneion. These buildings must have been prytaneia in all but name, or else they existed in addition to the prytaneion at each city and were used in some auxiliary way. The former must have been the case at Halos in Thessaly, for Herodotus tells us specifically that the prytaneion there was called the λήιτον (A 324).

Tosi has suggested that the difference between the buildings listed above and the prytaneion is not derived from local variations in official names (e.g., hierothytes vis-à-vis prytanis). Rather, Tosi believes the difference to stem from those buildings' lack of the common hearth.[17] This is an argument from silence, and a dangerous one. For example, the relevant passage from the decree of Karpathos mentioned above reads: καλέ[σαι] δὲ αὐτὸν καὶ ἐπὶ ξένια εἰς τὸ ἱεροθυτεῖο[ν]. This is not sufficient grounds to exclude the possibility that the Hierothyteion

13 *IG* XII^1, 846–849, 853. For a suggested identification of the Hierothyteion at Lindos see A. DiVita, "Lindos," *EAA* IV (Rome 1961) 640. Another Rhodian building had been suggested as the Hierothyteion at Kamiros by M. Segre, "L'agora degli dei Camirese," *Athenaeum* 12 (1934) 147–150.

14 *Michel* 437.

15 *SGDI* 3501.

16 *SEG* XII, 343. Note also an invitation for Xenia, perhaps to the Delphinion at Hyrtakinia; cf. L. Robert, *Opera Minora* (Amsterdam 1969) 1052–1054.

17 *Tosi* 20, note 54. The common hearth is discussed more fully in the next section, on religion.

contained the common hearth. Of the 112 Athenian decrees in the period of the fifth to the second century B.C. which contain invitations to the prytaneion for Xenia or Deipnon, only 1 (A 192) mentions the common hearth. Moreover, the concept of guest-friendship which is embodied in Xenia is dependent upon the common hearth, not the prytaneion or whatever building housed the hearth.[18]

Before leaving the subject of those who dined in the prytaneion, we ought to mention the status of women in this respect. Athenaeus (A 367) tells us that in Naukratis it was not permitted for any woman other than the fluteplayer to enter the prytaneion. Other sources seem to confirm this principle on a wider scale, with only one exception. In the early Roman period Polygnota of Thebes was invited to the prytaneion at Delphi (A 302). Delphi may, however, have been unique, since the priestess of Apollo entered the prytaneion there at least once every month (A 304). Elsewhere there may well have been restrictions on the presence of women at entertainment in the prytaneion.

At least in Athens and probably all through the Greek world, the honor of Sitesis in the prytaneion became more and more common in the course of time. There is evidence of an attempt to place some restrictions on the awarding of this honor (A 253) and Aeschines indicates his disapproval of the abuses of the privilege (A 140, 141). The epigraphical records of the bestowal of Sitesis are in accord with this feeling, for the granting of Sitesis becomes more frequent in the late fourth and third centuries B.C. By the Roman period a double portion of Sitesis had to be awarded in order to signify any real honor in the grant (A 236, 237). It will be seen below that this decline in the importance of the honors awarded in the prytaneion corresponds very closely with a decline in the building as an important political institution.

The Menu

Very little is known about the food which was normally served to the various categories of diners in the prytaneion. An inscription from Epidamnos (A 313; cf. Philippi, A 391) would

18 That a prytaneion must have the common hearth as one of its attributes is true; that the common hearth must be located in a prytaneion is not true (cf. Pausanias VIII, 9, 5).

lead one to believe that Xenia regularly involved a sacrifice at the hearth in the prytaneion, followed by the bestowal of parts, or all, of the sacrificial animal to the honorees. Along with this went remuneration on a handsome scale for the expense of travel between the foreigners' city and the city which was making the award. That money was part of the normal grant of Xenia is attested elsewhere (A 326; cf. A 1) and some financial quality is perhaps to be understood in the common but not universal use of the phrase "to give the most Xenia established by custom."[19]

Athenaeus (A 17) records that the Athenians set out a lunch for the Dioskouroi in the prytaneion consisting of cheese, barley cakes, ripe olives, and leeks; while Solon ordered that a barley cake be provided for those eating (*τοῖς σιτουμένοις*) in the prytaneion, and that they be given wheat bread on holidays. That wine was also provided is well documented (A 361, 427, 440), but a barley cake and wine alone hardly make for the sort of meal which one would expect to be served to distinguished guests of the state. Yet Athenaeus may be correct with regard to a simple meal in the sixth and early fifth century B.C. even if one hesitates to connect the menu closely with Solon. Aristophanes (A 35) also implies that the bill of fare in the Athenian prytaneion was not luxurious, at least down through the time of Perikles. After that the menu apparently was expanded, for Kleon can leave the prytaneion with a belly full of wheat bread, meat and fish.

At the prytaneion in Naukratis there were feasts on the birthday of Hestia, and at the festivals of Dionysos and Apollo every year (A 367). The participants in these feasts received a pint of wine, wheat bread, pork, barley gruel or a vegetable, two eggs, cheese, dried figs, and a flat cake, while the priests of Dionysos and Apollo received a double portion of everything. This seems like a respectable banquet, but there is no way of knowing if it reflects the normal menu for guests of the state. Athenaeus proceeds to say that on every other day of the year anyone who wished might eat in the prytaneion, and was to receive there a half-pint of wine if he had brought along some beans and smoked or fresh fish and a small piece of pork to share with the

19 *δοῦναι ξένια τὰ μέγιστα ἐκ τῶν νόμων* (A 433); cf. *Michel* 179, 197, *et al.*

others eating there. Such a "potluck" system cannot have been responsible for the provision of the Sitesis or the Deipnon which the state awarded its benefactors, but the wording of Athenaeus is interesting: "ἔξεστι τῶν σιτουμένων τῷ βουλομένῳ ἀνελθόντι εἰς τὸ πρυτανεῖον δειπνεῖν." Could the use of the words σιτουμένων and δειπνεῖν be related to the categories of Sitesis and Deipnon discussed above? Although Athenaeus cannot be describing the method by which guests were fed in the prytaneion, is it not possible that the kinds of food which he enumerates—beans, fish, pork, wine—were part of the regular menu for citizens honored with Sitesis and Deipnon? This can hardly be regarded as proven, but it seems a possibility, especially when one considers that in the late fifth century B.C. at Athens the food provided in the prytaneion, as seen above, included fish, meat, and, by inference, wine (A 35). This is not a precise correspondence to the food mentioned by Athenaeus, but it is close enough to permit us to see within the items listed the core of the regular bill of fare for those honored with entertainment in the prytaneion.

Religious

To this point our discussion has touched only one of the two most important functions of the prytaneion. We have considered the "prytaneion . . . at which dine those coming on a public embassy and those thought worthy of Sitesis because of some deed, and he who was aeisitos from honor" (A 466). There was another function performed by this building, equally important in the life of a city, which has been implicit in many of the sources already mentioned. In the prytaneion was the eternal flame, burning on the common hearth, which signified the life of the polis. Thus Pollux (A 465) calls those places upon which sacrifices were made or fires kindled, the "altar, censer, hearth; . . . Thus one would most correctly call that in the prytaneion on which the eternal fire burns." The nature of this fire as a perpetually alive flame could be used metaphorically for insomnia (A 448); and just as the hearth, and by extension the prytaneion, symbolized the life of the city, so other metaphors could arise: Athens was called the "hearth and prytaneion of Greece" (A 227, 228, 233).[20] It is quite understandable then if colonists took with them a spark of fire from the hearth in the prytaneion of their mother city (A 21, 257, 258) as a symbol both of the life of their new foundation and of the source of that life.[21] The prytaneion, as the residence of the perpetual flame, was more than any other building the symbol of the city (see A 11, 12, 227) and Livy (A 276) can rightly define the prytaneion as the core of a city (*id est penetrale urbis*).

There was a religious quality about the hearth in the prytaneion which was associated with the titular goddess of the hearth, Hestia. Dionysios of Halikarnassos may overstate the situation when he calls the prytaneion a specifically religious building (A 460), yet its religious character is to be noted in the mention of priestly conferences in the prytaneion at Andania (A 6), in the numerous religious processions from various prytaneia (A 2, 28, 179, 308, 359, 449), in the official sacrifices which took place there (A 195, 196, 293), and in the oaths which were sworn by Hestia in the prytaneion (A 307). Also testifying to this religious quality is the fact that at Olympia the ritual at the hearth in the prytaneion included songs sung in the presence of people such as manteis, exegetai, and flute-players. It would seem, however, that there was always a political flavor to these religious exercises, as is seen perhaps best in the role which the hearth in the prytaneion played in the entrance rites of the ephebes to citizenship (A 2, 195–202).

Considering that she was the goddess of the hearth and one

20 Plato (A 69) uses just such a figure of speech for the house of Kallias where men of intellectual rather than political or athletic achievement were accustomed to gather for meals. Certainly the equation between Athens and the "prytaneion of Greece" was a well-known metaphor by the time of Plato, which enables his use of it with reference to the house of Kallias. This is shown by the fact that Theopompos (A 121) can use the figure, with a malicious twist, as a vehicle for his opinions regarding contemporary Greek life. Such a device would have no force if the standard version of the metaphor were not commonly known.

21 It is interesting to speculate that, if colonies universally took fire from the hearth in the prytaneion of the mother city along to the new foundation, then the attested existence of a prytaneion in a colony implies the existence of a prytaneion in the metropolis. Thus, for example, Corinth and Sparta, although not having attested prytaneia, must have possessed the building since their colonies did have prytaneia; e.g., Korcyra (A 340), Syracuse (A 431, 432), Tarentum (A 434).

of the daughters of Kronos, Hestia has remarkably few material remains to testify to her importance. There have been no temples to her excavated, and it is unclear what is to be understood by the references to a ἱερὸν τῆς Ἑστίας since this may be the prytaneion itself or a specific part of that building.[22] On the other hand, it is clear in some cases that a "shrine of Hestia" must be an independent structure and not a prytaneion.[23]

Cult images of Hestia are not abundant either, although one hears of their existence in Athens (A 221) and Paros (A 381) as well as that which Pliny attributed to Scopas,[24] and two statues of the goddess are mentioned in the inventories from Delos (A 286, 287). One of the latter is seated on an omphalos, the other on an altar.[25] This sparsity of visual representations is apparently due in part to the fact that Hestia was a relatively late, and never completely anthropomorphized, development in Greek religion.[26] Thus the hearth alone may have provided an adequate symbol of Hestia's presence. Nevertheless, Hestia does have an all-pervasive quality—a hearth was common to all homes and many public buildings—and she seems to have

22 See Appendix D.

23 See *Tosi* 12, and notes 20–22. The sanctuary of Hestia in Peiraeus (*IG* II^2, 1214) cannot have been a prytaneion since we are told by Thucydides (A 11) that there was only one prytaneion for all of Attica.

Tosi places a proper emphasis on the importance of the hearth and suggests that, although every city-state had its own common hearth, this was not necessarily located in a prytaneion. If the polis did have a prytaneion, the *koine hestia* was to be found therein, but lacking a prytaneion, the hearth might be located elsewhere. Note the case of Hyrtakinia (*ICr* II, xv, 2, 18; see also note 16) where the common hearth was located in the Delphinion.

24 Pliny, *NH* XXXVI, 25; cf. G. Despinis, "Τιμητικονψήφισμα ἐκ Πάρου," *ΔΕΛΤΙΟΝ* 20 (1965) 119–133.

25 See W. Fuchs, "Hestia," *EAA* IV (Rome 1961) 18–22, for a collection of ancient representations of Hestia. To that collection add the relief from Pharsalos now in the Volos Museum; see S. G. Miller, "Hestia and Symmachos," *Opuscula Romana* IX:19 (1973) 167–172. Add also, quite probably, a figure on a classical relief from Phaleron; see M. Guarducci, "L'offerta di Xenokrateia nel santuario di Cefiso al Falero," *ΦΟΡΟΣ* (Festschrift Meritt, Locust Valley, N.Y., 1974) 64–65.

26 Hestia is not mentioned by Homer and there are few myths which deal with her. Thus Ovid (*Fasti* VI, 254) can say of her: "*te, dea, nec fueras aspicienda viro.*" Again, Pausanias (II, 35, 1) mentions that at Hermione there was a shrine of Hestia, but it contained only an altar and no image: ἄγαλμα μέν ἐστιν οὐδέν, βωμὸς δέ. Cf. Preuner, *Hestia-Vesta* (Tübingen 1864).

been mentioned regularly in prayers to the other Olympian powers.[27]

Another characteristic associated with Hestia, and her namesake the hearth, was the right of asylum and supplication. This custom was already known in Homeric times for Odysseus, at the court of King Alcinoos, seats himself by the hearth immediately upon his entrance into the megaron, having stopped first only to supplicate Queen Arete.[28] In later times one reads that the prytaneion at Naxos provided sanctuary for Neaera, who had fled from her husband and who, at his approach, "sat as a suppliant at the hearth in the prytaneion" (A 368). But asylum at the hearth in the prytaneion was only part of the larger concept of asylum at any hearth, for refuge was sought at hearths other than that in the prytaneion.[29]

Other deities are also associated with the prytaneion. At both Olympia and Athens there was a connection between the prytaneion and Artemis Agrotera (A 196–198, 200, 201, 374). In both places, however, a shrine or altar of Artemis lay outside the prytaneion proper, and the connection of Artemis with the building seems to have been incidental to the sacrifices performed by the ephebes as a part of their entrance into citizenship. An inscription from Cyrene (A 271) speaks of sacrifices to the gods in the prytaneion, and Hermes and Apollo were both represented in the Delian prytaneion along with Hestia (A 286, 287). Part of the annual festivals of Dionysos and Apollo were celebrated in the prytaneion at Naukratis (A 367) and Pan had an altar in the building at Olympia. None of these, however, seems to be any more than a secondary connection between the various deities and the prytaneion.

Archives and Museum

In addition to providing the city with a dining hall and a home for the state hearth, the prytaneion seems to have served also

27 *RE* VII, "Hestia," cols. 1272 ff. Note in particular the use of the expression ἀφ' Ἑστίας ἄρχεσθαι in prayers; cf. *Homeric Hymn to Hestia* (XXIX) 4–6, and Cicero, *De natura deorum* II, 67–68.

28 Homer, *Odyssey* VII, 153.

29 Notable among these was that of Hestia Boulaia in the Athenian bouleuterion where Theramenes once attempted to take asylum. The sanctity of this hearth was not respected, however, by the murderers of Theramenes, nor defended by the other Athenians present; cf. Xenophon, *Hell*, II, 3, 52, and Diodorus Siculus XIV, 4.

as a quasi archives, more for interesting memorabilia of past events in the city's history than for historical or political documents. At Athens the laws of Solon were preserved in the prytaneion (A 25, 211, 221, 231), but these were displayed more as historical artifacts than as current documents; the latter reposed in the Bouleuterion-Metroon complex at least from the end of the fifth century B.C. Pliny tells us that the stone which the Argonauts had used as an anchor was leaded in place in the prytaneion in Cyzicus since it was apt to wander away if not held firmly (A 277). The letter which the Rhodian admiral sent to his city announcing the events of the battle of Lade in 201 B.C. was preserved in the prytaneion of Rhodes (A 420), while at Imbros a stele with a particular *psephisma* was set up in the courtyard of the prytaneion (A 331). The Cretan copy of a treaty with Miletus was to be set up in the prytaneion of Phaistos (A 390), while a treaty between Lato and Gortyn was to be copied and set up in the prytaneion of each city (A 321). At Delos a room in the prytaneion bore the name *archeion* which almost certainly reflects the use of the room as an archives (A 286, 287).

Just as the prytaneion was a repository for such articles of interest to the city, so it also housed figures of both historical and allegorical significance for the community. At Athens, for example, the prytaneion contained statues of Demosthenes and Demochares (A 173, 262), Autolykos, Miltiades, and Themistokles, among others, along with statues of symbolic importance such as those of Hestia and Eirene (A 221). At Ptolemais, the statue of Lysimachos was to be erected in the prytaneion (A 415). Even as late as the third century A.D. such displays were being augmented by those of benefactors, such as Ulpius Eubrotos who had helped Athens during a famine (A 236, 237).

Of either historical or religious significance were the graves of eponymous heroes at Megara (A 356) and there are hints of the existence of hero cults in the prytaneion at Sikyon (A 428) and at Delphi (A 305). While the connection between such heroes and the prytaneion is too hazy to permit generalizations, one might remember the close topographical ties between the tholos (or "prytaneion-annex") and the monument of the eponymous heroes at Athens as described by Pausanias (I, 5, 1) and verified by archaeological discoveries.

Law Court

One other activity which took place in the Athenian prytaneion was that of a law court. The *testimonia* concerning this court seem to fall into two groups. In the first, one learns of murderers being condemned by a court in the prytaneion (A 13, 56, 220, 263), while the second group of ancient references concerns judgements about the guilt of inanimate objects which had caused death (A 106, 224). (A roof tile, for example, which had fallen from a housetop and killed a person below would be taken to the prytaneion for trial and punishment.)[30] The element common to both is homicide, and Pollux (A 230; cf. A 254) actually connects the two groups of *testimonia* by informing us that the trials in the prytaneion were conducted by the Phylobasileis and that they "concerned murderers and inanimate murderers".[31] If one is struck by nothing else about this court, one must certainly be aware of the primitive quality of judgements concerning inanimate objects, especially when one reads (A 230) that the guilty objects were to be expelled from the boundaries of the country.

The late reference (A 240) to a court near the prytaneion which was called the Ἐπάλξεις may reproduce the actual name of this court. If so, one would have to posit a physical addition to the prytaneion for the purpose of housing the law court. Such is not only implied by the meaning of the name, but even stated in the source: "ᾠκοδόμηται δὲ πρὸς τῷ πρυτανείῳ." The source is not particularly trustworthy, however, since the Ἐπάλξεις law court could be quite another entity, physically

30 Although he does not specifically mention the law court in the prytaneion, Aristotle, *Ath. Pol.* LVII, 4, probably refers to it when he mentions the trials of inanimate and non-human murderers undertaken by the Basileus and the Phylobasileis: δικάζει δ' ὁ βασιλεὺς καὶ οἱ φυλοβασιλεῖς καὶ τὰς τῶν ἀψύχων καὶ τῶν ἄλλων ζῴων.

31 We might well think that judgements περὶ τῶν ἀποκτεινάντων had been removed from the jurisdiction of the court in the prytaneion by the fourth century B.C. This would explain how the *testimonia* came to be of two types. The first of these was dependent upon sources from the time when the court still had jurisdiction over actual murderers, while the second comes from a date later than the transfer of such jurisdiction away from the prytaneion. See C. Hignett, *A History of the Athenian Constitution* (Oxford 1952) 311–313, who implies that the court in the prytaneion had given up any real jurisdiction (i.e., over human murderers) in homicide cases at least by the late fifth century B.C.

connected to the prytaneion only in the mind of a very late scholiast. Even if the topographic placement of the law court is correct, there is surely no reason to see this as a second court in the prytaneion distinct from that already discussed.

Social Welfare Institution

Among the sources there are traces of the use of the prytaneion, at least in Athens, as a social welfare institution. Such a use is vaguely implicit in the awards of maintenance in the prytaneion to athletes, statesmen, and their descendants discussed above. Even more intriguing is the story told by Plutarch and Aelian (A 215, 216) of the mule who had worked especially hard on the construction of the Parthenon and was to be fed "at public expense, voting it as they would Sitesis to an athlete exhausted by old age." Both the mule and the old athlete are beneficiaries of a sort of "social security" program, awarded on the basis of merit, which is channeled through the prytaneion. But the mule surely is not to be invited into the prytaneion, so that one must imagine a "prytaneion fund" into which monies were paid, usually for actual meals in the building, but occasionally for expenditures of a similar nature outside the prytaneion.

It might seem that the suggestion of a welfare system channeled through the prytaneion is based on an apocryphal story of a mule and not to be taken seriously. Yet it is just such a system which must be understood as the means by which the daughters of Aristides (A 18) were married out of the prytaneion with a dowry of three thousand Drachmai each. Even more conclusive, however, is a recently discovered decree of the end of the fifth century B.C. (A 59). This inscription is concerned with the provision of maintenance to the children of those killed by the Thirty Tyrants, and contains a reference to the prytaneion. Although this reference occurs in a sadly fragmentary area, the editor has suggested, correctly I believe, that the sense should be: "to give the children of all those killed by the Thirty an obol of sustenance every day just as it is given to war orphans from the prytaneion."[32] It is interesting to note

32 R. Stroud, "Theozotides and the Athenian Orphans," *Hesperia* 40 (1971) 280–301.

that Aristotle (A 146) links the prytaneion and orphans as two responsibilities of the public funds.

The conclusion seems secure that, in addition to the meals provided in the prytaneion for adults such as athletes and statesmen, there was also provision made for certain categories of minors to be fed at public expense with the financial arrangements made through the prytaneion. The actual meals took place outside the building and were continued for each orphan until he entered manhood, made his initiation sacrifices at the hearth of Hestia (see A 195–202), and could enter the prytaneion as a full-fledged citizen, probably no longer a responsibility of the state.[33]

The principle behind the connection between the prytaneion and such a social system is surely that the hearth in the prytaneion is the symbol of the state, the "home" of the city. As such, the prytaneion is the obvious means through which to arrange for the maintenance of wards of the state.

Personnel

There must have been a number of people who had various duties to fulfill in the prytaneion. Although there may well have been servants or slaves behind the scenes, one also hears of functionaries with such titles as the *οἰνοχόος* (A 361),[34] the *μάγιρος*[35] or the *ἀρχιμάγειρος*,[36] and the *αὐλητής* (A 367, 375) who must have had certain responsibilities in the prytaneion with regard to dining activities. Care of the building and its equipment resided, at least in Roman Athens, with the *ἐπιμελητὴς τοῦ πρυτανείου* (A 209), and care of the fire on the hearth apparently belonged to women past the age of marriage

33 The sources cited in the discussion above show that there was no permanent funding of the maintenance provided in or through the prytaneion. It seems rather that each case was a separate financial responsibility voted by the Demos. Perhaps indicative of the breakdown in the original functions of the prytaneion (see below, pp. 23–24, 126–127) is a parallel change in the method of financing, for in the mid-third century after Christ an endowment for Sitesis in the prytaneion could be bequeathed to the Council of the Areopagus by the terms of the will of an individual citizen (A 239).

34 See *Miller* 82.

35 *IG* XIV, 617.

36 See *Miller* 82.

(A 212).[37] Generally, however, the staff of the prytaneion is not well covered in the sources.

For the purpose of receiving foreign guests there must have been a citizen-host in the prytaneion of each city. This function was performed by the stephanephoros at Magnesia (A 348, 350–352), and by the archons at Kimolos, Paros, and Philippi (A 338, 379, 391). Otherwise, in the majority of *testimonia*, it is not specified who is to "καλέσαι δὲ αὐτοὺς ἐπὶ ξένια εἰς τὸ πρυτανεῖον" and one might take it to be a herald or some such person. A recently published inscription, however, mentions an official in Hellenistic Athens who is "elected for the reception of friends and allies" (A 203). In the new text, this Athenian official is to invite a group of men from Stiris to Xenia. Are we to suppose that, unless otherwise specified, there was always ὁ κεχειροτονήμενος ἐπὶ τὴν ἀποδοχὴν τῶν φίλων καὶ συμμάχων who is to be understood as the subject of καλέσαι? Such an assumption is unproven but attractive.

Evolution

The law court in the prytaneion for inanimate murderers is not the only characteristic which attests to the great age of the institution but, in the words of Frazer, "few bear the marks of a hoarier antiquity than the court in the prytaneion."[38] Frazer concluded that the prytaneion was the direct heir to the royal palaces of Homeric times.[39] Indeed, the two buildings and their hearths share many functions which have been discussed above —the entertainment of foreign guests and local dignitaries, the provision of asylum at the hearth, and the designation of the seat of administration of the government. Then too, the name prytanis, and therefore prytaneion, has a royal as well as a governmental connotation.[40] It was, in some places, synonymous

37 In the passage cited Plutarch does not make specific mention of the prytaneion, but the perpetual fire is surely that in the prytaneion.

38 J. Frazer, "The Prytaneum, the Temple of Vesta, the Vestals, Perpetual Fires," *JPh* 14 (1885) 147, note 1.

39 *Ibid.* 145–148.

40 That the office of the prytanis gave its name to the building was pointed out long ago by Hagemann, *De Prytaneo* (Breslau 1880) 13, but a certain confusion had existed in late antiquity. Typical of this is the passage in the *Etymologicum Magnum* (A 266) from the twelfth century A.D. which depends on a

with king, as Aristotle says: "... the officials ... (who) derive their honor from the common hearth; some call them Archons, others Kings, and others Prytaneis."[41]

That the prytaneion was a venerable building is shown by the appearance of the word on stone in the mid-sixth century (A 275, 427). The easy familiarity of Herodotus (A 14, 15, 324, 428, 429) with the prytaneion as an institution indicates that it was well established by the time of his writing. The many literary ties between the prytaneion and Solon (A 13, 17), while not necessarily to be taken as actual connections with the man, show that, by the fifth century B.C., the building could be thought to belong to a significantly earlier time. Thus the tradition which connected the inception of the Athenian prytaneion with the Attic synoecism attributed to Theseus was accepted already in the fifth century (A 11). To another such misty figure—Keleos—was attributed the foundation of the first prytaneion (A 462). Obviously one cannot establish any precise time for the inception of the institution, but it can be maintained, and will be argued in chapter three, that the Athenian prytaneion existed first in the Geometric period; that is, in the ninth and eighth centuries B.C.

As discussed above, the prytaneion was of importance in two major areas, religion and politics. A clear distinction between the two areas was probably never made since hospitality, or Xenia, was a custom prescribed by religious considerations, with political aspects originally of secondary importance. The

---

tradition which can be traced to late Roman times. If, as a scholiast to Aelius Aristides (A 256) says, Athens was, at a time somewhat after *ca* A.D. 200, the only city which "tends the hearth and the prytaneion unmoved and unchanged just as they preserve their original constitution," it would be easy to understand why little connection was seen or comprehended between the prytaneion and the prytaneis: no such connection had existed at Athens for centuries (the prytaneis were located in the tholos) and all other possible sources of information regarding a prytaneion-prytaneis connection at other cities had ceased to exist. It was, then, natural for etymologies to be formed on the basis of the function of dining—the function which literature most clearly designated for the prytaneion. Thus the prytaneion was understood as a treasury of grain, a pyrotameion as it were (A 257, 265). Another such etymological possibility was pyrotameion as a treasury of fire, and literature told the late lexicographers and scholiasts of the eternal fire which was housed in the prytaneion (A 257, 264).

41 Aristotle, *Politics* 1322b28; cf. Pindar, *Pythian* VI, 24, *et al.*

religious aspect of the prytaneion remained a constant centered on the hearth of Hestia with the perpetual fire symbolic of the life of the city-state, but as the Greek city-state became more important during the Archaic period, so the symbol of the life of the polis, together with the prytaneion in which that symbol was housed, acquired an increased importance. Hospitality extended by host to a visiting guest-friend was projected to the political level with Xenia offered in the prytaneion, the symbolic House of State, to other cities as represented by their ambassadors.

On this political plane, the prytaneion was a flourishing institution throughout the Classical period, but already in the fourth century B.C., its significance had begun to wane (see A 140). During the Roman period it became necessary to explain to one's readers just what a prytaneion had been (A 241 ff.) and at Ephesos in this period the building became more important as the center of religious activity concerning Hestia than as the center of the city's political life.[42]

It is quite understandable that the importance of an institution bound so intimately with the concept of Greek inter-polis relations would, along with the polis, decline as an international force during the Hellenistic era. One may note the series of three decrees on the same stone which honor ambassadors from Kos to Amphipolis, Cassandria, and Philippi.[43] These three northern towns set forth separate decrees which have much in common, including the honor of Xenia to be granted to the Koan ambassadors. Amphipolis, a Greek town taken over forcibly by Philip of Macedon, makes no mention of the place where the Xenia is to be given. Cassandria, a foundation of Cassander, grants the honor to be in the Archegeteion. Philippi alone invites the ambassadors to the prytaneion, where it is to

42 Hestia appears to have had a religious significance for the Ephesians of the third century A.D. far surpassing that which she held among the Greeks of Classical times: see *Keil* 128. It is interesting that in one of the inscriptions which Keil presents (p. 119), Hestia received the appellation ἀειπάρθενος which is, so far as I know, unique for her. Later it is frequently used of the Virgin Mary. One wonders if their common virginal purity had not caused some equation of these religious personalities in the pagan Greek town. For a similar transferal of Mary's iconography to Hestia in the fifth century A.D. see Fuchs, *op. cit.* (note 25) 22.

43 *SEG* XII, 373 (A 391).

be expected that the other towns would normally also have invited them. Although it is an argument from silence, might we not think that Philippi, originally the Greek town of Krenides which was taken over peacefully by Philip, had preserved its old forms of government even while paying service to the Macedonian king Antigonos; but that new settlements founded by the successors of Alexander, as well as towns which were directly under their rule as a result of seige and conquest, were not allowed as much independence as the existence of a prytaneion might imply?

The prytaneion, however, continued to play a religious role, and it remained an important establishment for activities within the city. This shift of emphasis back to the religious was evolutionary and cannot be precisely dated, but is most obvious in the Roman period when it became more complete and formal. People are no longer invited to Xenia or Deipnon in the prytaneion, at least not in the extant sources; the honor awarded in the prytaneion is exclusively Sitesis (e.g., A 236, 382, 383, 422, 423). At the same time, the lists of personnel connected with the prytaneion have become heavily religious in nature. At Ephesos, for example, the architectural members of the prytaneion (see below, chapter five) are inscribed in the third century A.D. with annual lists of officials whose titles are: *πρύτανις, κούρητες, ἱεροσκόπος, (ἱερὸς) ἐπὶ θυμιάτρου, σπονδαύλης, ἱεροκῆρυξ, ἱεροφάντης, ἱεροσαλπικτής.*[44] Although the prytanis and kouretes were essentially political offices, the religious character of the whole list is obvious.[45]

Whether the change in the predominant function of the prytaneion from political to religious had an influence on the architectural form of the building is a question not easily answered. A proper consideration of this question must await our examination of the remains of the various buildings.

44 F. Miltner, "Vorläufiger Bericht über die Ausgrabungen in Ephesos," *Jahreshefte* 43 (1956) Beiblatt, cols. 30 ff.; also see note 12 above and sources listed there.

45 The same shift in emphasis from political toward religious seems to occur in the Athenian tholos. Compare the earlier titles of the aeisitoi of the tholos with those of the Roman period as summarized by Dow, *op. cit.* (note 11) 22.

CHAPTER II

The Form of the Prytaneion

HAVING considered the various roles which the prytaneion played in ancient Greek cities, our next step is to examine the information to be derived from the *testimonia* regarding the form of the structure. Certain architectural elements are implicit in the functions of the prytaneion discussed in chapter one; other elements are specifically mentioned in the sources. The end result should be some idea of the plan of the prytaneion.

In the past, however, scholars have used the principle that similar functions for two buildings demand similar forms. Since the prytaneion is a building whose functions go far back in time, with even Mycenaean roots, the application of this principle would yield one of two results. First, the Mycenaean hearth was round;[1] the Temple of Vesta, the Roman equivalent of Hestia, was round; the prytaneion "annex", the tholos, at Athens was round: therefore, the prytaneion was also round. This was the general conclusion of earlier scholars,[2] but it was

1 See C. W. Blegen and M. Rawson, *The Palace of Nestor at Pylos* I (Princeton 1966) 85–87, for references to the circular hearth in the megaron at Pylos and other circular Mycenaean hearths.

2 Frazer, *JPh* 14 (1885) 150; K. Lange, *Haus und Halle* (Leipzig 1885) 80 ff.; G. Leroux, *Les Origines de l'Édifice Hypostyle* (Paris 1913) 183. Hagemann, *De Prytaneo* 37, reaches the ultimate compromise by proposing that the chamber of Hestia was round, but that the prytaneion which surrounded this chamber was

partly based on a late and confused tradition which equated prytaneia with tholoi (A 241, 255, 259, 264). Since the discovery of the buildings at Lato and Olympia (see chapter four) this earlier theory of a circular prytaneion has had to be abandoned in spite of the *testimonia* mentioned above.[3] It has been pointed out that even if the hearth of the Mycenaean palace, or that of Hestia, was round, this form was not necessarily reflected in the building sacred to that goddess; that the cults of Hestia and Vesta are not so identical as to imply identical sanctuary forms; and that the shape of the Athenian tholos is not necessarily based upon the shape of the prytaneion of that city, even if the tholos did take over part of the functions of the prytaneion there.[4]

The second possible conclusion regarding the form of the prytaneion based on the assumption of a continuous tie with pre-historic times is that, as the functions of the prytaneion reflect those of the megaron, so does the form of the building. The securely identified examples of prytaneia militate against this conclusion of a megaron-prytaneion architectural identity, and we will see that the sources indicate that the prytaneion had a form which was not identical with that of the megaron.[5]

Rather than relying upon misleading analogies of function (and presumably therefore form) to other architectural types, such as the megaron/oikos or the Hestia/Vesta/tholos parallels to prytaneia, our approach will be to utilize the sources for specific parts of the prytaneion, as well as for more general

---

rectilinear. The most prominent advocate of the circular prytaneion in this century is F. Robert, in his *Thymélè* (Paris 1939) 394.

3 E. Vanderpool, "Tholos and Prytanikon," *Hesperia* 4 (1935) 470–475, has shown that this tradition arose at a time when only the tholos at Athens retained any functions resembling those of a prytaneion, and that it arose because the area around the tholos was called the prytanikon (an area for the prytaneis) which was misunderstood by late writers as prytaneion.

4 J. Charbonneaux, "Tholos et Prytanée," *BCH* 49 (1925) 159–175, conclusively disproved the theory of the round prytaneion. For divergencies between Hestia and Vesta note, among other things, the difference in attendants: Plutarch, *Numa* IX, 5, as opposed to Dionysius of Halicarnassus II, 67; cf. Preuner, *Hestia-Vestia* 266.

5 M. Guarducci, in the commentary to *ICr* II, xv, 2, suggested that the ultimate derivation of the prytaneion was from the Mycenaean megaron by way of the Cretan Geometric temple, which served as an intermediary stage in the development. This suggestion is amply refuted in *Tosi* 153.

descriptions of the building, in order to see what sort of structure is to be expected in the remains. Explicit references to these elements are not numerous. If we assume some common denominator, however, and combine what we do possess with a few logical inferences, we may be able to visualize, even though in a somewhat incomplete fashion, the ground plan of a Greek prytaneion. In order to do this, we will have to use *testimonia* which refer to different buildings at different dates in time. The validity of the conclusions will therefore rest on the assumption that there was a generic architectural form for the prytaneion. It will not be easy to test such an assumption since securely identified prytaneia are few, but if it can be shown that these buildings do agree in essential details with one another and with the ground plan derived from the *testimonia*, then the original assumption will be justified. Then too, the way in which some of the sources, although late, mention the prytaneion would lead one to believe that an ancient Greek would form a mental image of a building with certain architectural characteristics if he heard the word prytaneion, just as he would if he heard the words "temples," "gymnasia," "agoras," "harbors," "docks," etc. (see A 461).

One should not, however, expect that the correspondence between any two excavated buildings to be identified as prytaneia would be as exact as, for example, that between two peripteral temples. Rather, one should look for a similarity of details peculiar to a civic building such as the prytaneion and to its functions. An analogous situation exists with respect to another type of Greek civic structure—the bouleuterion. Two bouleuteria, no matter how dissimilar in outline of plan, will at least share certain features of seating arrangements and a speaker's area.[6]

General Plan and Construction

There is no express evidence regarding the quality of the construction of the prytaneion, yet is it not logical to assume that the construction was of a substantial nature? Certainly the prytaneia at Siphnos and Syracuse (A 429 and 431) would support such an inference since the former was covered with

6 See *McDonald*, *passim*.

marble and the latter is described as "*ornatissimum*." Then too, a building of such civic importance, located in the center of the community and which was the place of entertainment of foreign visitors would very probably be better built than an ordinary private home. This is precisely what Dio Chrysostomos implies (A 217) when he sets off house and workshop against agora, bouleuterion, and prytaneion.

Since the demise of the theory of the round shape of the prytaneion, it has been the general assumption that the form of the prytaneion, as well as its quality of construction, was essentially that of a private house.[7] This idea seems to be supported by the scholiast to Thucydides (A 242) who calls the prytaneion an *οἶκος μέγας*. But this term is sufficiently vague to allow a variety of ground plans for our building type. In fact, the word *oikos* does not have to refer exclusively to a structure used for dwelling, and even if oikos in the reference cited does mean "house," it may still allude to the function of the building rather than the form.[8] That is, the prytaneion was an oikos in that it was the "house" of the prytaneis, or the "House of State," regardless of the architectural form. One might naturally expect that there would be little correspondence between the prytaneion and the house since the two buildings shared only the function of dining, and perhaps that of sleeping. Indeed, the tholos in Athens, the only place where we know that people both ate and slept in an official capacity, has a form obviously unlike the form of either house or prytaneion.[9] Nor would one expect there to be dining facilities in a private house to compare with those in a prytaneion, not to mention the divergencies between the two buildings made necessary by different requirements for a sacrificial area around the prytaneion's common hearth.

7 See Hagemann, *De Prytaneo* 34–36, for reference to the exterior; T. Wiegand and H. Schrader, *Priene* (Berlin 1904) 234; D. S. Robertson, *A Handbook of Greek and Roman Architecture*[2] (Cambridge 1943) 388; R. E. Wycherley, *How the Greeks Built Cities*[2] (London 1962) 134. The single exception, to my knowledge, has been *Tosi, passim* (but especially pp. 163–164).

8 See Liddell and Scott, *A Greek-English Lexicon*[9] (Oxford 1940), under *οἶκος* for documented meanings of the word as diverse as assembly hall, treasury and temple; but the primary meaning is, of course, that of a place of dwelling.

9 Aristotle, *Ath. Pol.* XLIV, 1; Andocides, *De Mysteriis* 45.

Location

The position of the prytaneion in the city is clearly indicated by the *testimonia*; the prytaneion should, generally, be found on or near the agora.[10] Herodotus may imply that the prytaneion and agora at Siphnos were near one another when he relates that both were adorned with Parian marble in the late sixth century B.C. (A 429), and one may sense an implicit topographical connection between the agora and the prytaneion in the sequence in which Philo lists the parts of a city to be laid out by an architect (A 461). More obvious information comes from Astypalaea, where an agoranomos was to have a monument in the agora near the stoa which was beside the prytaneion (A 10). Cicero also locates the prytaneion of Syracuse in the agora along with stoas, a bouleuterion, and a temple (A 431). An inscription from Crete (A 455) which records a treaty between Knossos and Gortyn established a boundary for the two towns which ran through a third town. This boundary line was to go beside the stoas, through the agora, and keep the prytaneion on its left as it ran in a straight line up a cart track. It is clear that the prytaneion of this town was on the edge of the agora. The inscription which orders the decoration of the stoas and the prytaneion at Cyrene (A 272) would also indicate a connection between the placement of the agora and the location of the prytaneion of that city if one assumes that stoas are typical of (though not limited to) agoras.

If the conclusion that the prytaneion was normally situated close to the agora is correct, one must still admit the possibility of exceptions to the rule. Pausanias tells us that the Athenian prytaneion was on the northern slopes of the Acropolis, not in the agora (A 221).[11] This situation probably came about because the prytaneion was established at Athens before the agora and, rather than move the common hearth of the city (see A 255) the prytaneion remained in its original location (although

10 See Hagemann, *De Prytaneo* 16–22.

11 D. Levi, "Il Pritaneo e la Tholos di Atene," *Annuario* 6 (1923) 1–6, hypothesized that this was the original site of the Athenian prytaneion; his views will be maintained and expanded in chapter three. The evidence of Pollux (A 466) cannot be used for Athens or any other city, for the context of his remarks shows that the prytaneion which he located on an acropolis refers to an ideal city, not to Athens or necessarily to any other existing city.

certain of its functions had to be transferred to the tholos in the agora). At Delphi the prytaneion was located within or very near the peribolos of the sanctuary (A 289), as one would expect at a center of religious activity.

In cities of great age or of singular religious importance the prytaneion might not be close to the agora, but in a city where the planning had been unencumbered by pre-existing structures, as in a colony or a city rebuilt after widespread destruction, one can expect to find the prytaneion in or near the agora.

Specific Elements

Courtyard

Despite certain fundamental differences between the prytaneion and the house as outlined above, various components were common to both. At least some prytaneia had courtyards which were presumably interior ones of the peristyle type so well known from domestic architecture (A 286, 287, 331). The vagueness of the word (*αὐλή*) is of such a degree, however, as would permit this courtyard to have been an area in front of the building which was marked off by a wall. In any event, there must have been an area within the prytaneion precinct open to the air but clearly defined as part of the prytaneion, for Herodotus mentions the establishment of a temenos for Melanippos in the prytaneion at Sikyon (A 428). It is certainly more usual to consider a temenos of that sort as being hypaethral rather than in a covered area.

Perhaps to be associated architecturally with the courtyard in the prytaneion is a gate (*πυλών*) which is mentioned as being in front of the prytaneion at Ephesos (A 311), although the source may refer to a separate structure.

Prostas

A more ambiguous architectural member of the prytaneion is the *προστάς* (A 415). The confusion surrounding the precise meaning of this term arises from the different uses of the word by both ancient and modern writers, but it would appear, considering the date and place of the source, that prostas must refer to a vestibule or anteroom in front of a larger, architecturally more significant room.[12] The meaning can be expanded further to indicate a room which not only opens into another room behind, but one which also has its front facing onto a courtyard. The prostas, then, is any area connecting a courtyard with a large room off the courtyard.[13]

The most complete description of any single prytaneion comes to us by way of two complementary inventory lists from Delos (A 286, 287). In these are mentioned items of value stored in five distinct parts of the prytaneion: the room called simply the prytaneion; the prodomos of this room; the room called the archeion; the prodomos of this room; and the courtyard. From the inscription one receives the impression that the list was made by a scribe who began in the room called the prytaneion, passed through an anteroom (prodomos), and then into the courtyard. He next turned out of the courtyard into the archeion, first passing through its anteroom, which he listed in his inventory only on his return to the courtyard from the archeion. Thus there was a central courtyard with two main rooms, the prytaneion and the archeion, each separated from the courtyard by its own prodomos. These prodomoi might very well be the architectural equivalent of the prostas in the prytaneion at Ptolemais which was discussed above.

Dining Room

In addition to the elements of the Delian prytaneion mentioned in the inventories cited above, there was another room called

12 See N. Lewis, "New Light on the Greek House from the Zenon Papyri," *AJA* 37 (1933) 397–399. Originally, as the etymology of the word would suggest, *προστάς* referred to a porch which stood in front of a building. In this sense *πρόστασις* is used of the porches of the Erechtheion (*IG* I², 372, lines 58, 62, 77, 83), and thus it might refer to something like the gate mentioned at Ephesos (A 311). But Lewis has shown that by the third century B.C. *προστάς* could be applied to any anteroom; cf. Photios: "'prostasia'... that which Homer called a prodomos, some call a pastas, others a prostas" (*ἔνιοι μὲν παστάδα, τινες δὲ προστάδα προσαγορεύουσιν, ἥν Ὅμηρος πρόδομον εἴρηκεν*).

13 See Vitruvius VI, 7, 1 (on private houses): "The peristyle has three sides with colonnades and on the side facing the south are two antae... the space between which is equal to two-thirds of the space behind. Some call this place the prostas, others the pastas" (*Id peristylum in tribus partibus habet porticus inque parte, quae spectat ad meridiem, duas antas inter se spatio amplo distantes... ex eo tertia adempta spatium datur introsus. His locus apud nonnullos prostas, apud alios pastas nominatur*).

the hestiatorion (A 278).[14] That we should find a room in a prytaneion known as the hestiatorion or banquet hall is not surprising. Pausanias (A 376) mentions one such hall in the prytaneion at Olympia where the victors at the games dined. It is, therefore, safe to assume the presence in every prytaneion of at least one room which could be called a hestiatorion.[15]

An attempt has been made in Appendix B to define the criteria for identification of a dining room. In sum, since a prytaneion was built with knowledge of its intended use, there should be present in every prytaneion a room of the proper size and shape to accommodate precisely a determinable number of couches of a standard size. The couches themselves may also appear, or supports for couches, or a raised border around the perimeter of the room.[16]

Certain questions arise concerning the hestiatorion in the prytaneion: how large was this room? Were there one or more such rooms in each prytaneion? To a great extent, the answers will be conditioned by our views as to whether or not all the people honored are together in the prytaneion at one time, or in some rotation. Unfortunately, there is sufficient evidence to answer these questions only with regard to the tholos in Athens. Although there are some literary indications that those eating in the tholos did so together and at the same time,[17] it will be argued in chapter three that dining in the Athenian tholos was done in two or more phases and that the use of words such as *συνδειπνεῖν* in the sources refers only to a joint meal of many of the prytaneis, not to a single meal of all the prytaneis at the same time. Elsewhere there are no criteria

14 For a discussion of the building at Delos in which these various rooms are to be found, see chapter four.

15 Note also the hestiatorion built by Romulus for each Roman assembly hall (A 454). While one may well doubt the historicity of the attribution of such construction to Romulus, the explicit connection between an eating and a governmental business area is indubitable.

16 For reference to raised borders in dining rooms see Appendix B, notes 2 (Vergina), and 9 (South Stoa I, Athenian Agora), and Table 2, note 6 (Perachora); also D. M. Robinson and J. W. Graham, *Olynthus* VIII (Baltimore 1938) 174–175.

17 E.g., Pollux VIII, 155: "The tholos in which every day fifty, that is, the tribe which is prytanizing, of the boule of five hundred dine together" (*ἡ θόλος ἐν ᾗ συνεδείπνουν ἑκάστης ἡμέρας πεντάκοντα τῆς τῶν βουλῆς, ἡ πρυτανεύουσα φυλή*); cf. Aristotle, *Ath. Pol.* XLIII, 3; Demosthenes, *De falsa legatione* 190; Timaeus (A 261).

for determining the size of the hestiatorion, even if one knew the number of people to be accommodated for a given meal in that prytaneion.[18] Still, may one not assume that there was only one room for dining in each prytaneion? An increase in the number of diners at meals in the prytaneion would entail only an additional dining period, not necessarily another room. Remembering the divisions of the prytaneion at Delos discussed above, and Pausanias' use of the singular *ἑστιατόριον* for the dining area in the Olympian prytaneion (A 376), one would expect to find a prytaneion with one room for dining rather than a building with two or more dining areas.

In addition to couches and tables, other indications of function in a dining room might be found. Refuse from dining is to be expected, and the presence of eating and drinking utensils is not only a logical inference, but is actually documented for the prytaneia at Cyzicus, Delos, Rhegium, and Sigeion (A 276, 281, 416, 427, respectively). Along with the dining area would naturally go a place for the preparation of food. Although there is no literary or epigraphical evidence for such facilities, analogous situations exist in the kitchen area next to the tholos in Athens,[19] and in the stoa at Brauron and South Stoa I in the Athenian Agora.[20] In the latter two cases, the evidence consists of areas of burning in the middle of the dining rooms themselves, apparently caused by the cooking of food on the spot. Such a situation is more formalized in the Asklepieion at Corinth where one finds regular stone-lined pits in the center of each room, most likely for cooking purposes.[21] One might expect that in a prytaneion there were cooks and servants to do

18 That the number of potential diners was quite large is shown by the case of Athens where, by the early third century B.C., there is good evidence for there being at least forty diners in the prytaneion. These are as follows: men or their descendants honored with Sitesis (A 26, 107, 139, 149, 150, 154, 158, 159, 160, 163, 169, 170, 172–177); hierophantes and manteis; an indeterminable number of Panhellenic victors; strategoi; and, in the month of Hekatombaion of Panathenaic years, the games directors (cf. chapter one, pp. 4–11). This reckoning of a minimum of forty takes into account neither those occasional diners who had received grants of Deipnon or Xenia, nor the unattested men and their descendants (Perikles for example) who almost certainly had been granted Sitesis.

19 H. A. Thompson, "The Tholos and its Predecessors," *Hesperia*, Suppl. IV (1940) 73–84.

20 See Appendix B, notes 9 and 10, respectively.

21 See Appendix B, Table 2, note 3.

this chore in a separate area, but there is no evidence permitting a choice between the two possibilities.

Hestia Hall

The presence of dining areas alone can never be adequate evidence for the identification of an excavated building as a prytaneion. There are too many other types of Greek buildings which also had dining facilities, such as the *καταγώγιον* or the *πανδοκεῖον* or "hotels" for visitors to shrines (e.g., that at the Asklepieion in Corinth), as well as private homes.[22] It has already been noted that, in the case of the Delian prytaneion (A 286, 287), there was a second room which must have been equal, or nearly equal, to the dining area in architectural importance. This room, called the prytaneion at Delos, contained the common hearth and thus was the area sacred to Hestia and concerned with the official cult. The nature of this room would have been a reflection of the cult inasmuch as the equipment required by the cult will be found in this room, but our knowledge of the cult is very limited. Central to it was the undying fire, so one expects a hearth, but even here there is ambiguity since there are references to a lamp (*λύχνιον*) in the prytaneion (A 206, 434, 448). It is tempting to suggest that such a lamp was used to keep the fire alive between periods of sacrifice at the hearth when the lamp would provide the spark for the sacrificial fire. Certainly, regardless of the presence of the lamp, there must have been an altar-hearth in every prytaneion as the constant use of the words *κοινὴ ἑστία* signifies, and Pollux (A 465) defined the *ἑστία* in the prytaneion in terms of *ἐσχάρα* and *βωμός*. That one such altar-hearth was of some size can be seen in the case of Olympia where the ashes from it were sufficient for use in annual repairs to the Altar of Olympian Zeus (A 373, 374), but Pausanias also tells us that the hearth

22 W. A. McDonald, "Villa or Pandokeion?," *Studies Presented to David M. Robinson* (St. Louis 1951) 365–367, and notes 5–8, offers a more complete discussion of buildings of this type, although a thorough study of ancient eating establishments is, at present, non-existent. Certain buildings where dining took place have been presented by R. A. Tomlinson in more recent years; see Appendix B, note 2, and Table 2, notes 4 and 6.

in the prytaneion at Olympia was made of ashes. Such a hearth might leave no trace of its existence.

Since it was in the Hestia Hall that the religious sacrifices took place, there should appear traces of fire and bones along with vessels characteristic of religious activities (e.g., phialai, oinochoai). Dedications of various types may also be found in such a room, although their precise nature cannot be indicated without better knowledge of the cult.

What other characteristic elements are to be associated with this hearth room are not clear, but the size of the room must have been large enough to permit a considerable number of people to participate in and observe the sacrifices performed there. The ephebes at Athens sacrificed, presumably in a group, in the prytaneion (A 195–202), there were many religious processions starting from or going by way of prytaneia (A 2, 28, 179, 308, 359, 449), and there was a relatively large body of officials concerned with the cult of Hestia in the prytaneion at Ephesos[23] and at Olympia (A 375).[24] In addition, the room may have contained provisions for the accommodation of spectators at the sacrifices.

Subsidiary Rooms

There were sundry subsidiary rooms and pieces of equipment in addition to those parts of the prytaneion already discussed. These include small rooms for the storage of table service, extra couches and tables, couch coverings, and other necessary paraphernalia.[25] One might like to think that the official weights and measures of the city were normally kept in the prytaneion, but there is no express reference to such storage in any prytaneion; one must rely solely on the analogy to the tholos at Athens.[26] It is also possible that such storage closets as there were

23 *Keil* 119–128.

24 *Miller* 82.

25 The presence of *στρώματα* in the tholos in Athens is epigraphically attested; see Thompson, *op. cit.* (note 19) 145, line 14.

26 See chapter three. The fragmentary mention of the *ὄργυια* in the Delian prytaneion (A 279) is not clear on this point, but it seems that this measure had particular reference to the Temple of Apollo and was not used except with respect to that building. Thus the orgyia belongs more to the category of mementoes than to that of weights and measures. Hagemann, *De Prytaneo* 48, however, took this inscription as evidence of a more extensive use of the prytaneion for the storage of official weights and measures.

in the prytaneion were in the form of wooden cabinets now long destroyed rather than in the form of separate rooms.

As already discussed, the prytaneion served as an archives of some sort and there existed an area in the Delian building specifically called an archeion. A smaller room to serve this purpose, or perhaps a limited space within a larger area, can be sought in suspected prytaneia.

One might also expect to find a room for the use of the custodian of the prytaneion. However, this official is attested only at Athens in the Augustan period (A 209). It would seem rather more likely that the prytaneis and the titled functionaries (see chapter one) normally exercised guardianship over the prytaneion during their period in office (see A 460); facilities for them have already been noted. Considering the unique situation of the Athenian prytaneion vis-à-vis the tholos and the residence of the prytaneis, it is possible that the *ἐπιμελητὴς τοῦ πρυτανείου* was likewise unique to Athens.[27] The tasks of cooking and cleaning would have been done by menials who could expect no lodging or especial facilities in the prytaneion.

Movable Contents

In addition to various objects considered above with regard to their appropriate part of the prytaneion (e.g., couches, pots, bones, ash), there may be other artifacts which have no obvious relevance to the prytaneion or to Hestia. In the Delian inventories (A 286, 287) there is documented the presence of statues of Hermes and Apollo in the prytaneion, and at Olympia there was an altar of Pan inside the prytaneion in addition to the normal hearth (A 374). The statues of Eirene, Demosthenes, and others in the Athenian prytaneion have already been mentioned (A 221). Obviously, unless documented in the ancient *testimonia*, it is not possible to foretell what extraneous material will be discovered in a specific prytaneion.

Summary

One should expect with some probability a prytaneion to have two main rooms (the dining room and the room of the hearth),

27 Hagemann, *De Prytaneo* 55, hypothesized a "thyroreion" for the lodging of the custodian in every prytaneion, but evidence for such a room is non-existent.

a courtyard (perhaps with anterooms connecting it with the two large rooms), and some indeterminable number of subsidiary rooms. These buildings will be well constructed, located on or near the agora, and will contain certain typical movable objects.

CHAPTER III

Athens: The Prytaneion and the Tholos

NOW that the tholos has been proved not to be the prytaneion but rather the "prytaneion-annex," there is no building at Athens which can be identified as the prytaneion. Nevertheless, a certain periodic scholarly debate has taken place concerning the location of the prytaneion. It is not unfitting in the present study to review the evidence and to indicate the area where future excavators might seek the prytaneion of Athens. At the same time a discussion of the Athenian tholos is germane because of the similarities of function between the tholos and prytaneia elsewhere. A clear presentation of the Athenian situation is desirable, moreover, since old theories still are current, and one often sees a general confusion between tholos and prytaneion, and between bouleuterion and prytaneion.[1] Let it be stated again that the Athenian tholos and the

1 For example, the confusion between tholos and prytaneion has recently appeared again in a discussion of *IG* I^2, 77, by W. E. Thompson, "The Prytaneion Decree," *AJPh* 92 (1971) 228, notes 11 and 12, where the aeisitoi of the Roman period are placed in the prytaneion. Both the aeisitoi and the prytaneis, who are honored in the same texts cited by Thompson, dined in the tholos, not the prytaneion. See above, chapter one, p. 9 and note 12. T. H. Price, "An Enigma in Pella: The Tholos and Herakles Phylakos," *AJA* 77 (1973) 66–71, completely confuses the Athenian tholos and the prytaneion. She further confounds the function of the bouleuterion with both that of the tholos and that of the prytaneion. The latter two buildings were, at Athens and elsewhere, separate and distinct structures, and neither served as the meeting place of the council.

prytaneion were two separate and distinct buildings which shared the functions fulfilled by the prytaneion alone at other cities.

The Athenian Prytaneion

It would be superfluous after Judeich's presentation to examine in detail the different opinions regarding the position of the prytaneion at Athens.[2] The present discussion will, therefore, be restricted to noting the chief proponents of the several views and the followers of these views since the publication of Judeich.

The problem centers around the location of the prytaneion in the centuries before the visit of Pausanias to Athens. His evidence (A 221) is incontrovertible as to the placement of the building on the northern slopes of the Acropolis in the second century A.D. Some scholars have hypothesized, however, one, and even two, predecessors to the building which Pausanias visited. These hypothetical prytaneia are to be located on the Acropolis and/or in "old Athens" on the southern or western slopes of the Acropolis.

The Acropolis Site

The advocates of the Acropolis as the site of the earliest prytaneion use as evidence a supposed continuity from the Mycenaean megaron on the Acropolis to a later prytaneion.[3] That some of the functions of the megaron were continued in the prytaneion is undoubtedly true (see chapter two, p. 26), but no continuity of location need be therefore assumed. In fact, the testimony of Thucydides, followed by Plutarch (A 11, 12), that Theseus founded one prytaneion for all of Attica at the time of the synoecism, would indicate that there was a new building and probably a new location at that time.

The same passage of Thucydides, coupled with his famous localization of the original Athens on the Acropolis and the area to the south (II, 15, 3), has been taken to show that the prytaneion in the time of Theseus was in that area defined by

2 W. Judeich, *Topographie von Athen*[2] (Munich 1931) 63, 296–297, 304.

3 E. Curtius, *Attische Studien* II (Göttingen 1865) 55; cf. L. Holland, "The Hall of the Athenian Kings," *AJA* 43 (1939) 289–298.

Thucydides.[4] There are, however, two points which have not been properly noted by the Acropolis site proponents. First, Thucydides, having described the synoecism and the establishment of one prytaneion, begins immediately his discussion of the original place of the city of Athens by saying: "Before this [the synoecism], the city consisted of the Acropolis and the part beneath the Acropolis especially toward the south" (*τὸ δὲ πρὸ τοῦ ἡ ἀκρόπολις ἡ νῦν οὖσα πόλις ἦν, καὶ τὸ ὑπ' αὐτὴν πρὸς νότον μάλιστα τετραμμένον*). Second, Plutarch (A 12), in following Thucydides, says about the prytaneion that it is where the town is now (*ὅπου νῦν ἵδρυται τὸ ἄστυ*).[5] Plutarch obviously is not referring to the Acropolis, and Thucydides quite clearly states that the prytaneion founded by Theseus was in some area other than the original city. To paraphrase the passage, Thucydides says that originally Athens was on the Acropolis and the area to the south, when Theseus synoecized Attica and established one prytaneion for all. The topographical indications are clear; from the time of Theseus, no prytaneion had existed on the Acropolis or in the area to the south. If a prytaneion had ever existed on the Acropolis or its southern slopes, it appears to have been unknown to Thucydides.

The fact that Pollux (A 466) places the prytaneion on the acropolis has also been cited as evidence. But Pollux is not alluding either to Athens or to any other real city. Rather, he is describing his idealized concept of where the prytaneion ought to be placed in an imaginary city.

An inscription from a seat in the theater of Dionysos has been held to prove the existence of the prytaneion on the Acropolis. The text of this inscription certainly does provide evidence for a cult of Hestia, Livia, and Julia on the Acropolis (*ἱερῆας Ἑστίας ἐπ' Ἀκροπόλει καὶ Λειβίας καὶ Ἰουλίας*),[6] but, considering the Imperial date of the inscription, and the names of the latter two deities, one might better think of a cult of Vesta, Livia, and

4 By using the expression "the time of Theseus" we may leave deliberately vague the absolute date for the establishment of a prytaneion in Athens. On the other hand, a date before the fifth century B.C. is obviously indicated, as is even a pre-sixth century date if one trusts the sensibilities of Thucydides.

5 Holland's rendering of this passage (*op. cit.* 291) as the "upper town", referring in his context to the Acropolis, seems inaccurate.

6 *IG* II², 5096.

Julia. Moreover, it was noted in chapter one that the presence of Hestia does not necessarily imply the existence of a prytaneion. Finally, by the time of the inscription cited, the prytaneion was surely on the north slope of the Acropolis, awaiting visits by Plutarch and Pausanias.

There is, then, no evidence for a prytaneion on the Acropolis later than the time of Theseus (i.e., the time when Thucydides thought Theseus to have lived), and there is only the general theory of continuity between the functions of megaron and prytaneion to support any argument for a pre-Theseus prytaneion on the Athenian Acropolis.

The "Old Athens" Site

The theory which places a prytaneion in the "Old Town" section of Athens was first formulated more than a century ago by Curtius.[7] Having hypothesized an older agora to the south of the Acropolis, and realizing the usual topographic connection between agora and prytaneion, Curtius felt obliged to place a prytaneion near this agora. As already seen, the evidence of Thucydides makes impossible any post-Theseus prytaneion here.

Is there evidence for an earlier prytaneion in the "Old Agora"?[8] The only evidence placing the prytaneion at the foot of the Acropolis on any side but the north involves two other buildings: the Boukoleion and the sanctuary of Dionysos in the Marshes (ἐν Λίμναις). About the latter we know that Thucydides (II, 15, 4) placed it within the confines of his original

7 E. Curtius, *op. cit.* (note 3) 54–68. One might better call this section "The Prytaneion on the South, or West, or Northwest Slopes of the Acropolis" because the building has gradually been moved clockwise around the Acropolis toward the site where Pausanias saw it. Dörpfeld, *Ath. Mitt.* 20 (1895) 188–189, moved the prytaneion to the vicinity of his Dionysos sanctuary southwest of the Areopagus. A. N. Oikonomides, *The Two Agoras in Ancient Athens* (Chicago 1964) 21 and map facing page 1, has pushed this hypothetical early prytaneion around even closer to where Pausanias saw it.

8 The problems of where, when, and if this "Old Agora" existed fall outside the scope of this discussion, and, moreover, have very little relevance to the question of the location of the prytaneion. The resemblance between such an "Old Agora" of the seventh century B.C. or earlier and the Classical or Hellenistic agora would be slight, and any connection between agora and prytaneion at that time is undocumented. For a summary of the problems and sources pertaining to the "Old Agora," see R. E. Wycherley, "Archaia Agora," *Phoenix* 20 (1966) 288–293.

Athens on the south side of the Acropolis.[9] We also know that the wife of the Archon Basileus annually went through a ritual marriage with Dionysos in the Boukoleion, and that the stele carrying regulations about this ceremony was set up in the sanctuary of Dionysos in the Marshes (*καὶ τοῦτον τὸν νόμον γράψαντες ἐν στήλῃ λιθίνῃ ἔστησαν ἐν τῷ ἱερῷ τοῦ Διονύσου παρὰ τὸν βωμὸν ἐν Λίμναις*).[10] Thus there was a religious connection between the Boukoleion and the sanctuary of Dionysos in the Marshes, and the assumption has been that they were located near each other. By this reasoning, the Boukoleion would have been in the old part of Athens to the south of the Acropolis. It would follow that, since Aristotle (A 143) testifies to the proximity of the Boukoleion and the prytaneion, the latter should also be sought in this area to the south of the Acropolis.

It has been noted, however, that by the time of Thucydides, not to mention Aristotle, the prytaneion was not and had not been for some time in the area south of the Acropolis. Furthermore, even if the Boukoleion and the sanctuary of Dionysos are connected by a ritual marriage, there is no reason to connect the two topographically. One might rather expect a religious procession from the Boukoleion to the sanctuary of Dionysos in the Marshes to have been an intrinsic part of the ceremonies.

The North Slope Site

If there is no evidence for a post-Theseus prytaneion elsewhere than where Pausanias saw it, and only an inference as evidence for a pre-Theseus prytaneion on the Acropolis, can one document the continuous location of the prytaneion on the north slopes of the Acropolis from the time of Theseus to that of Pausanias? Such a position was argued long ago,[11] and again more recently by Levi.[12] But these arguments have rested

9 Dörpfeld, *op. cit.* (note 7), believed that he had found this sanctuary at the southwest foot of the Areopagus. The identification is not secure, however, and the precise location of the sanctuary is not important to the following discussion.

10 [Demosthenes] LIX, 75–76; cf. Aristotle, *Ath. Pol.* III, 5.

11 T. H. Dyer, *Ancient Athens* (London 1873) 263–267; C. Wachsmuth, *Die Stadt Athen im Alterthum* I (Leipzig 1874) 462–484.

12 D. Levi, "Il Pritaneo e la Tholos di Atene," *Annuario* 6 (1923) 1–6.

largely on negative grounds in much the same way as the discussion to this point has shown only the lack of evidence for other locations for the prytaneion. Because this view of a constant location has not gained universal acceptance,[13] it would be better to have some positive evidence that the building seen by Pausanias was in the same location eight hundred or more years before his visit.

Unfortunately this positive proof is lacking, but there are certain indications that the prytaneion did not change its place from at least the Classical through the Roman periods. First of all, it is disturbing to imagine the common hearth—the visual symbol of the city—being moved around. One would rather think of the hearth as a fixed point possessing a certain sanctity. That this was so can be inferred from Aelius Aristeides (A 226; cf. A 256, 257) who talks of the "unmoved hearth of the prytaneion" (*ἑστίαν ἀκίνητον πρυτανείου*).

Another hint of this immovability of the hearth is provided by the passage of Plutarch mentioned above (A 12). There Theseus is described as making one prytaneion common to all Attica "where the town is now located" (*ὅπου νῦν ἵδρυται τὸ ἄστυ*). That this is a topographical reference, albeit vague, is indisputable, and it shows that Plutarch knew, or thought he knew, where the prytaneion of Theseus was located. Since Plutarch had seen (A 211) the Athenian prytaneion of his and, doubtless, Pausanias' time, it is tempting to think that Plutarch believed that the building which he had seen and the prytaneion of Theseus were one and the same. Of course, even if the beliefs of Plutarch were established, the validity of his opinions could not be proven.

Another indication of a permanent location for the prytaneion from at least Classical times to the Roman era is the fact that one can trace the presence there of the laws of Solon back from Pausanias (A 221) through Plutarch (A 211) and Polemon (A 190) to, most probably, Cratinus (A 25).[14] The continued

13 See Judeich, *op. cit.* (note 2) 297, note 2.

14 The fragment cited (A 25) contains an unmistakable allusion to the prytaneion. If Plutarch's attribution of it to Cratinus is correct, the presence of these laws in the prytaneion by the third quarter of the fifth century B.C. is documented. In arguing that Plutarch and Cratinus refer to the same objects, called *axones* and *kyrbeis* by them respectively, there is intended no claim that

presence of these κύρβεις or ἄξονες in the prytaneion does not necessarily suggest a stable location for the building, since the laws could have been moved along with the prytaneion, but the easier inference is that both the laws of Solon and the building which housed them remained on the same site throughout historical times. It is particularly unfortunate that Pollux (A 231) does not give a date for the shift of certain ἄξονες and κύρβεις to the agora and the prytaneion.[15] With a date for this transfer would have come a more secure *terminus ante quem* for the location of the prytaneion.

Finally, if the prytaneion can be assigned a permanent location by the time of Aristotle, it will have been in the midst of a cluster of old buildings. These include the Boukoleion, which has already been discussed (A 143), and the Basileion, which was near the Boukoleion and therefore near the prytaneion.[16] These two buildings, the Boukoleion[17] and the Basileion,

---

the two words actually have the same meaning, but rather that the ancient confusion which existed regarding the precise definitions of the two words allowed the same objects to be called by these different names. Plutarch himself (*Solon* XXV, 1–2) acknowledges the difficulties in terminology and we need not suppose that the *kyrbeis* of Cratinus and the *axones* of Plutarch were not the same physical objects. For the ancient debate about the meaning of the names, see especially Harpocration, *s.v.* ἄξονες.

15 Anaximenes (*apud* Harpokration, *s.v.* ὁ κάτωθεν νόμος) does give, however, a date for the move of some laws to the *bouleuterion* and the agora: "Ephialtes shifted the upper *axones* and *kyrbeis* from the acropolis to the bouleuterion and the agora" (τοὺς ἄξονας καὶ τοὺς κύρβεις ἄνωθεν ἐκ τῆς ἀκροπόλεως εἰς τὸ βουλευτήριον καὶ τὴν ἀγορὰν μετέστησεν Ἐφιάλτης). If Anaximenes and Pollux refer to the same event, which cannot be securely established, Pollux is probably wrong in mentioning the prytaneion as one of the destinations of the laws. There would have been no reason for Ephialtes to deposit the laws in two such disparate locations, and Pollux may have been confused by his knowledge of other laws (e.g., those of Solon) which were certainly in the prytaneion. Another possible source of the confusion could have been that Pollux misunderstood his own source's phrase εἰς τὸ πρυτανικὸν καὶ τὴν ἀγοράν (see chapter two, p. 26, note 3). Such an emendation in the text of Pollux would bring his topographical references into accord with those of Anaximenes, but since there is no manuscript evidence for such a change, and since πρυτανικόν is too rare a word to be lightly restored in a text, the suggestion can only be regarded as attractive.

16 Pollux VIII, 111.

17 The place of discovery of a large relief figure of a bull may be an indication of the location of the Boukoleion; see S. Miller, "Old Discoveries from Old Athens," *Hesperia* 39 (1970) 230–231.

housed, respectively, the Archon Basileus and the Phylobasileis[18] and one is entitled to associate with such ancient offices buildings of equally venerable age. There was, then, a group of very old buildings located on the north slope of the Acropolis from very early times.[19]

Where was this area? It is only for the prytaneion that any indications exist. The points from which to work are these:

1. The prytaneion was near the sanctuary of Aglauros and the place where the Persians climbed into the Acropolis in 480 B.C. (A 221).

2. The Street of the Tripods began from the prytaneion (A 222).

3. A dedication by an Epimeletes of the prytaneion was found built into a modern house at 20 Tripod Street (A 209).[20]

4. The sanctuary of Sarapis was below the prytaneion and on the way between it and the temple of Zeus Olympios (A 221).

5. The "Field of Famine" was behind the prytaneion (A 219).

Let us examine these topographical points and fix them on a plan of the area (fig. 1). The shrine of Aglauros is to be found at the base of one of the two stairways leading down from the Acropolis on the north slope.[21] There is no compelling reason

18 Aristotle, *Ath. Pol.* III, 5 and Pollux VIII, 111. The assumed proximity of the Basileion to the prytaneion is further supported by the judicial connection of the former's tenants, the Phylobasileis, with the court in the prytaneion; see chapter one, pp. 18–19 and note 31.

19 In addition to the prytaneion, Basileion, and Boukoleion, the Theseion and the Dioskoureion (following the account of Pausanias I, 17, 2–18, 2) should have been at no great distance from the prytaneion. With regard to the proximity of the prytaneion and the Dioskoureion, note the lunch set out in the prytaneion for the Dioskouroi (A 17).

20 Last seen in this house, to my knowledge, by S. Dow, *Hesperia* Suppl. I 192. The stone has since been removed in the interest of its preservation, and now resides in the Roman marketplace.

21 More properly, "Agraulos"; see M. Ervin, "The Sanctuary of Aglauros," *ΑΡΧΕΙΟΝ ΠΟΝΤΟΥ* 1958, 138–139, who explains the confusion of the two names Agraulos and Aglauros. I have retained the reading of Pausanias' text rather than further confuse the problem. The area to which he refers is quite clear.

FIGURE. 1. Map of the Plaka Area of Athens.

for choosing between them, but the western of these is perhaps preferable, for that would seem to be an area more easily climbed by the Persians (fig. 1, A).[22]

Next, Pausanias begins from the prytaneion going into the

22 This is also the better of the two places with regard to the sack of the Acropolis as described by Herodotus VIII, 53; see *scholion* to Demosthenes XIX, 303; Plutarch, *Alcibiades* XV, 4; Pollux VIII, 105; see also J. Travlos, *Pictorial Dictionary of Ancient Athens* (London 1971) p. 8, fig. 5, no. 11, and p. 72.

lower city (ἐς τὰ κάτω τῆς πόλεως) where he sees the sanctuary of Sarapis and a temple of Eileithyia, finally coming (I, 18, 6) to the Hadrianic gate near the Olympieion (fig. 1, K). Of these points, only the Olympieion entrance can be fixed with absolute certainty. On the other hand, there are some indications of the general area for the other points. An inscribed base of Roman times found near the Metropolis church (fig. 1, B) once carried a dedication to Eileithyia.[23] In the foundations of the same church was built another inscribed block concerning the cult of Isis and Sarapis.[24] Thus these two sanctuaries ought to be somewhere in the vicinity of this church, but other dedications to the Egyptian deities have been discovered in disparate directions. One of these was recently found at 4 Xenophon Street (fig. 1, F),[25] another was discovered much earlier near the south end of the Stoa of Attalos,[26] while a third was brought to light more than a century ago in the since-destroyed church of St. John Mankoutes (fig. 1, C).[27] These discoveries can obviously be used only as a general indication of the topographical situation of the Sarapeion.

Pausanias next retraces his steps to the prytaneion and starts out from it again, this time following the Street of the Tripods around the eastern foot of the Acropolis to the Theater of Dionysos. Here the topography is more secure since it has been shown that modern Tripod Street, at least for part of its length, follows the ancient route of the street of the same name. This route can be traced northwest from the monument of Lysikrates (fig. 1, G) to the foundations of another choregic monument discovered in the basement of 34 Tripod Street (fig. 1, H).[28] Beyond this point the course of the ancient street cannot

23 *IG* II², 4669.

24 *IG* II², 3565.

25 *ΑΡΧΑΙΟΛΟΓΙΚΟΝ ΔΕΛΤΙΟΝ* 20 (1965) *ΧΡΟΝΙΚΑ* 97.

26 *IG* II², 1612.

27 *IG* II², 4693. The presentation of inscriptions related to Sarapis is not intended to be exhaustive, but rather to show the dispersed area of their discovery places. For a fuller discussion of these, see R. E. Wycherley, "Pausanias at Athens II," *Greek, Roman, and Byzantine Studies* 4 (1963) 161–162. Travlos, *op. cit.* (note 22) 28, would place the Sarapeion in the area east of the Roman marketplace. Somewhere in the general vicinity of the "Diogeneion" (fig. 1, D) would not be too far wrong.

28 See Miller, *op. cit.* (note 17) 223–227.

be followed so certainly, but it does not seem unreasonable to suppose that it nearly followed the contours of the foot of the Acropolis, especially since it is said that the ancient Street of the Tripods was a favorite place for the promenades of fashionable Athenian youths, which suggests a nearly level road.[29] Following the contour of the slope toward the west, one comes out at about the southern side of the Eleusinion (fig. 1, E) where Travlos believes the Street of the Tripods joined the Panathenaic Way.[30]

Where along this street did the prytaneion lie? Travlos puts the building just off the Panathenaic Way east of the Eleusinion (fig. 1, P), but this does not accord well with the path of Pausanias. Coming through the agora to the Eleusinion (I, 14, 1), Pausanias then retreats to the Hephaisteion (I, 14, 6), and comes once more through the agora, exiting this time and passing the Gymnasion of Ptolemy,[31] the sanctuary of Theseus and that of the Dioskouroi (I, 17, 2 and 18, 1), before arriving at the Aglaurion (I, 18, 2). All these buildings are to be sought in the area between the Greek and Roman agoras and south of the latter. Since there must have been space for Pausanias to pass behind, or east of, the Eleusinion on his way to the Aglaurion, the buildings which he mentions must have stood east of the Eleusinion, and the prytaneion must be sought still farther to the east.

We are, then, in an area indicated long ago by Curtius (fig. 1,

29 Athenaeus XII, 542 f.

30 J. Travlos, *ΠΟΛΕΟΔΟΜΙΚΗ ΕΞΕΛΕΞΙΣ ΤΩΝ ΑΘΗΝΩΝ* (Athens 1960) 28, 106, 126, and fig. 7. Travlos, noting the two streets above and below the Eleusinion, chose the upper to represent the western end of the Street of the Tripods and thus located the prytaneion as one sees in fig. 1, P. However, neither of these two streets precisely follows the same contour line as the eastern part of the Street of the Tripods. Realizing this, Travlos has now, *op. cit.* (note 22) 1 and fig. 5, ingeniously hypothesized that these two streets represent the upper and lower forks of the Street of the Tripods which split apart to pass around the Eleusinion. His location of the prytaneion is now, therefore, slightly north of the earlier position.

31 It was once suggested that the Gymnasion of Ptolemy was located along the southern side of the agora; see H. A. Thompson, *Hesperia* 35 (1966) 40–43. This identification was never secure, however, and has now been repudiated by its author in *Agora* XIV 66, note 179. Travlos, *op. cit.* (note 22) 579, has suggested that the Gymnasion of Ptolemy be sought in the area east of the Roman marketplace.

O), which is close to the present 20 Tripod Street (fig. 1, J) where the inscription noted above (A 209) was found.[32] Although the north–south limits of the area of the prytaneion can be tied closely to the line of the Street of the Tripods, the east–west limits cannot be fixed so precisely. There is certainly justification for placing the prytaneion further east than Travlos, and perhaps even further east than Curtius did. The western end of the line of the Street of the Tripods will have been near the Eleusinion as Travlos maintains. The prytaneion, however, can be anywhere east of the Eleusinion with the choregic monuments beginning at the prytaneion and the name of the street changing at that point to the Street of the Tripods.

Identification of the Remains of the Prytaneion

Beginning in the early nineteenth century various scholars have attempted to identify different ancient Athenian remains as the prytaneion. Baron von Stackelberg, visiting Athens around 1810, drew a marble throne which he described as then standing on the site of the prytaneion.[33] Unfortunately, one knows neither what von Stackelberg had in mind as the site of the prytaneion, nor his reasons for so identifying the place where he saw the throne.[34]

32 E. Curtius, *Text der Karten zur Topographie von Athen* (Göttingen 1868) figure facing p. 55.

33 Baron von Stackelberg, *Die Gräber der Hellenen* (Berlin 1837) 33–35. This is the "Broomhall Throne" which is now in the J. Paul Getty Museum and which has been studied by C. Seltman, "Two Athenian Marble Thrones," *JHS* 67 (1947) 22–27, and most recently by J. Frel, forthcoming in *Ath. Mitt.* Von Stackelberg, publishing years after his visit to Greece, was unintentionally inaccurate when he discussed the throne: "*welche in Athen am Platze des ehemaligen Prytaneums stand, und sich wahrscheinlich jetzt noch dort befindet.*" We know that this throne left Greece nearly twenty years before von Stackelberg's publication; see A. H. Smith, "Lord Elgin and his Collection," *JHS* 36 (1916) 286, 294, and note 24.

34 Nor does one know why A. Michaelis, "Ancient Marbles in Great Britain," *JHS* 5 (1884) 146–148, calls this the site of the old Metropolis (fig. 1, B). That church is much too far north and too low on the slope for the location of the prytaneion, and if Michaelis was correct in his knowledge of the provenience of the throne, then von Stackelberg was simply mistaken about the site of the prytaneion. The error could have arisen from the portrayal in low relief on

The early epigraphist Pittakes held a life-long conviction that he had recognized the site of the Athenian prytaneion. Formulated at least by 1835,[35] this identification was repeatedly used by Pittakes as a reference point for the proveniences of various inscriptions,[36] but he envisaged an enormous structure which included the sites of the churches of Sts. John, Demetrios Katephoroi, Constantine, Panaghia Chryssocastrotissa, Theodore, Spyridon, and John Mankoutes. This is an area from a line drawn from O to D on figure 1, and including everything for about two city blocks to the north. In the autumn of 1857, the Greek government purchased a house at the eastern end of this area and excavated beneath it. This area is now known as the Diogeneion (fig. 1, D), but Pittakes always called it the prytaneion. If Pittakes had any evidence for this identification he never presented it, and the area he indicated is too far north and too low on the slope for the site of the prytaneion. Furthermore, Pittakes flatly contradicted the evidence of Pausanias when he identified the site of the Sarapeion with the church of St. Constantine which is the southernmost, or uphill limit of his prytaneion.[37] Pausanias clearly states that the Sarapeion lay below, or downhill from, the prytaneion (A 221).[38]

In the second edition of his *Topography of Athens*, Colonel Leake wrote: "recent excavations (in 1835) in building a house

---

one side of the throne of the tyrannicides whose descendants had Sitesis in the prytaneion (A 26, 70, 150).

It is reported (by Dr. Frel whom I thank for the information) that L. Beschi has discovered notes by Fauvel which would place the throne in the late eighteenth century at the Russian Church where other antiquities (including another throne) are now collected; see J. Lynch, *Aristotle's School* (Berkeley 1972) 17–21. If this is where von Stackelberg saw the throne, still he was mistaken about the site of the prytaneion, for the Russian Church lies outside the city walls of ancient Athens.

35 K. S. Pittakes, *L'ancienne Athènes* (Athens 1835) 131–139.

36 E.g., *'Εφημερὶς Ἀρχαιολογική* 1837–1861, nos. 285, 317, 631, 1464.

37 K. S. Pittakes, *'Εφημερὶς Ἀρχαιολογική* 1853, no. 1813.

38 Pittakes, *'Εφημερὶς Ἀρχαιολογική* no. 2595, note 1, and *op. cit.* (note 35) 133, further confused the issue by distinguishing another older prytaneion which lay further to the east. He maintained that this building was destroyed by an earthquake in the sixth year of the Peloponnesian War. This can only be based, although Pittakes nowhere cited his evidence, on the reference by Thucydides (A 384) to the earthquake which damaged the prytaneion at Peparethos, not at Athens.

adjacent to the church [Panaghia Vlastiki, fig. 1, Q] discovered some massive foundations, possibly those of the prytaneion."[39] This is in the region where it seems the prytaneion ought to be sought, but it is clear from his text that Leake called these remains the prytaneion because he, too, believed that the prytaneion had been in this area, not because there was found any objective material for identification in the excavations of the house.

Finally, at mid-century, Bötticher identified the prytaneion site with two rock cuttings which were visible to him.[40] These ran from northwest to southeast in the area between the churches of St. Soter and St. Simon, and at the rear of the chapel of St. Nicholas (fig. 1, R). These cuttings are no longer visible and Bötticher had no evidence for associating them with the prytaneion. Furthermore, the placement of the prytaneion in the area indicated by Bötticher is much too high above the level of the Street of the Tripods.

There are, then, no extant remains which can be identified with the Athenian prytaneion.[41] Nor can its probable form be suggested at this point in the development of our discussion. An inventory of the material objects known to have been in the prytaneion can, however, be presented. (The eventual discovery of architectural remains in association with any or all of these objects would, of course, help to identify the prytaneion of the Athenians.) First of all, the hearth of Hestia ought to be found in any prytaneion. The discovery of traces of couches and tables is likewise to be assumed, especially since Herodotus (A 15) specifically attests their presence in the Athenian prytaneion. Other uniquely Athenian discoveries should help to pinpoint the site of the building. While it is too much to hope that any remains should survive of the κύρβεις or ἄξονες (A 25, 190, 211, 221, 231), there is certainly the possibility that more durable objects might be found. These include the

39 W. M. Leake, *The Topography of Athens*[2] (London 1841) 270, note 1.

40 K. Bötticher, "Untersuchungen auf der Akropolis von Athen," *Philologus* Suppl. III (1863) 359–360.

41 The most recent attempt, to my knowledge, to identify any ancient remains as the prytaneion was by T. L. Shear in *Hesperia* 7 (1938) 328–329. Upon closer examination, these remains proved to belong to the Eleusinion; see H. A. Thompson, *Hesperia* 29 (1960) 334–338, and *Agora* XIV 150–155.

numerous statues which existed in the Athenian prytaneion (A 173, 221, 225, 236, 237, 262), as well as that of Agathe Tyche which stood in front of the building (A 238).

One can also estimate the age of the remains to be found on the site. It has been suggested that the building will have existed in the indicated area at least by the sixth century B.C. (see note 4 above), but the building may have been even older, for there are indications of a tie between the prytaneion and the inception of an aristocratic oligarchy in Athens. These indications are embedded in the several offices which Aristotle connects with what he terms the "oligarchic constitution": the Archon Basileus, Polemarch, Archon, and the Thesmothetai.[42] Another office, that of the Phylobasileis, is also mentioned by Aristotle as being equally venerable.[43] When did these offices arise? That is, when did the oligarchic aristocracy come into power? Questions such as these can be answered with neither precision nor security, but if one accepts the canonical date of 621 B.C. for the legislation of Draco, these institutions must have arisen in the eighth or early seventh century, for Aristotle regards them as a part of the constitution before the time of Draco.[44] Of significance for our purposes is that three of the offices mentioned were located in the three buildings which were situated on the northern slopes of the Acropolis: the Archon Basileus in the Boukoleion, the Phylobasileis in the Basileion, and the Archon in the prytaneion (see above, pp. 44–45 with notes 16 and 18). If these offices are correctly dated to the eighth or early seventh century, the earliest form of the buildings might likewise belong to this period.

There is no proof for this dating of the prytaneion and its neighbors, and the contention is obviously tenuous, but such a chronological point would accord with the archaeological evidence. This evidence is clearly not yet complete, but excavations in the Athenian agora have revealed what one may call the "direction of Athenian settlement." By this I mean the new

42 Aristotle, *Ath. Pol.* III, 2–3. The following argument assumes a basic historical accuracy by Aristotle.

43 *Ibid.* XLI, 2. Although there may be some hesitation in assigning a time for the inception of the Phylobasileis relative to the other offices mentioned, the antiquity of the former is assured by Aristotle.

44 *Ibid.* III, 1: *ἦν δ' ἡ τάξις τῆς ἀρχαίας πολιτείας τῆς πρὸ Δράκοντος τοιάδε.*

areas of expansion during the growth of Athens toward the end of the Dark Ages. These areas can be measured and defined by the presence of traces of habitation as opposed to graves. Thus it is not fortuitous that the earliest physical remains of a house in the agora area belong to the second half of the eighth century,[45] for it is just at this time that there is a push of settlement into the area north of the Acropolis and the Areopagus. This push is not immediate, but is rather the culmination of a gradual build-up of population pressure in the area, the evidence for which comes in the increasing ratio of wells (representing habitation) to graves with the passage of time.[46] The steady trend toward the settlement of the area north of the Acropolis and Areopagus is clear, and the use of this area by the late Geometric period (the mid-eighth century) is obviously turning from the funereal to the domestic.

It seems eminently reasonable that it was during this period of expansion that a cluster of buildings—Boukoleion, Basileion, and prytaneion—was established on the north slope of the Acropolis. The reason for this population expansion will have been the synoecism of Attica, as Thucydides (II, 18, 2–3) clearly implies, as well as an increasing prosperity.[47] The reason for the establishment of the prytaneion will have been the constitutional swing away from smaller "royally" governed units to the larger but oligarchic union of Attica. It might be wondered if the original prytaneis were not unlike feudal barons, brought together for mutual consultation in one building—the prytaneion.

If it is to be expected that the remains of the original prytaneion will go back to the late Geometric period, it can be

45 D. Burr, "A Geometric House and a Proto-Attic Votive Deposit," *Hesperia* 2 (1933) 542–551.

46 These wells-to-graves ratios, based on the map in E. Brann, *The Athenian Agora VIII: Late Geometric and Protoattic Pottery* (Princeton 1962) plate 45, are: Submycenaean, 2:14 or 12.5%; Protogeometric, 9:30 or 23%; Early Geometric, 3:5 or 37.5%; Middle Geometric, 7:11 or 38.9%; Late Geometric, 17:16 or 51.5%; Protoattic, 9:2 or 81.2%; Black Figure, 15:0 or 100%. Note the slow but uninterrupted progression.

47 The suggested dating of the synoecism of Attica, and thus of the prytaneion to the eighth century implies no date for Theseus. If Theseus existed, when Theseus existed, and whether Theseus effected the synoecism of Attica are questions irrelevant to our discussion.

definitely stated that the latest remains will be at least as late as the third century A.D. (A 239). The building may have been destroyed by the Herulian invasion of Athens in A.D. 267, for the only references to the prytaneion at Athens after this date are those of scholiasts and lexicographers (A 241 ff.). It is also possible that the prytaneion suffered during the sack of Athens by Sulla in 86 B.C. The evidence for such damage comes from the passage of Plutarch (A 206) where he states that the sacred lamp was extinguished during the tyranny of Aristion. This is hardly sufficient evidence to claim Sullan damages to the prytaneion, but it is interesting that the ephebes, who had sacrificed regularly in the prytaneion during the late second century B.C. (A 195–202), did not sacrifice there for a time shortly after the Sullan sack of Athens.[48] The reason for this might very well have been that the prytaneion was out of service due to the raid. If so, archaeological evidence will be found on the site.

The Athenian Tholos

Architecture and Date

Originally, the tholos was a simple circular building with an inside diameter of 16.90 meters.[49] There was a door of indeterminable width opening toward the agora on the east, and six columns within the structure. These columns were spaced in two clumps of three, one to the west and one to the east side of the north–south axis of the tholos (fig. 2). The pavement at that time was a hard-packed brown clay which sloped downward toward a drain at the east. The roof originally consisted of a very interesting, if difficult to reconstruct, combination of triangular and diamond-shaped terracotta tiles.

The kitchen was a less well-built structure on the northern side of the tholos. Although at times the kitchen assumed various shapes, there seems to have been a continuity of activity in this area, during the whole life of the tholos, where food was prepared for the prytaneis and the aeisitoi.

48 E.g., in 79/8 B.C.; see *SEG* XXII, 110.

49 H. A. Thompson, "The Tholos and its Predecessors," *Hesperia* Suppl. IV (1940) 45 ff., is the basic source for the whole of the discussion concerning the actual remains of the tholos and the surrounding structures. Only points of especial interest will be further footnoted. For the *testimonia* relating to the tholos, see *Agora* III 179–184.

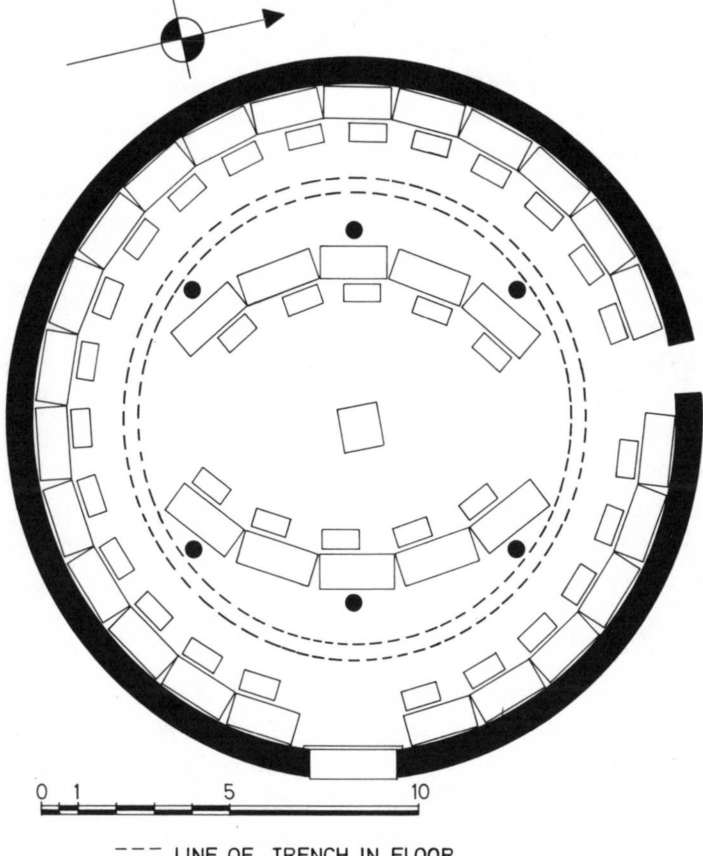

FIGURE 2. The Athenian tholos with couches restored.

With the identification of this area as a kitchen, and on the assumption of the desirability of easy communication between the two areas, a door has been restored on the north side of the tholos. Although the wall of the tholos is not preserved to a height sufficient to prove the presence of a door in this area,[50] the principal north–south axis of the building, as revealed by the arrangement of the interior columns, argues for an entrance along this axis. Moreover, a door to the north would be convenient for access to both the kitchen area and the Bouleuterion. Thus, the steps approaching the porch of the Bouleuterion extend almost up to the tholos and provide an easy means of

50 Thompson, *op. cit.* 56, 73, and fig. 56.

communication for the prytaneis from the north door of the tholos to the Bouleuterion.

Built in the period between the Persian sack of Athens and 460 B.C., the tholos retained the essential features described above throughout antiquity although various vicissitudes necessitated repairs and remodeling from time to time. Among these should be noted the destruction of the terracotta roof by fire at the end of the fifth century B.C. and its replacement, possibly by a bronze covering; the addition of a porch to the east façade in the time of Augustus; the laying of a mosaic floor in the mid-first century A.D.; and the replacement of this floor by another of marble slabs about a century later. When this latter floor was installed, the interior columns were removed from the tholos. After this time the tholos was almost certainly covered by a dome. Disturbed by the Herulian sack of Athens in the third century A.D., the tholos seems to have continued in use into the fifth century when it fell into complete disuse.

Function and Equipment

One of the functions of the tholos, or the Skias as it was called in official parlance, was that of storehouse. Here were kept small statues of silver[51] and weights and measures[52] of which several examples, marked *ΔΗΜΟΣΙΟΝ*, have been found in the area of the tholos.[53] Various religious activities went on there too, either in the tholos proper or in the surrounding area. Frequently attested, but enigmatic, are the Phosphoroi, connected to the tholos by their priest whose title was "*ἐπὶ Σκιάδος*."[54] This connection between the Phosphoroi and the tholos brings other religious celebrations to the area, for the prytaneis are attested as sacrificing to "Apollo Prostaterios and Artemis Boulaia and the other gods for whom it is customary, and they sacrificed to . . . [?] . . . and to Artemis Phosphoros and to Athena . . . ."[55] Thus a certain amount of religious activity, albeit with political overtones, has to be reckoned with in the area of the tholos. In this context there should be noted the

51 Pausanias I, 5, 1.

52 *IG* II², 1013, 37 ff.

53 Thompson, *op. cit.* (note 49) 141–142.

54 *IG* II², 1795, 51–52; cf. *IG* II², 1796 and 1798.

55 *IG* II², 902, 6–8; cf. *Hesperia* 26 (1957) 66–67.

fragment of a stone base found in the Hellenistic levels in the center of the tholos. This base is restored in figure 2 and while it was found obliquely oriented with respect to the axes of the tholos, and while evidence for its specific nature is lacking, it is most easily imagined as the base of an altar.[56] It is striking to note the relationship of the orientation of the base with the position of the restored north door. One is tempted to think, as already mentioned, that the north door provided communication not only for servants between tholos and kitchen, but also for prytaneis between tholos and Bouleuterion. The altar in the center of the tholos would have directly confronted prytaneis entering from the Bouleuterion.[57]

None of these uses of the tholos is as well documented as that of dining. This function is both mentioned by numerous sources[58] and presupposed by certain other evidence. Hesychios defines the tholos as, among other things, "the place in which the drinking-party vessels are kept" (. . . *τόπος, ἐν ᾧ τὰ συμποτικὰ σκεύη ἀποκεῖται*). From an inscription found within the tholos area[59] comes mention of just such vessels (*κοτυλίδα, ποτήρια*) as well as tripods and phialai which were being stored in the Skias. These are the sort of objects which are to be expected in an area used for dining, and the excavations complement our knowledge in this respect. In the tholos were discovered kylikes, kantharoi, skyphoi, and kotylai, as well as flatter shapes of pottery, mostly of plain black glaze.[60]

In any area where dining is known to have taken place, there are to be expected not only table utensils, but also couches upon which the diners reclined. The same inscription which lists the tripods, cups, etc. (note 59), also mentions couch-covers or mattresses (*στρώματα*) in the Skias. While it can be assumed that these were used on couches, there are no remains of the couches

56 So suggested by Thompson, *op. cit.* (note 49) 47; cf. *Agora* XIV 43.

57 This was not, however, the altar of Artemis Boulaia which would have been outside the tholos, although still in the vicinity. An inscription which was to be set up "in the agora by the altar of Artemis Boulaia," *Hesperia* 6 (1937) 448, indicates a separate existence for her altar. It is, of course, possible that the prytaneis did perform all their sacrifices, not just those to Artemis Boulaia, outside the tholos proper in the surrounding precinct.

58 E.g., Pollux VIII, 155; Suda, *s.v.* *θόλος*; Aristotle, *Ath. Pol.* XLIII, 3.

59 Agora Inv. no. I 5344; see Thompson, *op. cit.* (note 49) 145.

60 *Ibid.* 126 ff.

themselves or indications of their position in the building. This question of the number and position of the couches is of importance since it is only in the Athenian tholos that the number of daily diners can be determined. This number is a minimum of fifty-six and a maximum of sixty-two: that is, the fifty monthly prytaneis plus the aeisitoi (see chapter one, p. 9 and note 11) the number of which varied from six to twelve throughout the late Classical and Hellenistic periods.

Allowing for considerations of doors, traffic of prytaneis and servants, columns, and the like, I have not been able to find any reasonable arrangement of couches and tables which approaches the necessary number, and only a very few more than the thirty-four couch-table units shown in figure 2 can be fitted into the area of the tholos. In fact, there may have been even fewer since the central area of the tholos might not have had any couches.[61] The probable accuracy of the arrangement of the couches around the circumference of the tholos is shown, however, both by analogy to the normal lining of couches within the perimeter of rooms,[62] and by the fourth century

61 My arrangement of couches in the center of the tholos (fig. 2) is completely arbitrary. J. Travlos, *op. cit.* (note 22) fig. 693, doubts that there were ever any couches in the middle of the building, and he may be correct if one believes that the statuettes and weights and measures were kept in this area, or that some of the sacrifices mentioned above were performed there.

62 Twenty-five standard-size couches fit precisely around the interior of the tholos from the left to the right side of the east door. The north door, the position of which was restored without consideration of couch dimensions, coincides exactly with the position of one couch. The coincidence is striking and tends to confirm the restoration. For a discussion of couches lining the circumference of another circular room, see S. G. Miller, "Round Pegs in Square Holes," *AJA* 76 (1972) 78–79.

J. S. Boersma, *Athenian Building Policy from 561/0 to 405/4 B.C.* (Groningen 1970) 54–55, 212, has presented two restorations of couches in the tholos, one for dining, one for assemblies. His restorations claim to take account of, first, a need for quick change from dining to assembly activities in the tholos, and second, the irregular arrangement of the interior columns. By arranging the couches in a "meander" from wall to column and back again, Boersma does not abide by the mathematical principles outlined in Appendix B which, it seems to me, must be followed. Boersma fails to show that the irregular spacing of the columns was caused by demands of couch arrangement. Couches cannot be arranged to fit irregularities in a building without first showing that the irregularities were caused by the use of a predetermined couch size in planning the structure. If the principles are not followed, then one can restore couches in any fashion and in any building which one desires.

B.C. trench in the floor of the tholos discovered by the excavators. This trench describes a concentric circle about 2.40 meters in from the wall. It was filled with refuse typical of dining activities[63] and its distance from the wall is sufficient for couches, tables, and access space.

The conclusion, therefore, must be either that dining in the tholos was done in shifts, or else that it was not done on couches. Even if the latter were true, which is highly unlikely considering the normal Greek dining custom, couches must still have been brought into the tholos daily since some of the prytaneis slept there every night.[64] Moreover, in the absence of couches, the mention of *στρώματα* in the inscription noted above (note 59) would have to refer to something other than the usual meaning of couch-cover or mattress.

If it is necessary to conclude that dining was done in shifts, it must also be noted that meetings of the prytaneis as a political body probably did not take place in the tholos. The Bouleuterion was close at hand for such purposes, and there is no evidence for such meetings in the tholos. A passage from Aristotle, although not compelling, would seem to indicate that the prytaneis did no business whatsoever in the tholos: "Those among them [the Boule] who are prytanizing first eat together in the tholos, getting money from the city, then they assemble the Boule and the Demos."[65] Indeed, one never hears of the tholos as a place of explicitly political activity, and the prytaneis had their own "office space" reserved within the Bouleuterion.[66]

The validity of the arrangement and the number of couches restored in figure 2 is partly substantiated by Aristotle, who

---

Furthermore, it is nowhere attested that the prytaneis ever met within the tholos to conduct business. As evidence for his assembly arrangement of couches, Boersma can cite only Plato, *Apology* 32c–d, but does not note that the reference is to the Thirty Tyrants, not to the fifty prytaneis (see below, p. 60). Finally, Boersma's restoration of couches ignores the presence of the trench in the floor of the tholos to be discussed below.

63 Thompson, *op. cit.* (note 49) 60–61.

64 Aristotle, *Ath. Pol.* XLIV, 1.

65 *Ibid.* XLIII, 3: *οἱ δὲ πρυτανεύοντες αὐτῶν πρῶτον μὲν συσσιτοῦσιν ἐν τῇ θόλῳ, λαμβάνοντες ἀργύριον παρὰ τῆς πόλεως, ἔπειτα συνάγουσιν καὶ τὴν βουλὴν καὶ τὸν δῆμον.*

66 Lysias XIII, 37.

relates that every night the epistates for the day was to select a trittys of the prytany in office at that time to spend the night in the tholos, apparently so that they would be on hand in case of emergency.[67] A "trittys" might be explicable in constitutional terms, but it is equally possible that the whole prytany did not sleep overnight in the tholos because there was not enough room.[68] In fact, if the aeisitoi also spent the night in the tholos—and surely some of them, such as the herald, would have been as necessary as the prytaneis in an emergency—one can understand why the fraction of the prytany which slept in the tholos was one trittys. Any higher proportion could not have been accommodated. That the Thirty Tyrants could carry on business in the tholos in 404 B.C. means only that they were a small enough group to be accommodated by the building while the larger group of the prytaneis could not.[69]

Relevance of the Tholos to Prytaneia

There are many differences between the functions of the tholos and those of a prytaneion. For example, there is no evidence of a cult or a hearth of Hestia in the tholos,[70] and the entertainment of state guests as opposed to civil authorities is not attested

67 Aristotle, *Ath. Pol.* XLIV, 1. Although C. W. J. Eliot, "Aristotle Ath. Pol. 44.1 and the Meaning of Trittys," *Phoenix* 21 (1967) 79–84, believes that the τριττὺν τῶν πρυτάνεων of Aristotle refers to the political entity known as a trittys and not to the fraction $\frac{1}{3}$, the fact remains for us that the tholos would never have had to accommodate more than twenty-seven prytaneis for sleeping plus, probably, the aeisitoi. This number (27) is, according to Eliot, the maximum number of prytaneis which has been observed to be from any one political trittys in the prytanizing tribe during the fourth century B.C. See P. J. Rhodes, *The Athenian Boule* (Oxford 1972) 24–25.

68 Implicit in this discussion is the suggestion that the prytaneis did not originally stay overnight in the tholos. Although it was a feature of the constitution in Aristotle's day for a trittys of the prytaneis to sleep in the tholos, it seems to have been an extraordinary event in 415 B.C. (Andocides I, 45) when the prytaneis spent the night in the tholos. This means that the tholos was not built for sleeping purposes, and that the size of the building placed a restriction on the size of a group sleeping there. The constitutional fraction (a trittys) will have been a consequence of the pre-existing architectural form.

69 Plato, *Apology* 32c–d.

70 The hearth of Hestia Boulaia is to be found in the Bouleuterion; Aeschines, *De falsa legatione* 45; *Hesperia* 12 (1943) 64–66; Diodorus Siculus XIV, 5, 3; *et al.* See Rhodes, *op. cit.* (note 67) 33–34.

in the tholos before the third century A.D.[71] Just as their functions differed, so did the architectural forms of the tholos and a prytaneion.

The differences were not, however, more significant than the similarities. Both had a hestiatorion and a kitchen, and in some ways the precinct surrounding the tholos is like the courtyard of the prytaneion. It was in this area of the prytaneion that inscribed stelai were sometimes set up (A 331); and at Athens the tholos precinct yielded great quantities of inscriptions, many with the provision that they be set up in the prytanikon (*στῆσαι ἐν τῷ πρυτανικῶι*).[72] The tholos at Athens and the prytaneion elsewhere are also both close to the agora.

Perhaps the most basic question regarding the tholos is why the circular shape was chosen for the dining area of the Athenian prytaneis. If it is true that the Athenian prytaneion antedated the tholos and the agora as a center of Athenian political activity (see p. 53 above), there was an obvious necessity for the erection of a building nearer the Bouleuterion, and thus the agora, in the fifth century B.C. It was shown in chapter two that the generic form of the prytaneion elsewhere was certainly not round, and the assumption is justified that the same was true of the prytaneion in Athens, although the evidence of the building itself has not been found. If the Athenian prytaneion did not serve as the model for the tholos, it is fruitless to speculate on some other, unknown archetype for the building.[73]

71 A 236, 237. There may be an exception in *IG* II², 3735, when a Sophronistes of the Ephebes in the second century A.D. was "honored with a Herm and in the tholos" (---*τετειμη/μέννον Ἑρμᾷ καὶ ἐν τῇ / θόλῳ* . . .).

72 For the inscriptions see Dow, *Hesperia* Suppl. I, nos, 5, 20, 29, 30, 31, 37, *et al.* It was the preponderance of such decrees in the area of the tholos which led Vanderpool, *Hesperia* 4 (1935), to solve the confusion which exists in the later sources between tholos and prytaneion. F. Robert, *Thymélè* 123, expresses doubts about this identification of the prytanikon with the tholos precinct. While it is true that prytanikon inscriptions were found as far away as the Tower of the Winds, these were surface finds, and the concentration of excavated inscriptions which were to be set up in the prytanikon was in the tholos area. Moreover, the word coincides so well with the known purpose of the tholos and its precinct (i.e., a "prytaneion-annex") that there need be no hesitation in applying the name prytanikon to the area around the tholos. See *Agora* XIV 41–42.

73 Two possible prototypes for the tholos in the agora should, however, be mentioned, although there is no proven connection between either of them

On the other hand, the building must have been constructed at a time when its ultimate purpose was known and the design chosen intentionally even if the reasons for this choice are obscure to us. The size of the tholos will have been limited to less than the most desirable by structural problems of roof support over a large span. Its actual size may well have been determined by making the circumference large enough to hold couches for twenty-five, or half the prytaneis.

The Archaic "Prytaneion-Annex"

Before leaving the west side of the Athenian agora, two more buildings ought to be considered under the heading of prytanikon. These are, in chronological order (see fig. 3) the complex FGHIJ located beneath the tholos, and Building D under the Old Bouleuterion. It has been suggested that each of these buildings was at one time the predecessor of the tholos-prytanikon as a dining hall for the prytaneis.[74] Were this true, important implications for the genesis of the prytaneion form would emerge, since these buildings might reflect the form of the prytaneion on the north slope of the Acropolis. The sole basis of such an identification is, however, the assumption of a logical progression of buildings on the same site dedicated to the same purpose. Thus the Classical Bouleuterion was preceded by the Archaic Old Bouleuterion which was preceded in turn by Building C, or the "Primitive Bouleuterion." By an analogous theory the tholos would have been preceded by buildings D and FGHIJ.

It has been pointed out that such an assumption of orderly progression is not necessarily valid,[75] and that the buildings are

---

and the tholos. One is the orchestra, presumably of Archaic date, which is attested in the agora by Photios (*s.v.* Ὀρχήστρα). The other is a Persian tent suggested as the model for the tholos by D. B. Thompson, "The Persian Spoils in Athens," *The Aegean and the Near East, Studies Presented to Hetty Goldman* (Locust Valley, New York 1956) 282–283.

74 Thompson, *Hesperia* Suppl. IV 40–44. For Building FGHIJ, *ibid* 15–38; for Building D, *ibid.* 12–15, and H. A. Thompson, "Buildings on the West Side of the Agora," *Hesperia* 4 (1937) 122; see *Agora* XIV, 25–29, 42.

75 O. Broneer, review of Thompson's "Tholos and its Predecessors," in *AJA* 45 (1941) 128.

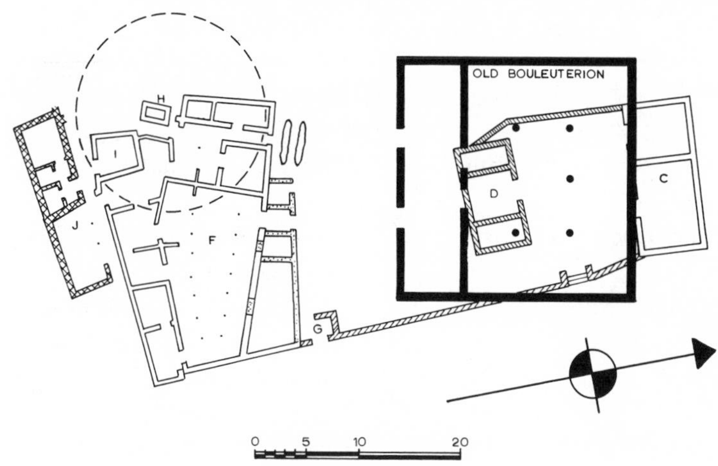

FIGURE 3. The structures beneath the Athenian tholos.

not at all well suited to the provision of prytaneion-like facilities for the prytaneis.

Table 1, along with the plan (fig. 3), elucidates a simple fact: Building F was constructed before Building D and lived on after it. Therefore, even if Building F was the Archaic "prytaneion-annex," Building D could not have been.

The other point which emerges from table 1 is that at the very time when the Old Bouleuterion was being constructed, the north side of Building F was destroyed. Building J, erected at the same time, may have been intended as a replacement for the northern part of Building F, but it seems strange that Building F should so suffer just at the time of the rejuvenated democracy if it had been intended as a prytaneion-annex.

The date of Building F seems secure as the decade following 550 B.C. This was a period of political instability which saw the

TABLE 1. Construction on West Side of Agora

First quarter sixth century B.C.	Building C constructed
550–540 B.C.	Building F constructed
Early third quarter sixth century B.C.	Building D constructed
Early fourth quarter sixth century B.C.	Building D demolished; Buildings C and F linked by wall
510–490 B.C.	Building C demolished; Old Bouleuterion constructed; Building F curtailed on north, but Building J added on south
479 B.C.	Building F reconstructed after the Persian sack
470–460 B.C.	Building F demolished; tholos constructed

final victory of Peisistratos. It is therefore a difficult period within which to imagine the construction of any building as politically significant as a prytaneion-annex. If the building is much later than 550 B.C. (i.e., 546/5 or later), it probably would not have been intended as a prytaneion-annex at all. Even if Peisistratos did not disturb the existing magistracies,[76] he cannot be expected to have constructed a building for the convenience of the prytaneis. Furthermore, there is no evidence as to when the prytaneis assumed their role as a standing committee for the Boule. If Solon did provide for such an arrangement, or if such a provision was made at any time before Kleisthenes, we hear nothing of it. The point is that, until the prytaneis became part of the Boule, there was no need for them to be located near the Bouleuterion.

On the other hand, the construction of Building F is better than a normal private dwelling, and the long wall which was built to connect Buildings F and C in the fourth quarter of the sixth century B.C. shows a close relationship existed between the buildings at that time, and marks off an area between them as reserved for special activities. Furthermore, the prompt reconstruction of Building F after the Persian Wars shows that

76 Herodotus I, 59, 6.

the structure was needed. The nature of that need is indicated by the immediate construction of the tholos over Building F when the latter was dismantled about a decade later. While Broneer (note 75) is correct in characterizing Building F as not well suited to the needs of the prytaneis, it may be hypothesized that Building F, of some different original designation, was taken over by the re-established democracy as a prytaneion-annex near the new center of the government.[77] That take over is represented archaeologically by the wall connecting Buildings F and C. This wall clearly delineated an area of the recently defined agora as being reserved for the future growth of the center of everyday Athenian politics.

The theory postulated above—that the prytaneis dined in shifts in the tholos—gains some force from the use of Building F by the prytaneis in the late Archaic period. There is no room in Building F which has sufficient space for all the prytaneis to dine together. This means that at least a generation of prytaneis had dined in smaller groups before the tholos was constructed.[78]

Conclusions

The examination of Athens with regard to the prytaneion and related buildings has yielded certain information which will be useful in identifying buildings at other sites. We have seen the

77 So suggested by Professor Thompson in a conversation, but he would identify the original purpose of Building F as a sort of Peisistratid townhouse; see *The Athenian Agora; A Guide*² (1962) 21. Boersma, *op. cit.* (note 62) has adopted this idea of the "House of Peisistratos" taken over by the prytaneis in 507 B.C. In *Agora* XIV, 28, the question of the original purpose of Building F is not treated, but the problem of pre-Kleisthenic prytaneis is finally realized. The existence of prytaneis much earlier in Athenian history can probably be taken for granted on analogy with, for example, the previous existence of archons. But when did the prytaneis become part of the constitutional scheme; when did they become a committee of the Boule? Since even the existence of a Boule before Kleisthenes is not secure, one cannot assume that there was a committee of prytaneis as a part of such an earlier Boule. The identification of Building F as originally intended for the use of the prytaneis in the 540's B.C. is, therefore, hypothetical and extremely dubious.

78 But Rhodes, *op. cit.* (note 67) 16–19, maintains that the prytaneis did not become a committee of the Boule until the time of Ephialtes and that the tholos is an architectural manifestation of that constitutional change. If this is correct, then the prytaneis were never housed in Building F, and Building F was neither designed nor ever used as a prytaneion-annex.

types of small objects, such as drinking and eating utensils, which should be found in prytaneia, and it has been shown that a prytaneion need not have had a dining room large enough to accommodate all the possible diners at one time. In cities where the prytaneion preceded the formal demarcation of the political agora, it has been noted that there may exist near the agora a prytanikon, or "prytaneion-annex," while the prytaneion itself could be situated at any distance from the agora. As a corollary to this, we have theorized that the prytaneion and its hearth remained at a fixed point throughout the life of a city, and it has been seen that no evidence exists at Athens to contradict this. Finally, it may be noted that while a prytaneion-like structure might be necessary to the functioning of a democracy, a prytaneion proper is not. It would appear that the prytaneion at Athens pre-dated the democracy there, but it is obvious that the democracy could function without the prytaneion itself. Thus a prytaneion may have existed in any city, regardless of the form of government of that city.

Plate 1

a. Delos: General view of the prytaneion from the south.

b. Delos: Room II with herm against line of north wall, from southeast.

c. Delos: Room II and northern closets, from southwest.

Plate 2
a. Delos: Stylobate of southern façade with dedicatory bases on steps, from east.

b. Delos: Columns and frieze blocks from southern façade, now lying in Room I.

c. Delos: Doric capitals from southern façade, now lying in Room I.

Plate 3

a. Delos: Bench supports in eastern end of Room I, from northwest.

b. Delos: Threshold block of door between Rooms III′ and III, from east.

c. Delos: Juncture of northwest corner of prytaneion with walls 1 and 2, from north.

Plate 4

a. Delos: Juncture of walls 1 and 2 with wall 3, from northwest.
b. Delos: Wall 4 passing beneath altar, from southwest.
c. Lato: General view of northern part of agora, from south. Great steps in center and prytaneion above.

Plate 5

a. Lato: Great steps from southeast with front wall of prytaneion at top and back wall of prytaneion above.
b. Lato: Stone border on east side of room 36 from south with threshold of door to Room 44 in foreground.
c. Lato: West side of Room 37 with steps and projections.

Plate 6

a. Lato: Room 36 with raised border in background and central stylobate in center, from southwest.
b. Lato: Room 37 with central hearth in foreground and door to Room 38 in upper right corner, from southeast.
c. Lato: Room 37 with central hearth in foreground, from northeast.

Plate 7

a. Dreros: General view of the building, from northeast.
b. Dreros: Room III, from east.
c. Dreros: Room IV, from east.

Plate 8

a. Dreros: Room V with wall B in left center, from northeast.
b. Dreros: Hearth in Room V.
c. Ephesos: Beginning of the *Clivus Sacer* with carved bases of processional arch on either side, from east.

Plate 9

a. Ephesos: Doric columns of portico, from south.

b. Ephesos: Part of north wall of portico, from south.

c. Ephesos: Entrance into Room II from Room I, from north.

Plate 10

a. Ephesos: Room III, from south.
b. Ephesos: Earlier square structure in center of Room III, from southwest.
c. Ephesos: Composite capital of northwestern column in Room III.

Plate 11

a. Ephesos: Southeast corner of east court with Odeion wall in left background, from north.

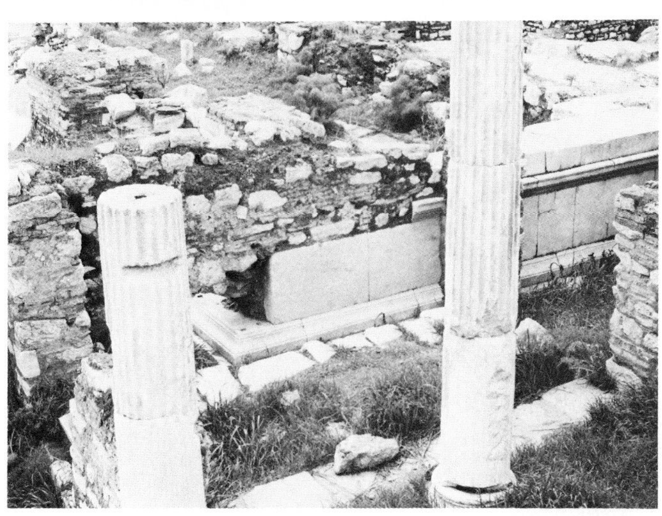

b. Ephesos: Northeast corner of altar (covered by later wall) in east court, from north.

c. Ephesos: Northeast corner of altar in east court with first step and western return of base moulding, from south.

Plate 12

a. Ephesos: Southwest corner of Room II, from northeast.
b. Ephesos: Ionic capital from east court peristyle.
c. Ephesos: Ionic column base from east court peristyle.

Plate 13

a. Kolophon: General view of agora, from south.

b. Kolophon: Area of building, from south. Arrow at central structure in east room.

c. Kolophon: Central structure in east room, from southwest.

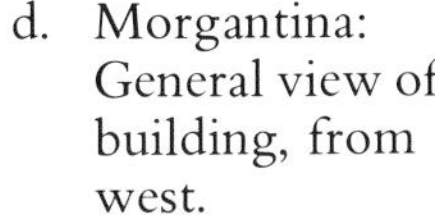

d. Morgantina: General view of building, from west.

Plate 14

a. Priene: Threshold block of door between building and Sacred Stoa, from east.
b. Priene: Doorway of Room V with Doric capital re-used as base for inscribed column at upper right, from south.
c. Priene: Juncture of northeast corner of the Sacred Stoa and bedrock cutting for east wall of building, from southeast.
d. Priene: Door from Room I to courtyard, from north.

Plate 15

a. Priene: Room III with bedrock floor on left, steps in doorway on right, from south.
b. Priene: Inscribed column in courtyard of building.
c. Priene: Bedrock hearth in Room VIII, from southwest.
d. Priene: Northwest corner of Room III and east wall of Ekklesiasterion, from southeast.

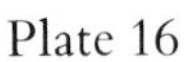

Plate 16

a. Priene: Water basin and trough in northwest corner of courtyard, from southeast.
b. Delphi: General view of Building XIV, from northwest.
c. Delphi: Juncture of north wall of Building XIV and peribolos wall, from south.
d. Megara Hyblaea: Eastern rooms of building, from southeast.

CHAPTER IV

Delos, Lato, and Olympia

THE purpose of this chapter is to examine the remains of the three excavated buildings which can be securely identified as prytaneia. The identification of these buildings is based on specific evidence, valid only for each individual building, without regard to more general considerations of architectural form or location. These buildings can, therefore, be studied and used as reference points to generate evidence for the identification criteria which we have developed from the *testimonia* and from analogies of function with the Athenian tholos. The result will be a more clearly defined idea of the generic form of the prytaneion as an architectural entity.

Delos

Location

The prytaneion of Delos lies about twenty meters southeast of the temple of Apollo.[1] The building faces south, however, away from the sanctuary, and its west and north walls are

1 For relevant *testimonia*, see (A 278–287). For all three buildings discussed in this chapter, see appropriate parts of the Site Bibliography. R. Étienne of the French Archaeological School in Athens is now undertaking a complete study of the Delian prytaneion. Hopefully his published results will be able to answer some of the questions raised in the following discussion.

shielded from the sacred area by a group of altars and the so-called bouleuterion, respectively. The façade of the building commands a moderately broad open area which contains the altar of Zeus Polieos and which is defined to the south and west by the rear walls of two stoas.[2]

The Remains

A rectangle measuring 15.12 × 25.78 meters, with its longitudinal axis running north–south, the building's state of preservation ranges from foundation courses in the southeast to a wall height of about one meter above the floor level in the northwest. The wall construction above floor level consists of a marble orthostate course whose visible surfaces are carefully worked and whose joints are regular and squared. The inner faces of the blocks in the core of the wall are very rough and irregular. This orthostate course is 0.31 to 0.35 meters high toward the interior of the building, while the corresponding course on the exterior is significantly higher, 0.38 to 0.41 meters. Above this course comes the typically Delian rough ashlar masonry of gneiss set back *ca.* 0.05 meters from the face of the lower marble course (pl. 1b). A rigid economy has been observed in the construction, for in those areas where the walls would not be visible (as behind the subsidiary rooms at the back of Room III, see pl. 1c) this marble course is absent and the gneiss walls begin directly above the foundations.

Room I.—This area (see fig. 4), best defined as a porch or vestibule, is 3.25 meters deep. Its southern wall forms the principal

2 See P. Bruneau and J. Ducat, *Guide de Délos* (Paris 1965) Plan I facing page 75. Only R. Vallois, *L'Architecture Hellénique et Hellénistique à Délos* I (Paris 1944) 172–175, provides any discussion of the architectural remains of the building. The only detailed plan of the building, drawn in 1910, was published by Vallois nearly half a century later: *Les Constructions Antique de Délos: Documents* (Paris 1953) pl. IV. Because certain details of construction and plan of the building ought to be better known, the discussion which follows gives considerable detail.

This same principle will be followed for other buildings presented in chapters four and five. Detailed presentations will be made whenever none is now available elsewhere. Measurements and observations which are not to be found in the cited sources will be based on visits to the various sites by W. A. McDonald in the early 1950's, and on visits from 1967 to 1970 by myself, during which measurements were checked and the accompanying photographs made.

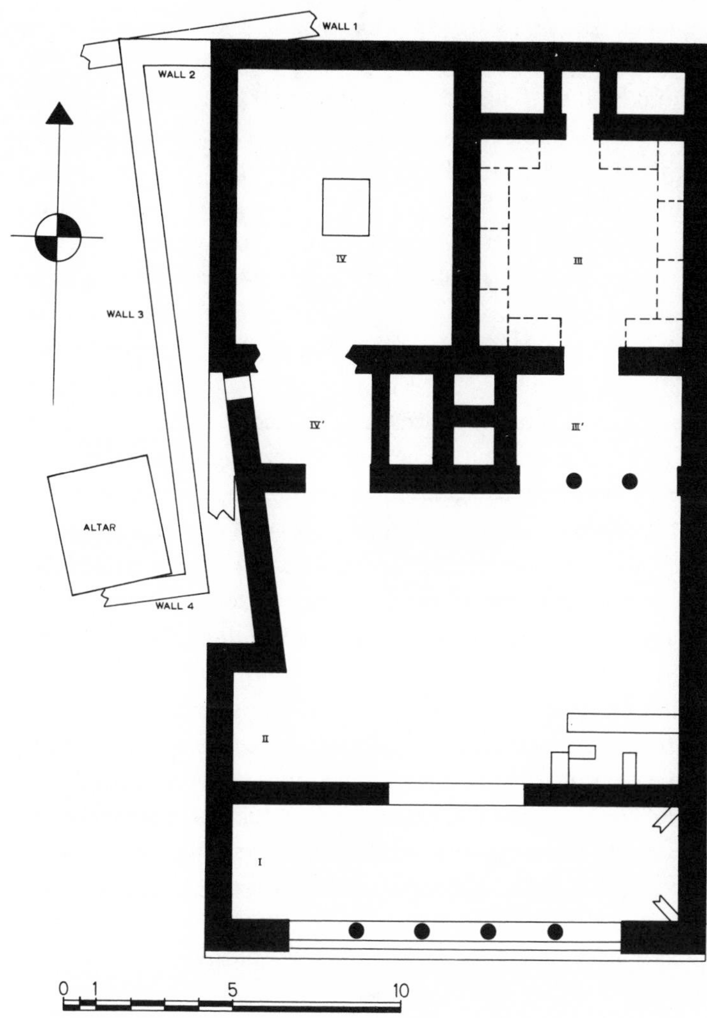

FIGURE 4. Plan of the prytaneion at Delos.

façade of the building, and is approached by a three-step krepidoma. Heavy spur walls from both ends give the whole a tetrastyle in-antis arrangement, although the spur walls are rather heavier than normal antae. In between these, and resting on the lower steps, there are now a series of eight bases which carried dedications by other cities[3] or by private citizens.[4] The

3 E.g., *IG* XI[4], 1132.
4 E.g., *IG* XI[4], 1171.

stylobate shows clearly the positions of four columns (pl. 2a) and several architectural members of the façade are now lying within Room I. These consist of several fragments of a triglyph-metope frieze, eight rather stylized Doric capitals, and fragments of three pseudo-Ionic columns (pls. 2b, 2c). That the column members belong together is shown by the fact that the preserved lower diameters of the columns match precisely the traces on the stylobate (0.375 meters in diameter), while their upper diameters (0.30 meters) and empolion cuttings match the lower surfaces of the capitals. The absence of fluting on the capitals below the echinus is another indication that the capitals and columns are to be associated.

In addition to these elements, another column shaft, of much smaller dimensions (0.24 meters top diameter; 0.28 meters bottom) was found in the building. Several inscriptions covered the surface of this column[5] and Vallois[6] associated with it three or four small capitals whose present location and precise identity I do not know. Using these, Vallois reconstructed a loggia over Room I with a balcony suspended, in cantilever fashion, and projecting past the lower colonnade by about 0.50 meters; that is, a projection of the loggia equalling the projection of the antae toward the south beyond the line of the stylobate (see fig. 4). Access to this loggia would have been by means of a stairway in Room II. The reasoning of Vallois is that there is no possible structural position for the inscribed column other than in an upper storey, and that there must have been a projecting balcony to enable access to all sides of the column for the inscriber and the readers of the texts.

This arrangement is not well documented, and is difficult to visualize. One would like to see the smaller capitals, or at least drawings of them, so as to study their profiles.[7] Of the eight capitals now lying in the building (pl. 2c), the seven well enough preserved to yield accurate measurements are nearly equal in size, and are certainly too large to be associated with the

5 *IG* XI², 105–108, 110, 111, 113; cf. R. Vallois, *L'Architecture Hellénique et Hellénistique à Délos* II (Paris 1966) 104–105.

6 *L'Architecture* I 173.

7 Vallois, *L'Architecture* II 103–105, gives their dimensions and later (p. 133) discusses their profiles which are, he claims, the same as the larger capitals of the façade.

inscribed column. Since four of these capitals belong to the southern façade of the prytaneion, there are four more which find no place in the reconstruction proposed by Vallois. One might wish to place them between Rooms I and II, but the remains in that area are too meager to provide evidence as to whether the line of division between the rooms was a wall or a stylobate. It will be seen that two of these capitals could belong to a small portico between Rooms II and III′.

One other feature can be assumed in Room I, although it is never mentioned and is now partially destroyed. On the 1910 plan of the actual state of the building (see note 2) there were present in the two eastern corners of Room I two marble slabs, set on end and placed diagonally out from the corners. These blocks, still near their original positions (although no longer *in situ*; see pl. 3a), served as the supports for a bench 0.64 meters wide which ran around the three sides of the small alcove formed here by the anta and the eastern exterior wall of the building.

Room II.—As one enters this room the most striking attribute is the tall herm which has been re-erected in the center of the northern side of the area (pl. 1b). In the southeast corner of the room are the scanty remains of what has been called a stairway foundation. Such an identification is based on the hypothetical existence of an upper storey over Room I, and while the dimensions of the remains (about 1.96 × 3.90 meters) are not unsuitable for a stairway, the foundations are too poorly preserved to justify any secure identification of their purpose.

Room II was originally paved with large slabs of gneiss, many of which remain in the northeast corner of the area, while a few similar pieces survive along the western wall. This paving, along with a drain in the southwest corner and the room's large area (7.83 × 13.65 meters), shows that the room was probably hypaethral. (The peculiar zig-zag of the western wall of Room II will be discussed below when we consider the history of the building.)

Rooms III′ and IV′.—These two areas will be discussed together because they performed the same function, and because the small, closet-like rooms between them are preserved only in their foundations. Thus the line of separation between

Rooms III′ and IV′ is unclear, as is the placement of doors into these "closets."

In spite of the similarity of function, differences do exist between the two rooms. In the southwest corner of Room III′ there is a marble herm base, and communication between Rooms II and III′ is by a distyle in-antis arrangement. The stylobate for this small portico still retains traces of the two columns which once rested upon it along with cuttings for a metal gate between them. The dimensions of the column traces (0.37–0.38 meters in diameter) are such that two of the four capitals left over from the southern façade of the building ought to belong here.

In Room IV′, on the other hand, a large threshold block indicates that the entrance here from Room II was different from that in Room III′. Not only are the cuttings in the threshold block suitable for a swinging door, but the block itself is a course higher than the level of the floor in Room II, whereas the block in the entrance of Room III′ has its upper surface at a height equal to the paving.

One other noteworthy feature exists in Room IV′. A door pivot and stop is cut into the upper surface of the northernmost exterior orthostate of the zig-zag section of the western wall. The pivot is 0.06 meters in diameter and the cutting for the stop indicates a door valve width of 0.67 meters. The narrowness of this door and its height above the floor (*ca.* 0.40 meters) show that this was a subsidiary door cut into the western wall sometime after the building was erected.

Room III.—This room was entered from Room III′ by a double door whose threshold block indicates a total door opening of 1.56 meters (pl. 3b). Although the sockets for the receipt of door pivots and the central door catch on the inside of the block are clear, the purpose of the two rows of three circular cuttings each—one row on the upper surface of the tread, the other on a lower lip on the south side of the block—is not. These holes are too small (0.04 meters in diameter) for normal door pivots, and are perhaps better seen as cuttings for metal grills which were in front of the doors.[8]

8 For details of a similar arrangement at Lykosura, see B. Leonardos, "*Λυκοσούρος Ψήφωμα,*" *'Εφημερὶς Ἀρχαιολογική* 1899, plate 3.

Room III is smaller than its western counterpart, Room IV, because of the construction along its northern side of three small "closets." Room III measures 6.47 × 5.88 meters, while the closets have a uniform depth of about two meters, including wall thickness. These closets were a part of the original construction as is shown not only by the bonding of their walls into the exterior walls of the building, but also by the fact that marble orthostates appear on their southern wall, thereby providing Room III with a wall surface like that of the other rooms of the building. Since the north wall of these closets does not possess these marble orthostates, this face of the wall was never visible from the main room (pl. 1c).

The central of the three closets was entered from Room III by a doorway 1.11 meters wide. The sill of this doorway is preserved and shows that the doorway was open, without a swinging door. Access to the two flanking chambers will have been from this central room, for the marble orthostates of the southern wall of the eastern closet are preserved in an unbroken line.

Room IV.—Measuring 7.93 × 6.55 meters, this room has its marble orthostate course preserved for the entire length of its northern and western sides (pl. 1b). The other two walls are preserved only in their foundations so that the position of the entrance into this room from Room IV′ can only be estimated. In the center of the room are the foundations of a structure of unknown shape, size, and function. Its identification as the hearth of Hestia[9] is dependent upon the identification of the whole building as a prytaneion.

Date

If little has been published about the building as an architectural entity, discussions of the evidence for its date do not exist. It is generally held that the original construction belongs to the end of the Archaic or the beginning of the Amphictyonic Period (the first decade following the Persian Wars), while repairs were effected at the end of the fourth century B.C.[10] The

9 Vallois, *L'Architecture* I 173; Bruneau and Ducat, *op. cit.* (note 2) 89.

10 Vallois, *L'Architecture* I 64, note 6, 109; H. Gallet de Santerre, *Délos Primitive et Archaïque* (Paris 1958) 298; Bruneau and Ducat, *op. cit.* (note 2) 88.

evidence for the latter date is epigraphical, for there are records of work done to the prytaneion at that time (A 278).

Lacking excavation reports, the only dating evidence available is the series of columns, capitals, and frieze blocks discussed above. All these elements indicate a Hellenistic date. The upper ends of the glyphs on the triglyphs are squared off in section, not undercut below the taenia as is common earlier. The column-capital mixture of pseudo-Ionic and Doric is anything but canonical for the Classical period, and the profiles of the capitals are certainly later than the Classical type. Vallois compares the latter, with reason, to three capitals from the Heraion at Olympia;[11] unfortunately, the Olympia examples are not dated.[12] However, if the smaller capitals which are associated with the inscribed column do in fact have the same profile as the capitals of the façade (as Vallois asserts, see note 7), they must all be from the late fourth or early third century B.C. at the latest. One of the inscriptions on the column records the acts of the archon of 284 B.C.[13] If this building is the prytaneion, as will be argued below, a late fourth century date for the capitals of the southern façade would agree very well with the recorded repairs to the south part of the prytaneion in the last years of the fourth century (A 278).

For the original construction date there is very little evidence. It is customary to term the structure late Archaic or early Classical, but no evidence has ever been presented to document such a contention. There is available, however, one vague indication of date. West of the building is a wall (fig. 4, wall 3) which runs obliquely to a north–south line and has an overall length of about 15.50 meters. This wall turns at a right angle to the west at its southern end (wall 4), and turns east at its northern end, thus forming a zig-zag. The northern arm has two periods of construction with a slightly different orientation for each. Wall 1 is oblique to the line of the north wall of the building,

11 *L'Architecture* II 133.

12 See F. Adler *et al.*, *Die Baudenkmäler von Olympia* II (Berlin 1892) pls. XXII, S3 and S4, XXIII, S11.

13 *IG* XI², 105. In fact, the whole series of archons listed in the inscriptions of this column belong to the first half of the third century B.C. Theoretically the capitals and columns could be much earlier, but stylistically they cannot be placed in the Classical period.

while wall 2 is a western extension of the line of the building's north wall (pl. 4a). The earlier wall 1 must pre-date the construction of the building, because the latter's northwest corner is built up against it. Wall 2, on the other hand, is constructed up against this same northwest corner of the building and consequently must post-date it (pl. 3c). The bonding of wall 3 into both walls 1 and 2 (at different levels) shows that wall 3 was both original to the period of wall 1, and later re-used in the period of wall 2. Wall 4, since it is bonded into wall 3 in its lower courses, likewise belongs to the earlier period. There is, then, the following relative chronology: (a) wall 1-3-4; (b) the building; (c) wall 2-3-4.

Wall 1-3-4 would give a *terminus post quem* for the building, but it has never been dated. Sometime after its original construction, wall 4 was cut off on the west by an altar.[14] This marble altar has foundations of large blocks of gneiss beneath which passes the lowest visible course of wall 4 from the earlier period (pl. 4b). The altar has been aptly compared to another altar at Delos which can be dated to the late sixth or early fifth century B.C.[15] This suggests that the altar west of wall 4 should be dated to about 500 B.C. and wall 1-3-4 sometime earlier. This obviously gives only the vaguest of dates for the building: later than a wall which is earlier than an altar of *ca.* 500 B.C. Since, however, wall 4 of wall 1-3-4 was encroached upon by the altar around 500 B.C., a similar date for the encroachment upon wall 1 by the construction of the building is at least possible, and may even be close to the true date.

An epigraphical reference of the late fourth century B.C. notes repairs to "the wall by the prytaneion" (A 278). If wall 1-3-4 is the wall indicated in the inscription, here is a possible explanation of the zig-zag in the west wall of the building. This zig-zag encroaching upon Rooms II and IV′ is not original to the construction, for there is still visible a part of the foundations of an earlier west wall which continued directly southwards

14 This altar is labeled 23B in the general plan of Delos in Bruneau and Ducat, *loc. cit.* (note 2).

15 This, the altar of Apollo Genitor, is situated northeast of the Agora of the Italians in front of the so-called Temple of Anios; see R. Vallois, *BCH* 53 (1929) 198–200; H. Gallet de Santerre, *BCH* 71–72 (1947–1948) 408, and *op. cit.* (note 10) 300.

from the start of the zig-zag of Room IV′ (fig. 4). The original western wall of the building was in a straight north–south line. One might, then, imagine the building (and the altar) as having been constructed at a time when wall 1-3-4 was in a ruinous condition. At a date in the late fourth century B.C. (i.e., the time of the inscription) it was decided to repair this wall. The reasons for such a decision after nearly two centuries of disuse are not clear, but the effect was to force a zig-zag into the western wall of the building to correspond with the zig-zag of the rebuilt wall 2-3-4.

Identification

Originally called a temple of Dionysos,[16] this building was first identified as a prytaneion by Roussel.[17] It has already been seen how well the contents of the "repair" inscription fit with the archaeological evidence for this building (A 278; cf. pp. 74–75). A dedication to Hestia made by the archon of 287/6 B.C. was discovered in the building.[18] The inscribed column which has been mentioned before contains an inventory of the table service which each archon received and then passed on to his successor (including such items as σκύφοι, κύαθοι, φιάλη, οἰνοχόη, etc.), and this is only one of a series of similar inventories found in this building.[19] These range from 268 to 170 B.C. While there is no mention of the physical location of any of the objects in the inventory of each archon, there is an inscription of 179 B.C. which specifically mentions silverware from the prytaneion (A 281). Furthermore, although some of these lists were found in places other than our building, the heaviest concentration of these lists was discovered in this building. Even if one assumes that the silverware handed from archon to archon was located in this building, it does not necessarily follow that this building has to be the prytaneion. However, it has been noted that such implements were appro-

16 E.g., by Bürchner, "Delos," *RE* IV (1901) 2468.

17 P. Roussel, *BCH* 35 (1911) 432, and *Délos Colonie Athénienne* (Paris 1916) 47, note 6, 221–222; see also F. Dürrbach, *IG* XI², page 1.

18 *IG* XI⁴, 1137. Four other dedications to Hestia (*IG* XI⁴, 1138–1141) may also have belonged here originally; see P. Bruneau, *Recherches sur les cultes de Délos à l'époque hellénistique et à l'époque impériale* (Paris 1970) 443.

19 *IG* XI², 110, 111, 113, 115, 122, 126, 128, 133.

priate to any prytaneion, and the inventory of 221 B.C. lists a "libation pourer with an inscribed legend: 'sacred to Hestia'."[20]

The identification of the prytaneion of Delos must ultimately rest, however, on whether or not one can identify individual parts of the building with parts of the Delian prytaneion which are known to have existed. Among the series of inventories made after the Athenians gained control of the island in the second century B.C. are two (A 286, 287) from consecutive years which list the contents of the prytaneion room by room. The rooms distinguished in these lists are: prytaneion, prodomos, courtyard, archeion, prodomos. Vallois has labeled the parts of the building under discussion in accordance with these texts: Room IV is the prytaneion, Room III is the archeion, Room II is the courtyard, and Rooms III′ and IV′ are the prodomoi of the archeion and the prytaneion, respectively.[21] This arrangement works very well, with the hearth of Hestia in the prytaneion proper (i.e., the room as opposed to the whole building). The closets in the back of Room III for the archives justify the appellation of archeion for that area. Moreover, the inscriptions tell us that there were four herms on stone bases in the courtyard and two herms on stone bases in the prodomos of the archeion. One of these may very well be that still standing in Room II (i.e., the courtyard) beside the low base of another, while one such base is still in place in Room III′ (the prodomos of the archeion; pl. 1b).[22]

There is a problem in the lack of a dining hall, or hestiatorion, which is to be expected in any prytaneion, and which certainly must have existed in the prytaneion at Delos (see A 280). This is also evidenced by the "repairs" inscription (A 278), which mentions work done on the wall south of the hestiatorion and the prytaneion. If this refers to the prytaneion in the same sense as the inventories discussed above (i.e., the room, not the building as a whole), the hestiatorion will have been a neighboring room. Vallois has suggested that Room III was called the hestiatorion in the late fourth century, but the

20 *IG* XI², 124: *σπονδοχοΐδιον ἐπιγραφὴν ἔχον ἱερὸν Ἑστίας.*

21 *L'Architecture* I 174.

22 For details of the heads of three other herms found in the prytaneion see J. Marcadé, *Au Musée de Délos* (Paris 1969) 146–152.

archeion in the mid-second century B.C.[23] Such a change in nomenclature presumes, however, a drastic change in the function of the room. In fact, both rooms must be present, and contemporary, in the Delian prytaneion; the archeion is epigraphically attested, and the hestiatorion is a necessary part of any prytaneion.

Might not the hestiatorion be Room III, while the archeion referred to in the inventory is either the set of closets at the northern end of Room III, or else the set of closets in the area between the two prodomoi (Rooms III′ and IV′)? Room III is suitable for ten standard couches 0.80 × 1.70 meters (see fig. 4). It is interesting to note, moreover, that the threshold block (pl. IIIb) which leads from Room III′ to Room III is much more worn on its right half than on its left. The left valve of the door was, then, normally kept closed and would not interfere with any couches to the left of the door. The couch to the right of the door is set back 0.60 meters from the door pivot and thus allows the door to open partially, but not to swing back fully against the wall. To prevent the door from banging into the couch, the threshold block is provided with a door stop cut at an angle oblique to the stop for the closed door. The maximum angle which the door could open before hitting the supposed couch is about 138°. The stop carved in the threshold allows the door to open only 132°. While one cannot be certain that a couch behind the door explains the existence of this stop, such an explanation fits well with the other observations made regarding this room. The epigraphical evidence from Delos concerning its prytaneion corresponds so well with the remains of this building that there need be no hesitation in identifying it as the prytaneion.

Lato

Location

The prytaneion at Lato is located at the head of a broad flight of steps which opens out onto the northern side of the agora.[24]

23 *L'Architecture* I 174.

24 See *Testimonia* (A 345, 346). The original report of the excavations in the building is by J. Demargne, *BCH* 27 (1903) 216–221. The results of a re-examination of the remains have recently appeared: P. Ducrey and O. Picard,

These steps were used as seats for open-air assemblies, and two flights of stairs with lower risers were cut into the seats to facilitate ascent.[25] The building holds, then, a commanding position over the agora as a whole and over the ekklesiasterion in particular (pls. 4c, 5a).

The Remains

The southern walls of the building are preserved only in their lower course, while, following the steep upward slope of the hill, the northern walls are in better condition, preserved as high as two meters in places. The building consists of four, or perhaps five, rooms built between two east–west walls which extend beyond the building on both ends (see fig. 5). The southern east–west wall has a thickness varying from 0.90 to 1.07 meters, while the eastern north–south wall averages about 0.57 meters thick. This difference was partly due to the use of the east–west walls as terrace walls to build up level areas on the side of the hill, which rises sharply to the north. The plan of the prytaneion was, then, influenced by the terrain upon which it was built.[26]

Room 44.—This triangular area at the eastern end of the building may not be a room at all. It has been labeled variously as a courtyard, porch, *recoin* and *avant-cour.* Its precise nature is difficult to determine, for the eastern end of its northern wall has fallen away as has its southern wall slightly to the east of this area. The space between these walls at their closest point is 1.30 meters, but it is impossible to say whether or not a door ever existed here. The northern wall is only preserved to a height of one or two courses and is not bonded into the exterior northeast corner of Room 36.

"Recherches à Latô. Le Prytanée," *BCH* 96 (1972) 567–592. I have derived great benefit from discussions with Mr. Ducrey, and the various similarities in our manuscripts when compared in the spring of 1972 was gratifying. Certain differences of interpretation do remain, however, as pointed out by Picard and Ducrey and as mentioned in the discussion below.

25 *McDonald* 32–35 discusses the evidence for identification of these steps as an ekklesiasterion; see also Ducrey and Picard, *op. cit.* (note 24) 591–592.

26 The influence of the terrain and other local problems upon the shape of the prytaneion at Lato has been ignored in the various theories which attempt to explain the derivation of the form of the building; see, for example, *Tosi* 153.

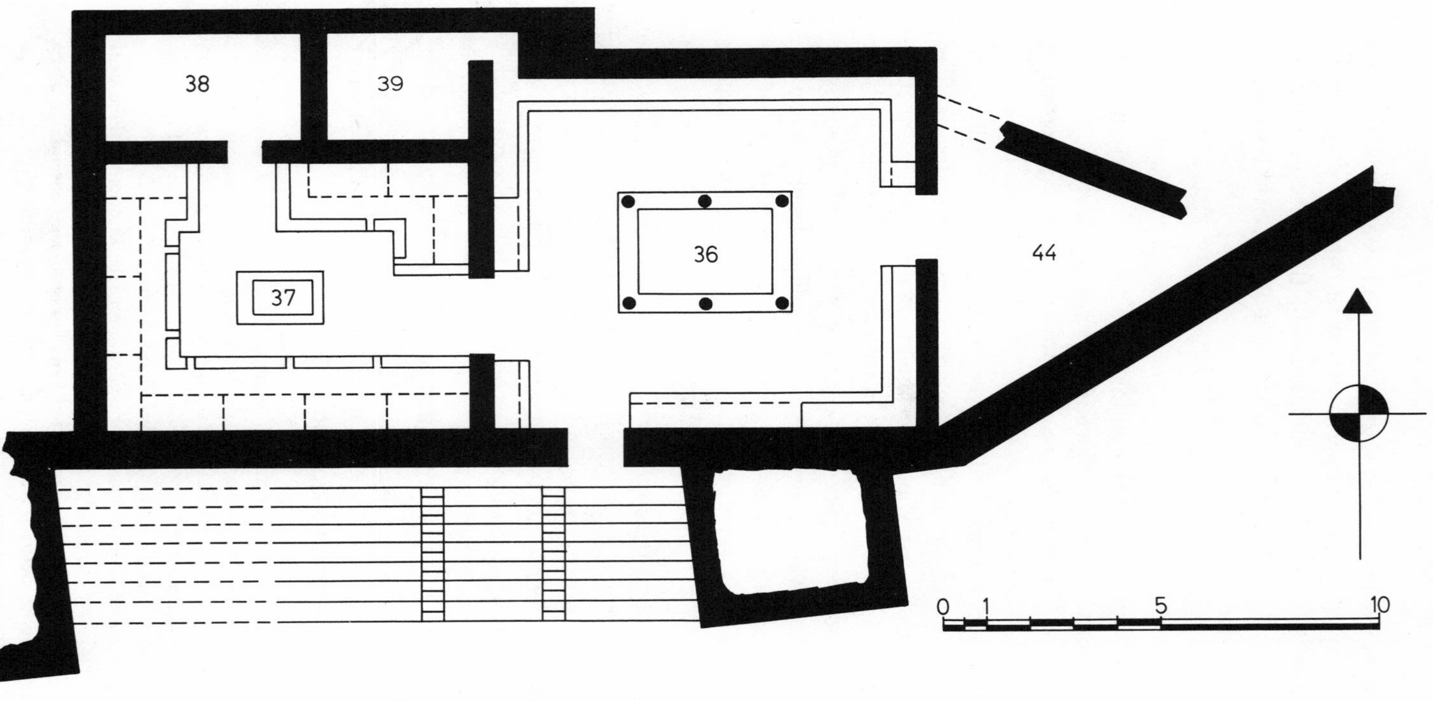

FIGURE 5. Plan of the prytaneion at Lato.

Room 36.—This large (8.20 × 9.85 meters) room has inside its perimeter, except where interrupted by doorways, a double step made of small rocks and protruding 0.78 to 0.84 meters from the inside face of the room (pl. 5b). The height of the lower riser averages 0.15 meters, while that of the upper is 0.20 meters. The width of the upper of the two steps from the inside face of the wall is 0.48 to 0.53 meters. In the areas where this upper step no longer exists it is probably to be restored (fig. 5). Since the height of these steps is not sufficient for seats—one's knees come nearly to one's chin—perhaps they formed an area for spectators to stand, rather than sit, around the perimeter of the room.[27]

In the center of the room is a rectangular structure built of large blocks, and measuring 2.97 × 3.92 meters. The top of this structure is about 0.20 meters above floor level.[28] In many places the inside surfaces of the blocks are not smoothly worked, which indicates that these surfaces were not visible and that the floor inside the structure was also 0.20 meters higher than the area which surrounded it. This structure has been called a hearth or altar,[29] but such a designation fails to take account of certain facts. First, the room as a whole is quite large and has a considerable ceiling span, and the central structure is very large for an interior hearth or altar. Second, no traces of burning, nor any remains of sacrifices, are reported as having been discovered in specific association with the central structure. Finally, the whole area was littered with fragments of columns when excavated. Since there are many holes on the upper

27 *Tosi* 152 wants to recognize this room as a bouleuterion based on the "seats" which line the room and on the presence of Hestia Boulaia in the prytaneion at Adramyttion (A 1). With the ekklesiasterion-step complex close at hand, this seems an unnecessary conjecture, and the presence of Hestia Boulaia in a prytaneion does not necessarily imply the use of that prytaneion as a bouleuterion, or the existence of a prytaneion-bouleuterion combination. The altar of Artemis Boulaia in Athens was probably near the tholos (see above, chapter three, note 57), and was certainly not in the bouleuterion. See *Agora* III, 55, no. 118, and below, Appendix C, *s.v.* Aigai.

28 This measurement is on the northern side of the structure. On the south the ground now slopes away, but a drafted line 0.21 meters below the top of the southeast corner indicates the original floor level on this side also. These blocks are in no way to be termed orthostates as they are called by *Tosi* 151.

29 E.g., Kirsten, "Lato," *RE* Suppl. VII 353, calls it "*eine herdartige Aufbau.*"

surface of the blocks of this structure (pl. 6a), it seems likely that this was actually the stylobate for an arrangement of interior supports.[30] Nonetheless, Room 36 should be understood as a room of religious or cult significance, for the excavator mentions the discovery here of three or four female terracotta figurines and several libation bowls.

Since there is no evidence for any drainage system, it seems unlikely that the central structure was hypaethral, for the higher floor level of the structure vis-à-vis the surrounding floor would have drained rain water out from the center into the surrounding lower parts of the room. Perhaps a clerestory system should be restored over the central structure, on which the hearth (the *κοινὴ ἑστία*) would rest (a smaller, less substantial hearth; see chapter two, pp. 34–35) with provision, by means of the clerestory, for smoke removal from the center of the room. The raised steps which line the room would then serve as an area for the observation of the sacrifices and libations in the center of the room at the hearth—rites such as those mentioned by Pausanias at the hearth in the Olympian prytaneion (A 375, 376).

Room 37.—This room is somewhat smaller (6.40 × 8.30 meters) than Room 36 and is entered from the latter. It too contained a central rectangular construction which is 2.00 meters long and has a width of 1.23 meters on the eastern face, 1.33 meters on the western. The top of the foundation course of this structure designates the level of the floor in the center of the room (pl. 6b). Resting on that foundation is a course of orthostates. Several of these have been removed since the time of excavation, but enough remain to show the careful fitting of the joints. While the exterior faces of these blocks are well worked, the interiors are so rough as to preclude the possibility of their having been visible when the structure was

30 The holes in the stylobate appear in many cases, however, simply to be weathering marks in the porous stone, and a systematic arrangement of cuttings for column placements is not easily extracted. Demargne, *op. cit.* (note 24) 216, seems to have felt the same difficulty: "*Tout autour les fouilles* (i.e., of the structure in the center of Room 36) *ont mis au jour des débris de colonnes, mais nous n'avons pas pu constater la place où elles se dressaient.*" Ducrey and Picard, *op. cit.* (note 24) 575, have recovered, however, traces of circular beddings for six columns, one at each corner, and one along each of the long sides. This scheme appears in figure 5.

in use. This construction, which "*manifestement est un autel*" in the words of the excavator, has also been called a hearth (Kirsten), a central serving table (Frickenhaus), and an eschara (Ducrey and Picard). Certainly, as is visible in plate 6c, the stones have a top surface dressed for the receipt of something above; the nature of that element is, however, enigmatic.[31]

The raised platform of packed stones which runs around the perimeter of the room is mounted by a double step of well-worked blocks. The platform has an average width, from the interior wall surface, of 1.38 meters (with variations of $\pm$ 0.04 meters); the lower step has a tread width of about 0.28 meters. The height of the risers is 0.25 meters. The upper surface of the platform was covered by a pavement of small stones embedded in white cement.[32] At irregular intervals blocks have been extended out from the platform level to fall flush with the riser face of the lower step. These projections vary in width from 0.18 to 0.21 meters and have shallow rectangular cuttings on top near the front edges (pl. 5c).[33] These projections are not easily explained. They are too small and irregularly spaced to have served as bases for roof supports, and they seem pointless as column or pier bases. Such piers might as well, and more easily, have rested directly on the lower step. It seems that the purpose of these projections must be understood as somehow related to the height and function of the platform.

One cannot be dogmatic about what that function was, but it seems more than fortuitous that standard couches (0.85 × 1.85 meters) fit precisely around the south and west walls on top of the platform. Since it is known that this building was a prytaneion, it requires no special pleading to interpret the platform as intended to receive couches. Unfortunately, the

31 The additional contention of Ducrey and Picard, *op. cit.* (note 24) 579, that the central construction in Room 37 was the common hearth is unnecessary and incapable of proof. The common hearth ought to have been in the center of Room 36 (see above, p. 82). Pausanias (A 376) tells us that the hearth was not in the hestiatorion of the prytaneion at Olympia, and the parallels cited by Ducrey and Picard are to cooking hearths in dining rooms, not to common hearths.

32 Ducrey and Picard, *op. cit.* (note 24) 576.

33 The projections along the southern side of Room 37 are no longer *in situ*, but a photograph made at the time of excavation clearly shows their positions; see Demargne, *op. cit.* (note 24) 217, fig. 4. The two projections in the northeast corner of the room have secondary cuttings toward the rear of the blocks.

couches do not fit quite so well in the northeast corner of Room 37. The overlap in that corner causes the occupant of the corner couch to recline on his right, rather than the more usual left side. I can offer no explanation for this phenomenon, but the precise fitting of the couches from the northeast corner of the room to the edge of the platform alongside the door to Room 36 makes me believe that such an arrangement of the corner couch was intentional.[34]

With the explanation of the platform as an area for dining couches, the projections become intelligible as some system of support for tables. Even this function is not completely clear since it is very difficult to correlate the positions of the projections with those of the couches; the projections do not consistently align with the head of every couch.[35] Then too, one would expect a double, rather than a single, support for the tables, like those at Corinth and Troizen.[36] Despite these problems, it seems best to see in the projections an arrangement for the support of tables.

The only artifact discovered in Room 37 was a perirrhanterion in the northwest corner of the room.[37] While its specific function and original position in the prytaneion at Lato cannot

34 With this restoration there are eleven couches, three more than the *οἶκος ὀκτάκλινος* which Frickenhaus, "Griechische Banketthäuser," *JdI* 32 (1917) 131, note 2, called this room, but he does not mention how he had arranged his eight couches. Perhaps he experienced the same difficulty in the northeast corner of the room and therefore omitted those three couches. Ducrey and Picard, *op. cit.*, (p. 579) imply that the couches were of a width equal to that of the platform (i.e., 1.35 to 1.40 meters) and suggest (p. 579, note 16) that their length was 2.10 to 2.20 meters. Such dimensions for dining couches are unknown; see Appendix B. It should be noted that the two-stepped platform around the perimeter of Room 37 in the prytaneion of Lato is quite different from the more typical raised borders in the rooms at other sites mentioned by Ducrey and Picard.

35 It might be thought that any restoration of couches in Room 37 ought to take into account some relationship between the supports and the number of couches; that is, the number of couches ought to be determined by the number of projections. The restoration offered in figure 5 does not suggest any such relationship because the principle of standard couch size as outlined in Appendix B, so eminently applicable here, seems to me preferable.

36 See Appendix B, Table 2, notes 3 and 7 respectively.

37 Demargne, *op. cit.* (note 24) 217–218. Other finds are mentioned by the excavator as discovered in a room of the prytaneion (which room is not specified): two bronze pins, the base of a lamp, and a stone catapult ball with the inscribed letters *ΓΟΡ*.

be ascertained, one might remember the epigraphically attested presence of a perirrhanterion in the prytaneion at Delos (A 286, 287).

Room 38.—This small room (2.60 × 4.60 meters) can be reached only from Room 37 and is perhaps a storage chamber servicing Room 37: Demargne mentions the discovery of pithoi and weapons in this room. That the room was not intended for heavy traffic is shown by the height of its threshold (about 0.45 meters) above the floor of Room 37.

Room 39.—This room is also small (2.48 × 3.17 meters) and like its western neighbor should be understood as a storeroom servicing Room 36 from which it was entered. Nothing of any distinguishing character now remains to help identify its specific function and none of its contents were published as such by the excavator. It is attractive to speculate that it was an archives room, or a storage chamber for the paraphernalia required at the ceremonies around the hearth in Room 36.

Date

The determination of the construction date of this building is exceedingly difficult. Weickert called it no later than the fifth century,[38] but did not believe that there was evidence for the Archaic date usually assigned to the building.[39] Various tests carried out by Ducrey and Picard were disappointing with regard to ceramic evidence for a construction date, but the interrelationship of building, steps, and towers has led them to argue that it was erected in the late fourth or third centuries B.C.[40] Their argument, if not conclusive, is persuasive and we ought to think of it as an early Hellenistic building.

Identification

The identification of the building as a prytaneion has rarely been questioned, and Kirsten's excellent discussion of its claim

38 C. Weickert, *Typen der archaischen Architecktur in Griechenland und Kleinasien* (Augsburg 1929) 174, note 1. He is followed by Kirsten, *op. cit.* (note 29) 349.

39 E.g., by F. Tritsch, "Die Agora von Elis and die altgriechische Agora," *Jahreshefte* 27 (1932) 83, note 22; and by R. E. Wycherley, *How the Greeks Built Cities*[2] (London 1962) 55.

40 Ducrey and Picard, *op. cit.* (note 24) 588–591.

obviates the need for all but a bare summary here.[41] That a prytaneion existed at Lato is attested by two inscriptions, and the provenience of one of these (A 321) is very instructive. This stone, which was to be set up in the prytaneion, was discovered broken into eleven pieces.[42] Of these, seven were found in the agora, two on the ekklesiasterion steps, and two in Room 37. It is quite obvious that the stone, broken and scattered downhill, once stood in the building which can be securely identified as the prytaneion of Lato.

Olympia

Location

The prytaneion at Olympia is located at the northwest corner of the Altis and forms the northern limit of the sacred area toward the west. The west wall of the Altis abuts, and is mortised into, the southwest corner of the building. To the southeast is the temple of Hera, and immediately to the south is the Philippeion. As one approaches the site today, the prytaneion lies just inside the entrance on the left, as in antiquity (A 377).

The Remains

The plan of the prytaneion at Olympia for any one period of time cannot be fully recovered. The structure was rebuilt many times in antiquity and the modern excavations were too early (1880's) to take full cognizance of all the complications on the site. In publishing the building, Dörpfeld resolved the problem by simply offering two plans, one for the Greek prytaneion, one for the Roman.[43] The former is the plan which one often sees reproduced in handbooks. A recent re-examination at the site has shown, however, that there were at least four major phases of construction, and that Dörpfeld's plan of the Greek prytaneion combined elements from all these periods, many of

41 *Op. cit.* (note 29) 352–355.

42 Not *in situ* as *Tosi* states (p. 151) nor in two pieces as she says in her footnote 67; see Demargne, *op. cit.* (note 24) 219–226.

43 W. Dörpfeld, *Die Baudenkmäler von Olympia* II (Berlin 1892) 58–61, 140, 180, and pls. 43–44. For *testimonia* regarding the Olympian prytaneion see (A 372–377).

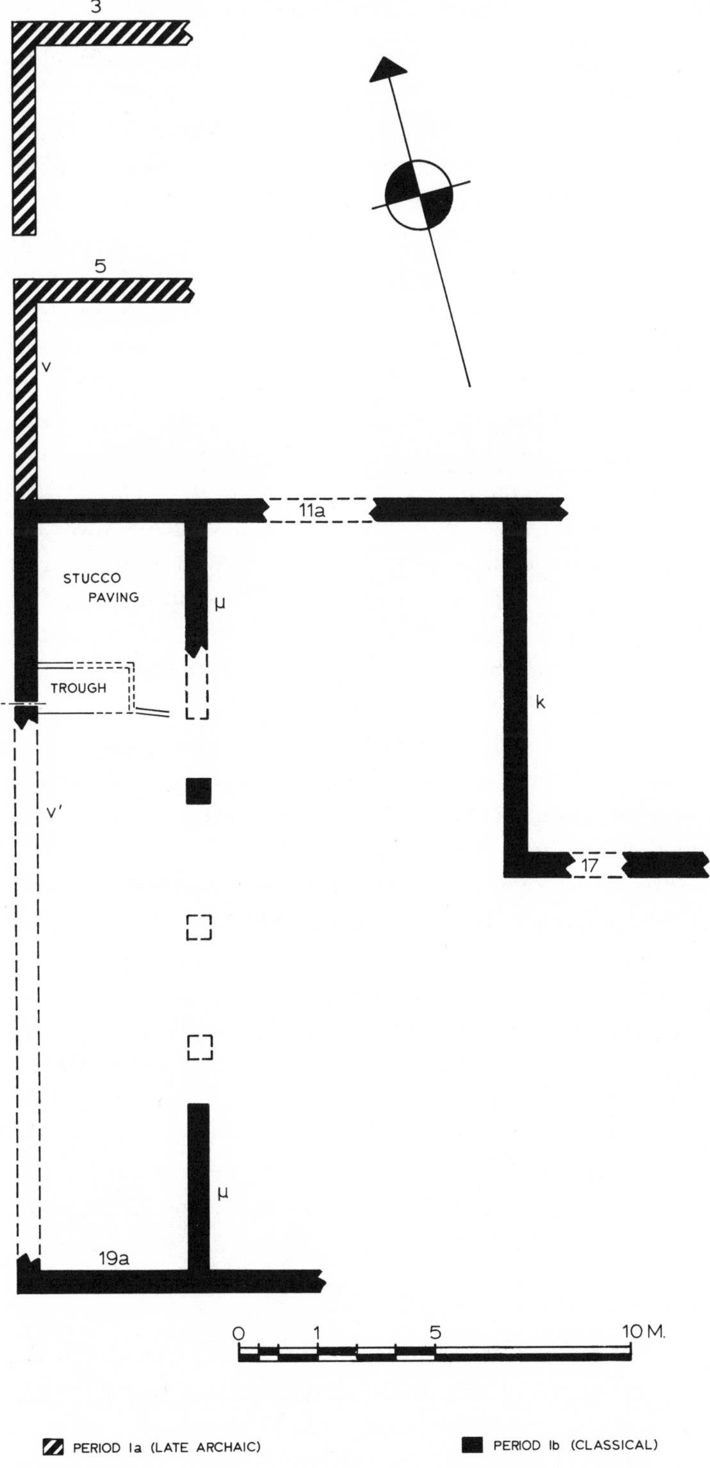

FIGURE 6. Plan of the Classical remains of the prytaneion at Olympia.

which could not have been in use at the same time.[44] In addition, there is reason to believe that the full extent of the earlier remains to the east has not been exposed.[45] A complete presentation of the remains would be superfluous here, but an outline of the results of the examination in the field may be useful.

Period Ia. The remains of this period (fig. 6) are three walls constructed of rubble in the northwestern area of the prytaneion (walls ν, 3, 5). They extend some 11.60 meters north–south, and 4.35 meters east–west, and limit two rooms the full dimensions of which cannot be recovered.

Period Ib. During this phase the walls of period Ia were still in use, but a much larger building was added on to the south. From this period there are preserved walls κ, μ, ν′, 11a, 17, 19a. The full north–south dimension of the prytaneion was then 30.94 meters, while the preserved east–west dimension is 19.40 meters; it was originally larger. The plan is necessarily incomplete, but certain elements are discernible. The two earlier rooms at the northwest remained in use, and their line was extended to the south bordering a long narrow room, with stuccoed water facilities in the north. This room opened out to the east onto what may have been a courtyard. There were at least two more rooms to the east, but their size, shape, and function cannot be determined.

Period II. The whole of the structure of period I was destroyed by fire, and a new building was reconstructed. This structure (fig. 7) followed the same lines as the earlier building, but was somewhat expanded so that the new north–south dimension was about 32.80 meters. Once again there was a series of smaller rooms in the northwest area, a long, narrow (but wider than the original) room in the southwestern area, numerous fragments of walls to the east which may have formed parts of as many as four rooms, a long and relatively narrow courtyard in the southwestern area, and a larger courtyard at the north central area.

Date

Period Ia can be placed on the basis of ceramic evidence in the early fifth century B.C., and period Ib commenced not long

44 *Miller* 79–107.

45 *Ibid.* 83–84 and note 10.

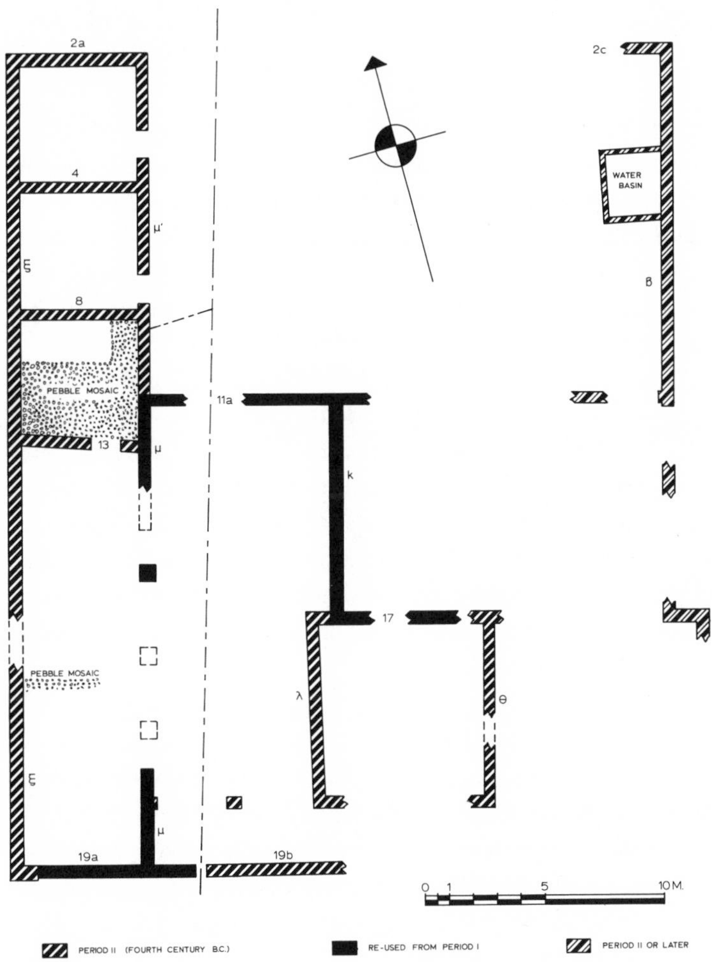

FIGURE 7. Plan of the Hellenistic remains of the prytaneion at Olympia.

thereafter.[46] The whole of the structure of period I was destroyed in the second quarter of the fourth century B.C.,[47] and the reconstruction of period II took place around the

46 Perhaps in 472 B.C., the date of the synoecism of Elis; see A. Mallwitz, *Olympia und seine Bauten* (Munich 1972) 128.

47 Two causes for this destruction and two dates have been suggested: an earthquake in 374 B.C. which is attested at Helike in Achaia (Pausanias VII, 24, 5 ff.) by Mallwitz, *op. cit.* (note 46) 98, 128; and the battle between the Eleans and the Arcadians in 364 B.C. (A 372) by *Miller* 104. The latter suggestion, involving the identification of the prytaneion with the shrine of Hestia mentioned by Xenophon, is further discussed in Appendix D.

middle of the fourth century B.C. This building stood, with many repairs and remodelings, until the second century A.D.

Identification

The basis for the identification of the prytaneion at Olympia is the account of Pausanias who located the building very closely: "The Eleans have the prytaneion inside the Altis; it was built by the exit which is beyond the gymnasion" (A 374), and "this building [the Philippeion] is on the left of the exit by the prytaneion" (A 377). A comparison of these statements with a general plan of the site will show the validity of the identification.[48] Other evidence for identification is in the form of lists of officials found in or around the building. Many of these officials are known to have been present in the prytaneion at least once a month.[49] Finally, the shrine of Hestia mentioned by Xenophon (A 372) is almost certainly the prytaneion, and his account of the battle between the Eleans and the Arcadians within the Altis would place the shrine of Hestia in the general area of the prytaneion.[50]

Conclusions for the Prytaneion at Olympia

Although the discussion presented above, taken together with the full publication of the re-examination of the remains at Olympia, tells the state of our knowledge at present about the building, certain facts should be reiterated here. Several previous theories about the building are no longer tenable: The eastern limits of the prytaneion are not known, and the northern limits in the original period were extended in a late Classical rebuilding (period II) some two meters to the north. There is, therefore, no known prytaneion of the Greek period which has the square shape and the *plethron* dimensions (*ca.* 32.80 meters) which were restored by Dörpfeld.[51] The central room in Dörpfeld's plan, the so-called Hestia Hall, does not belong to the original phase of the prytaneion, and it lost its form in the next large-scale remodeling of the building.[52] Thus the fre-

48 For the most recent site plan see Mallwitz, *op. cit* (note 46).

49 *Miller* 82.

50 See Appendix D.

51 *Op. cit.* (note 43) 60; see Appendix C, Thasos.

52 *Miller* 93, 95, 106.

quently repeated contention that this room was the central unchanged point of the Olympia prytaneion is incorrect,[53] and it is not at all clear that this was τὸ οἴκημα τῆς ἑστίας mentioned by Pausanias (A 376).

The earliest architectural structure on the site is to be dated to the early fifth century B.C. This was destroyed and rebuilt with an expanded plan in the middle of the fourth century B.C. The only remains known to be from an earlier period are those of the "ship-shaped structure" which may be a hearth of Hestia of the Geometric period around which the later prytaneion was constructed.[54]

Although securely identified as the prytaneion of Olympia, the remains of the building from the Classical and Hellenistic periods are so meager that there is little of use for comparison with other prytaneia. The rooms at the north of the building were subsidiary areas for cooking and storage.[55] On analogy with the plan of the Roman period, a courtyard may be postulated for the Greek period in the north central area of the building. Finally, even if they cannot be recognized in the remains, Pausanias (A 376) distinguished two major areas in the Olympia prytaneion: the room of the hearth of Hestia, and the dining room. If it is legitimate to combine the remains with the account of Pausanias, then the prytaneion at Olympia did contain the elements of Hestia-room, dining room, courtyard, and subsidiary rooms. Although precise details of plan and arrangement of these elements are lacking, the prytaneion at Olympia can be said to have had the essential elements of a prytaneion, as derived from the sources in chapter two.

Synthesis: *Testimonia* and Remains

A collation of the *testimonia* and evidence from the buildings discussed to this point show that a prytaneion must be located on or near the agora or, at religious sites, bordering the sacred

53 Dörpfeld, *op. cit.* (note 43) 60; cf. Weniger, *Klio* 6 (1906) 6; Gardiner, *Olympia* (Oxford 1925) 268.

54 *Miller* 84.

55 The southernmost of these rooms may be the site of the mixing of water from the Alpheios and ash from the hearth for repairs to the Altar of Zeus (A 373); see *Miller* 106–107.

area. When exceptions to this rule occur, as at Athens, there will be a "prytaneion-annex" on the agora which may have no architectural similarities to a proper prytaneion. While not necessarily as grand as other public buildings, the prytaneion will be substantial in its construction, and far better built than typical domestic structures. The prytaneia at Delos and Lato warn that the courtyard may be a simple hypaethral area rather than a formal peristyle court. On one point the *testimonia* and the remains agree and are unequivocal: the two principal functions of a prytaneion will have architectural manifestations in a dining room and a hearth room. The prodomos or prostas may or may not appear in the plan of a prytaneion, but there will always be subsidiary rooms for storage.

CHAPTER V

A Catalogue of Prytaneia

IN THIS chapter the remains of all those buildings which have, in my opinion, some reasonable claim to be considered as prytaneia will be discussed in light of the criteria of identification which have been developed in the previous chapters in order to establish the degree of probability with which they may be identified as prytaneia. The buildings to be considered are located at Dreros, Ephesos, Kolophon, Magnesia, Morgantina, and Priene. A number of other buildings have been suggested as prytaneia at one time or another. These buildings, however, either lack the necessary evidence to prove or disprove the identification, or else it can be shown that they certainly were not prytaneia. These buildings are gathered in Appendix C.

Dreros

Location

The building identified by the excavators as the prytaneion of Dreros[1] lies to the southwest and above the open area identified

1 Among the *testimonia*, (A 307) may apply to Dreros. For all of the buildings discussed in this chapter, see appropriate parts of the Site Bibliography. The principal report on the building at Dreros is that of Demargne and van Effenterre, "Recherches à Dréros," *BCH* 61 (1937) 16–26. The building discovered twenty years earlier by Xanthoudides, *ΑΡΧΑΙΟΛΟΓΙΚΟΝ*

as the agora of the city.[2] The agora area, never completely explored, was bordered along its southern side by a long flight of steps which return to the north on both ends. These returns suggest that the whole area was originally bordered on the east, south, and west sides by such a step arrangement. North of our building, and overshadowing the agora on its western side, is the Geometric structure identified as the Delphinion.[3]

The Remains

Any attempt to study the building at Dreros today suffers from serious handicaps. The area surrounding the building was refilled after the excavations in the thirties and has become very overgrown in the intervening years. In order to refill this surrounding area, parts of the south and east walls of the building were restored to a height of a meter and more. The present situation is, then, that of a relatively small hole in the ground with the walls of the building lining this hole (pl. 7a). There are, moreover, difficulties in ascertaining the heights of the south and east walls at the time of excavation, and it is impossible to study the walls which ran out further to the east and south since they are now covered by more than a meter of earth. One must hope that the excavators were correct in their assertion that the original extent of the building is complete as it now appears and that those presently covered walls had no functional connection with the building. However, the plan of the site produced by the excavators (note 2) shows several rooms and walls which appear to have been connected with or a part of the building.

The general technique of construction was rubble masonry and used local gray limestone. Cut blocks are rare, and squared or well-worked blocks non-existent, although some corner

---

ΔΕΛΤΙΟΝ 4 (1918) Suppl. 25 and fig. 10, on the western height of Dreros and obliquely suggested by Marinatos, *BCH* 60 (1936) 254, note 4, as a prytaneion is called an Andreion by Demargne and van Effenterre.

2 Demargne and van Effenterre, *op. cit.* 6, fig. 2, give a sketch plan of the area and, on plate I, a more detailed plan of the excavations in the vicinity of the building.

3 S. Marinatos, "Le Temple Géométrique de Dréros," *BCH* 60 (1936) 214 ff. The now partially reconstructed and roofed Delphinion is visible at the right side of plate 7a.

and threshold blocks are rough-hewn. The floors were apparently of beaten earth except in Room III (see fig. 8) where stone paving was found in the northeast corner at the same level as the threshold.[4] Elsewhere, the present ground level is about 0.60 meters below the thresholds so that the original floors are now destroyed.

Room I.—The size (*ca.* 1.00 × 2.50 meters) and location of the small room outside the entrance to the building signals its subsidiary role to the larger complex behind. Its particular function is hard to understand, however, as there is lacking here—as throughout almost all of the building—any record of the artifacts discovered within it.

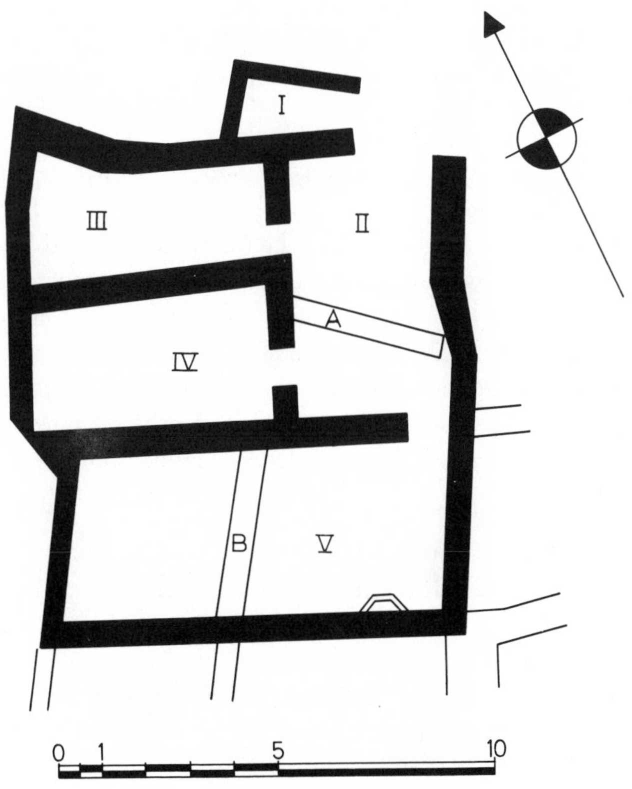

FIGURE 8. Plan of the building at Dreros.

4 Demargne and van Effenterre, *op. cit.* (note 1) 16.

Room II.—Measuring 3.30 × 5.70 meters, with a zig-zag in its east wall, this room was labeled a vestibule for the obvious reason that it served as the anteroom for the remaining three rooms. Wall A (fig. 8) obliquely bisects Room II and was constructed later than the building since its now extremely scanty remains are bedded higher than the top surfaces of the thresholds which opened onto this room originally.

Room III.—The entrance to this room from the vestibule (Room II) is in the extreme southeast corner and has a threshold of small stones (pl. 7b). The room is irregular in plan (2.03 meters wide at the east end, 2.90 meters wide at the west, and 5.50 meters long) and its function unknown. The presence in it today of several pithos fragments might indicate some storage use for the room, but one cannot know with certainty whether these fragments were found in this room or were deposited there after the excavations.

Room IV.—This twin of Room III is more regular in form (2.88 × 5.86 meters) and has its entrance more nearly in the center of its eastern side (pl. 7c). The threshold is a solid block which preserves what may be the pivot hole of a door. If so, the door would have been a single valve about 0.65 meters wide as indicated by the dimension from pivot to jamb cutting. The excavators do mention a few of the finds in this room such as a crude stone wash basin and a small steatite oil press, but these objects are not sufficient to define the function of Room IV.

Room V.—This is both the largest room (3.66 × 8.72 meters) and the one in which the most productive finds were made. Entered from the vestibule by a doorway at its northeast corner, the floor levels of the room, higher in the west, are divided by a north–south wall (wall B, fig. 8) which cuts across the width of the room (pl. 8a).[5]

5 The excavators described this as "a line of rocks", but the size of rocks involved, visible in plate 8a, surely indicates a substantial structure. One might think, noting the huge rock apparently in place in the face of the southern wall of the building and in line with wall B (i.e., a block bonding the two walls), that wall B was of some height and originally divided Room V into two smaller rooms.

Near the southeast corner of Room V was found a small trapezoidal area, limited by three stones, which contained a quantity of ash and bones (pl. 8b). Between this area and wall B were found an iron pruning hook, pithos fragments (see below), and several coins of the late fourth or early third century B.C. It would seem quite clear that at some time Room V was used as a cooking and storage area.

Date

The excavators of this building dated its original construction in the Geometric period,[6] but the connection which they saw between the building and its northern neighbor, the Delphinion,[7] make clear their belief that the building under discussion should have been built shortly afterwards: that is, sometime after the mid-eighth century B.C. Finds from the area of the building have been dated, however, to the mid-seventh century B.C.,[8] and we are entitled to wonder what evidence was available to the excavators for their earlier dating.

The building had a long life, for several coins of the late fourth and early third centuries B.C., as well as some Hellenistic pottery, were discovered within the structure. The excavators used this fact as evidence for the date of a remodeling which included the construction of wall A. How much later the building continued in use cannot be said; no evidence of discoveries of a later date has been published.

Identification

The original basis for identification of this building as a prytaneion was simply its domestic qualities and its proximity to the agora of Dreros. The agora, however, is not at all securely identified, while a domestic character in the plan of a building is, as we have seen, not a criterion of identification for a prytaneion.

The application of our own criteria, beyond that of location

6 Demargne and van Effenterre, *op. cit.* (note 1) 26.

7 Dated *ca.* 750 B.C. by Marinatos, *op. cit.* (note 3) 256.

8 I refer to the fragments of relief pithoi mentioned by Demargne and van Effenterre, *op. cit.* (note 1) 19, fig. 12, nos. 4 and 5. These fragments belong stylistically in the mid-seventh century B.C. according to J. Schaefer, *Studien zu den griechischen Reliefpithoi* (Stuttgart 1957) 17–18.

already mentioned, yields disappointing results. The quality of construction is not outstanding, although there is little else from Dreros with which to compare it. No courtyard is present, although Room II might be so called. The other rooms do not have indications of dining facilities and their irregular shapes do not easily accommodate couches. One might identify the hearth in Room V with Hestia and thereby allow the room to fit into the expected prytaneion plan as the area sacred to Hestia, but the hearth in the building at Dreros is a rather poor and crude structure which seems more likely a cooking area than a religious zone where sacrifices of state were conducted. On the other hand, both Rooms III and IV would satisfy the requirements for subsidiary rooms for storage, especially since one now contains large pithos fragments. There is, then, some correspondence between the building at Dreros and our criteria, but the differences are too numerous and there are too many unanswered questions (e.g., the identification of the agora) to regard this building as more than a possible prytaneion. Considering its proximity to the Delphinion, one might think of the building as a dependency of the temple such as a priests' house.

Ephesos

Location

The building identified as the prytaneion of Ephesos is located in the saddle which joins the two hills of the ancient city.[9] Situated on the north side of the agora, the building lies just west of the long-known Odeion, and at the head of a short street which turns slightly obliquely to the so-called Kuretes Street. The lower, western end of the latter street begins just

9 Such identification was made by F. Miltner, "Vorläufiger Bericht über die Ausgrabungen in Ephesos," *Jahreshefte* 44 (1959) Beiblatt 289 ff. with reference to earlier publications. See *testimonia* (A 310–312).

Two other, now discarded, identifications of the prytaneion at Ephesos should be mentioned here: the Roman House above the theater by *Keil* 123; and the "Theater-Gymnasion" by J. T. Wood, *Discoveries at Ephesus* (London 1877) 102. Cf. F. Miltner, *Ephesos* (Vienna 1958) nos. 18 and 14 respectively on the plan of the city. Neither of these suggested identifications had the authority of evidence at the time of proposal and they need not be considered further.

opposite the Library of Celsus, and it thus provides direct communication between the lower center of the Roman city and the building in question. At the juncture of Kuretes Street and the street to the building are the pedestals of an arch (pl. 8c). Two of the voussoirs of this arch have been found and will be discussed below. The base blocks of the arch are ornamented with reliefs of a sacred procession in which a ram and a goat are being led off. The street leading beneath this arch up to the "prytaneion" has thus been called the *Clivus Sacer.*[10]

The Remains

The area of the building is difficult to determine because there have been four major periods of construction. We may call these, for the sake of convenience, Hellenistic, Augustan, Severan, and Byzantine. Since the Severan seems to be essentially a rebuilding of the Augustan plan, we may group these two together and will refer to them without any chronological adjective, especially since they represent the largest part of the building extant. The Byzantine walls do not concern us, and the Hellenistic elements still discernible will be so designated.

The Forecourt.—The remains of the site are L-shaped (fig. 9) with three main parts.[11] The first of these is the open court in the southwest corner of the L. The remains of this are not plentiful, but enough is extant to restore a three-sided Ionic peristyle courtyard, open on its northern side, with an open drain running around the court just inside the colonnade stylobate.[12] Of these elements, enough of the drain and the stylobate blocks are still *in situ* to establish the inner dimensions of the court as about 13.00 × 14.50 meters. In the center of this courtyard are four large blocks which form a rectangular foundation 2.50 × 2.10 meters. Although the purpose of the foundation cannot be definitely determined, a copy of the

10 See A. Bammer, "Zur Topographie und städtebaulichen Entwicklung von Ephesos," *Jahreshefte* 46 (1961–1963) 151, fig. 98, no. 48.

11 The northeast corner of the building has never been excavated below Byzantine levels, and our picture of the structure is therefore necessarily incomplete, though clear in outline.

12 The building was plundered by the builders of the Baths of Scholastikia; see Miltner, *op. cit.* (note 9) 302–305.

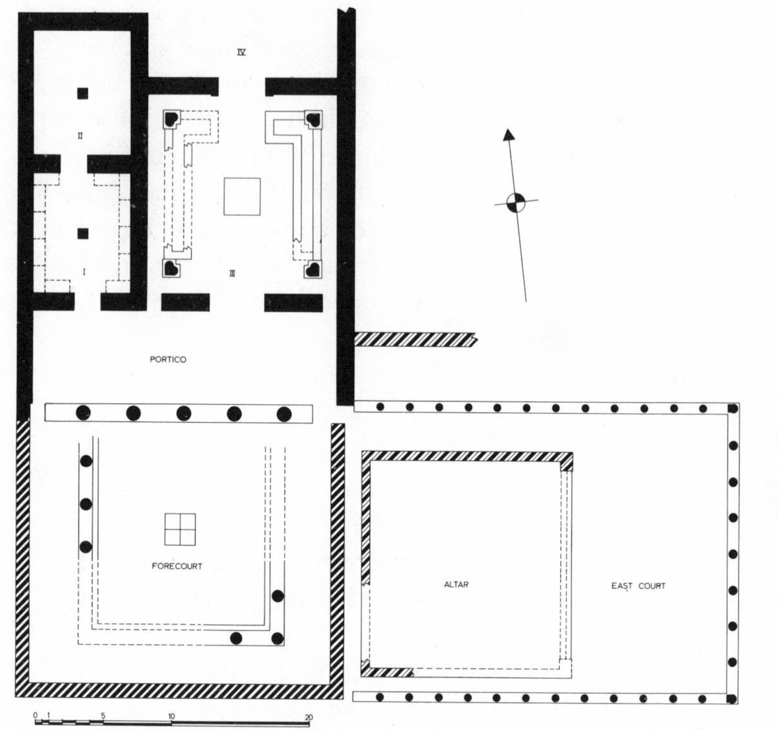

FIGURE 9. Plan of the building at Ephesos.

Ephesian Artemis (see note 23 below) was found nearby and may once have stood on top of these blocks.

The Portico.—On the northern or open side of the Forecourt lies a monumental colonnade which served as the porch of the building behind (pl. 9a). This Portico was of the Doric order and can be restored as pentastyle in-antis. The columns are unfluted and rise to a (restored) height of nearly 8 meters. Both these columns and the entablature above are completely covered with inscriptions, which will enter into the discussion of the building's identification.

The deep (7.35 meters) porch dates from the Severan remodeling in its present condition, although it seems to follow closely the Augustan lines. Such a chronology is indicated by the marble orthostates of the walls with the moulded string course above. These blocks (pl. 9b) are not in the same position which they occupied at the time of their inscription as is evidenced, for example, by the first complete block at the right side of plate 9b. The text of the top line reads -]*ου τοῦ Ἀρτεμι-δώρου*. The other half of the inscription is on another block several meters away which, although used in the same relative position in the height of the wall, was placed without regard for textual continuity. Miltner was able to date this inscription to early Imperial times, and we thus have a *terminus post quem* for the construction of the present wall, as well as a *terminus ante quem* for the original position of the blocks.[13]

Rooms I and II.—The Portico serves not only as a façade for the structure behind, but also as a common element which binds together the two non-communicating sets of rooms which comprise the building. The western of these sets consists of two rooms, one behind the other. The first of these, Room I, measures 6.65 × 8.35 meters; the rear one, Room II, while having the same width, has a length of 8.73 meters. Each room has a central columnar support, and the door between them was fitted with a large marble threshold and door jamb sockets (pl. 9c). Both doors of Room I are off-center, and on opposite sides of the main axis. Although it is impossible to prove that couches belong in Room I, the restoration of ten couches, each 0.85 × 1.88 meters, fits very well with the dimensions of this room.

Rooms III and IV.—East of Rooms I and II lies Room III, the dominant feature of the whole structure. This is a large (12.25 × 13.52 meters) room with four columns, placed toward the corners. Room III is now entered from the porch by a broad central doorway flanked by smaller openings, but the excavator considered that these two side doors had been cut into the walls some time later than the Severan remodeling of the building. Directly opposite the central entrance was, originally, another opening leading out of the northern side of Room III. This doorway was at least two steps up from the floor of the room. Blocked in Byzantine times, the outline of the doorway remains visible (pl. 10a), but the area beyond the door (Room IV) is obliterated by the Byzantine construction over it.

The floor of Room III is paved with large marble slabs and in

13 F. Miltner, *Jahreshefte* 43 (1956–1958) Beiblatt 33; for the complete text of this inscription see *ibid.* 31–32, no. 2.

the middle of the floor a square foundation protrudes slightly above the level of the paving (pl. 10b). This foundation must pre-date the marble floor since the latter is carefully laid up to it. It was taken by Miltner to represent the hearth which carried the eternal fire of Hestia, but since its superstructure is now completely missing, the original purpose cannot be proven.

The walls of Room III have a marble string course above carefully worked marble orthostates. Above the string course, the wall is of either crude ashlar masonry with some mortar between the stones, which is probably Augustan; or of nicely coursed brick and mortar (pl. 9b) which should belong to the Severan repairs. The construction of both periods will have been covered by marble revetment.

In the four corners of the room are the columns mentioned above, heart-shaped in section, and resting on Ionic bases with high pedestals. The monolithic shafts are of gray, veined granite, 4.16 meters high. The total height of the columns with pedestals and capitals is about 6.26 meters which is, therefore, the minimum height of the ceiling of Room III. The capital is of composite type (pl. 10c) and retains the heart-shaped section of the column. Miltner considered this capital to belong to the Severan rebuilding.[14]

Also of Severan date or later are two low parallel brick walls resting directly on the marble paving of Room III and stretching between the pedestals on either side of the room (fig. 9). Although not completely preserved, it appears that these walls originally turned the corners at their northern ends and met to form two short arms along the axis of the room. The function of these low brick walls is enigmatic, but Miltner took them to be underpinnings for seats where the Boule would gather.[15] The preserved condition of these walls helps to confirm this suggestion, since the wall nearer the center of the room is considerably lower than the wall behind it (pl. 10b). The identity of the group which would have assembled on these seats cannot, however, be confirmed as the Boule. Even if this building

14 *Ibid.* 33. If the association of Hestia with this building (to be discussed below) is correct, one might connect these columns with those dedicated by a certain Artemidoros to Hestia Boulaia; see W. Alzinger, *Die Stadt des siebenten Weltwunders* (Vienna 1962) 222.

15 *Op. cit.* (note 9) 298–299.

is the prytaneion, any connection between it and assemblies of the Boule is unattested.[16]

The East Court and the Hellenistic Altar.—East of the Forecourt there are traces of a north–south wall which served as the back wall of the Forecourt on this side. This wall also divided the Forecourt from another three-sided court which lies to the east, and has its open, non-columnar side on the west. Although the excavator closely associated this court with the building under discussion, the degree to which it was functionally and architecturally an organic part of the building is not clear to me. The open area of the court measures 26.97 × 19.86 meters and is lined on three sides by Ionic columns. The entablature of the eastern colonnade was at a higher level than that of the northern and southern sides as is indicated by the nature of the southeast corner column, a double column with two complete capitals at different heights (pl. 11a; note also the difference in levels of the bases).

Behind this eastern colonnade, the back or eastern wall of the court was formed, in part, by the retaining wall of the cavea of the Odeion. The original back wall consists of small stones laid in ashlar fashion (pl. 11a). This wall is terminated at the Odeion's southernmost buttress. The effect of the pre-existing east wall of the court upon the Odeion can be discerned in the vertical line in the wall blocks of the Odeion (to the right of the reconstructed column at the left in plate 11a) at a point where the curve of the Odeion wall was abruptly halted and forced into a straight line next to the eastern wall of the court.

Within the court is a large altar (pl. 11b) measuring 14.98 ×

16 Miltner's use (*Ephesos* 27), followed by Alzinger (*Die Stadt* 222), of the words prytaneion and *Rathaus* as though the latter were the equivalent of the former is unnecessarily confusing and without ancient authority. The ancient equivalent of *Rathaus* is, of course, bouleuterion. The confusion has been propagated by the suggestion that the bouleuterion and the prytaneion are to be recognized in the same building; see F. Eichler, *AAW* 1962, 41. The supporting evidence for this dual identification is the presence of Hestia Boulaia in inscriptions found in this building (see below), and the discovery of an inscription with mention of τὸ βουλευτήριον (Eichler gives no more of the text) which was re-used in a wall of Room III. Hestia Boulaia need not demand a combination prytaneion-bouleuterion (see above, chapter four, note 27), and the re-used inscription is not compelling evidence.

16.14 meters. The western side of the altar still preserves *in situ* most of the orthostate course as well as a few crowning blocks. It appears that there was a flight of steps up to the top of the structure from the east. This is shown by the moulded toichobate on the eastern side of the altar which turns westward about 1.40 meters south of the northeast corner of the altar (pl. 11c). This return continues on top of the first step, but is cut off for the second. In form the altar was like the Great Altar of Pergamon.

Date

No detailed discussion of the date of the building at Ephesos has been made, nor is any possible here without knowledge of the artifacts and the stratigraphy of the area. For the earlier phases, we have only the profiles of the mouldings of the large altar (fig. 10),[17] and the Ionic members from the court which surrounded it (pls. 12b, c).[18] These resemble others of the third or second century B.C.[19] Since the west end of the East Court northern stylobate is built up against the southeast corner of the east wall of the Portico, the lower levels of the Portico wall, and presumably of the whole structure westwards, must be at least as early as the East Court.

17 While mouldings similar to those of the altar are not easily found, despite Miltner's unhesitating attribution of them to the Hellenistic era, the cyma reversa of the base moulding (fig. 10, B) should be compared to a podium base from the theater of Segesta which is dated to the third or second century B.C.; see L. Shoe, *Profiles of Western Greek Mouldings* (Rome 1952) pl. XXIX, 2; and with a base moulding of the late fourth or third century B.C. from the Asklepieion at Corinth; see L. Shoe, *The Profiles of Greek Mouldings* (Cambridge, Mass. 1936) pl. XXXVIII, 8.

18 Eichler, *AAW* 1962, 40, states that the altar is from the Augustan period, and the surrounding colonnade about a century later. He further states that the altar has a poured foundation (*gegossenen Fundament*) which proves that it had no predecessors. The previous year (*AAW* 1961, 68) Eichler had said that there were earlier Hellenistic rubble foundations below the altar. At that time, he also mentioned pottery from a test trench in this area which ranged from Attic Black Glaze to Arretine, but he did not relate any of this pottery to its stratigraphic context. It is to be hoped that such a presentation will appear. Until it does, I prefer to place more weight on the chronological indications of the style of the architectural members.

19 Perhaps the greatest similarity to the rather low proportions of the capital is in the Great Altar of Pergamon; see J. Schrammen, *Der grosse Altar* (Berlin 1906) pl. X. The capitals of the inner pteron of the Temple of Apollo at Didyma are also close to ours; see T. Wiegand, *Didyma* (Berlin 1941) pl. 52, no. 409.

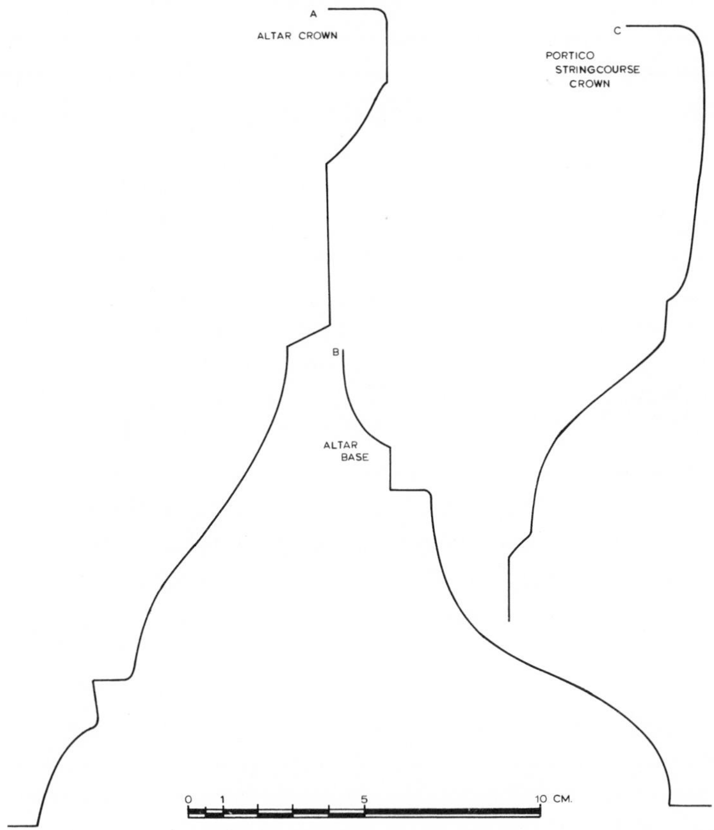

FIGURE 10. Profiles of mouldings at Ephesos.

There may be an indication derived from masonry style that other parts of the building should also be assigned to the Hellenistic period. In Room II (pl. 12a) three distinct types of masonry are visible. The uppermost of these is from the Byzantine period and is marked by the thinner walls which were set back on top of their predecessors. Beneath this type comes another which makes use of small stones and mortar in roughly ashlar coursing. This style is the same as that of the walls directly above the marble orthostates in Room III (pl. 10a) which we have associated with the Augustan work in the building. Beneath this Augustan construction, Room II has yet another style of masonry, quite clear in plate 12a, which consists of large well-cut blocks laid in pseudo-isodomic fashion. This section of the wall must be pre-Augustan and we might conclude that it belongs to the Hellenistic construction. Unfortunately, it is only in Room II that this style of masonry is visible, due probably to the heavy destruction and rebuilding in later times.[20]

Ample evidence exists for confirming an Augustan reconstruction date. First of all, there are architectural elements which bear inscriptions from the early first century A.D. and which have, therefore, a *terminus ante quem* for their erection.[21] Second, the profiles of the Doric capitals from the Portico are very similar to the capitals of the so-called Gate of Mithridates in Ephesos. This gate can be dated, on epigraphical evidence, to the end of the first century B.C.[22] Finally, a copy of the Artemis of Ephesos dated by Miltner to the first century A.D. on stylistic grounds was found in the southern part of the Forecourt.[23] If her place of discovery reflects her original place of dedication, which seems likely, she, too, provides a first century *terminus ante quem* for the building.

The Severan (or, more properly, first half of the third century A.D.) restoration of the building is attested by the style of the heart-shaped composite capitals (pl. 10c) and by the quality and quantity of brickwork which has already been mentioned. Then too, the inscriptions on the displaced blocks of the Portico (pl. 9b; see also pp. 100–101) give a *post quem* date for the brickwork above them, although this is only a general indication of a date sometime after the first century A.D.

The date for the building's final destruction at the end of the fourth century A.D. is well documented. At the foot of Kuretes Street there is a large bathing establishment called the Baths of

20 In 1961 and 1962 trenches dug to various earlier levels produced ceramic evidence of a Hellenistic date—the first half of the third century B.C.—for these walls; see F. Eichler, *AAW* 1962, 38–39, and *AAW* 1963, 46. However, in the next year Eichler (*AAW* 1964, 40) changed his mind and stated that nothing in the whole area of the building was to be dated before the Augustan period. The Hellenistic pottery which had been found earlier was now to be explained as part of a leveling fill which was laid before the building was constructed. Again (see note 18), neither pottery nor its stratigraphic context was presented, and I do not feel compelled to accept this undocumented statement.

21 Miltner, *op. cit.* (note 13) 33.

22 Miltner, *Ephesos* 27; cf. 24.

23 Miltner, *op. cit.* (note 9) 305–307.

Scholastikia, after the name of their ancient restorer.[24] The reconstruction of this complex near the end of the fourth century A.D. is indicated by the style of the statue of Scholastikia and the letter forms of the accompanying inscription. Since many architectural members of our building, such as one of the Doric columns and its capital, were built into the walls of the renovated baths, the building cannot have survived the end of the fourth century A.D.[25]

Identification

Since the building is recognizable, for the most part, only in the remains of Imperial times, we shall have to consider its identification with respect to that period. If, however, we find it likely that the building was the prytaneion of Ephesos in the Imperial period, the general principle of the immovability of the hearth of Hestia will indicate the same location for the earlier prytaneion. Before applying the architectural criteria, one ought to consider the strictly Ephesian indications of the site of the prytaneion.

There are two inscriptions from Ephesos which yield certain topographical information about the prytaneion. One of these (A 310) dates from around A.D. 230 and mentions a road down from the prytaneion to the entrance of the plateia. This, as Keil has pointed out, must put the prytaneion at some point higher than the library, theater, and forum of Ephesos which are the lower parts of the city during the period of the inscription.[26] The second inscription (A 311) is on two of the voussoir blocks from the gate of the so-called *Clivus Sacer* (pl. 8c). While the inscription is not complete because the adjacent blocks have not been found, enough of the text survives to indicate that it is the record of the erection of fourteen columns along with their stylobates, stone ambulatories, friezes, statues, and, most significantly, the gate in front of the prytaneion.[27] While there

24 Miltner, *op. cit.* (note 13) 22–24.

25 Miltner, *op. cit.* (note 9) 301–305. Miltner raises the question whether the building was still standing or was in disrepair at the time of this plundering. He opts for the former, although there is really no way to be certain about the condition of the building at that time.

26 *Keil* 123.

27 Miltner, *op. cit.* (note 9) 295.

is no indication of the location of the items mentioned, it seems quite likely that the gate in front of the prytaneion was the very gate which carried the arch bearing this record. Could the *κάθοδος ἀπὸ τοῦ πρυτανείου* in the first inscription be the road behind this gate, the *Clivus Sacer*? If so, the building under discussion must be very near the site of the prytaneion.

Although there is no explicit mention of the prytaneion among the many inscriptions found within the building, a number of them have a common element—references to Hestia. One of these, for example, records the thanks of various officials to Hestia Boulaia, the Undying Fire, Demeter, Kore, daughter of Demeter, Apollo Klarios, Kinnaios, and all the gods (*εὐχαριστοῦμεν Ἑστίᾳ Βουλαίᾳ / καὶ Πυρὶ ἀφθάρτῳ καὶ Δήμητρι / καὶ Δήμητρος Κόρῃ καὶ Ἀπόλ/λωνι Κλαρίῳ καὶ θεῷ Κινναίῳ / καὶ πᾶσιν θεοῖς*).[28]

The mere mention of Hestia, especially in company with so many other deities, could never prove conclusively the identification of the building as the prytaneion, even though Hestia is pre-eminent throughout these lists and the undying fire is particularly appropriate to a prytaneion. However, another group of inscriptions from the building list officials during given prytanizing periods.[29] The lists usually begin with the Kouretes, followed by the sacrificing priests (*ἱερουργοί*). Next comes a group of officials with titles such as: *ἱεροσκόπος, ἱεροφάντης, ἱεροκῆρυξ, σπονδαύλης, ἱεροσαλπικτής*, along with an official in charge of the censer (*ὁ ἐπὶ θυμιάτρου*). While the nomenclature is not precisely the same, we might recall the officials whose presence in the prytaneion at Olympia is attested both by Pausanias (A 375; chapter one, p. 9 and note 12) and the inscriptions found there. There is also a similarity between the Ephesian officials and the aeisitoi in the Athenian tholos in the Roman period. These parallels are not proof that our building at Ephesos was the prytaneion, but they are certainly suggestive.

28 *Ibid.* 292, note 66; see Miltner, *op. cit.* (note 13) 28–29, for other inscriptions from the building which record thanks to "Hestia Boulaia and all the gods," and which mention a female prytanis sacred to Hestia. Two more such texts have been presented by D. Knibbe, *Jahreshefte* 47 (1964–1965) Beiblatt 37–44.

29 Miltner, *op. cit.* (note 13) 30–32, and *op. cit.* (note 9) 366–371.

Architectural criteria also suggest that the building was the prytaneion of Ephesos. The courtyard, the principal rooms for Hestia and dining (Rooms III and I, respectively), and the subsidiary rooms are all present in the building. Its quality of construction is quite good—indeed monumental—and there are no difficulties in recognizing the building as a major civic structure. Given the location, the building may, in all probability, be identified as the prytaneion of Ephesos.

Kolophon

Location

The building at Kolophon is located at the northeast corner of an open area which may have been the agora of the ancient city. Situated on a spur of land projecting out from the northern slopes of the acropolis, the area is fairly level, but relatively small (about 50 × 120 meters), and was limited on north and west by an L-shaped stoa. The building with which we are concerned was a later addition to the east end of the northern arm of this stoa.[30]

The Remains

The history of the excavations, unfortunately tied to the political events of 1922 in western Asia Minor, did not include a careful survey of our building, and Holland was forced to piece together a plan based on notebook sketches. This history is important for us because the remains of our building were found directly below the modern ground level, and so close to the present surface that it was not clear that the floor of the building had been preserved.[31] This means that the preserved walls were mostly foundations, constructed of undistinguished rubble masonry with larger blocks used only to help bond walls at corners. Since the excavations, the now-exposed walls have crumbled and become amorphous lines of small stones (pls. 13a, b) which do not allow precise measurements. Where possible, I have checked Holland's sketch plan and have found

30 The only report on the building is by L. B. Holland, "Colophon," *Hesperia* 13 (1944) 103–106.

31 Holland, *op. cit.* 103.

it to be accurate to ± 0.20 meters, but more precision is neither possible nor implied in the plan presented here (fig. 11).

Despite these difficulties, the outlines of the building are clear. Added to an earlier stoa, the colonnade of the latter was extended eastwards to provide a common columnar façade for the stoa and our building. Behind this façade lay the three rooms of the building. The eastern of these was the largest (about 10.35 × 12.80 meters) and had the foundations of a pilaster preserved against the western wall. This pilaster is no longer discernible, but it was in line with a structure (about 1.40 × 1.50 meters) in the center of the room, which has been interpreted as a roof support. The southern and western sides of this central structure are still preserved (pl. 13c).

Adjoining this room to the west are two smaller rooms, the northern measuring about 3.85 × 5.70 meters, the southern about 5.25 × 7.20 meters. The means of communication between these rooms cannot be determined.

Throughout this area were found traces of earlier remains. The most notable of these was a paved north–south street which

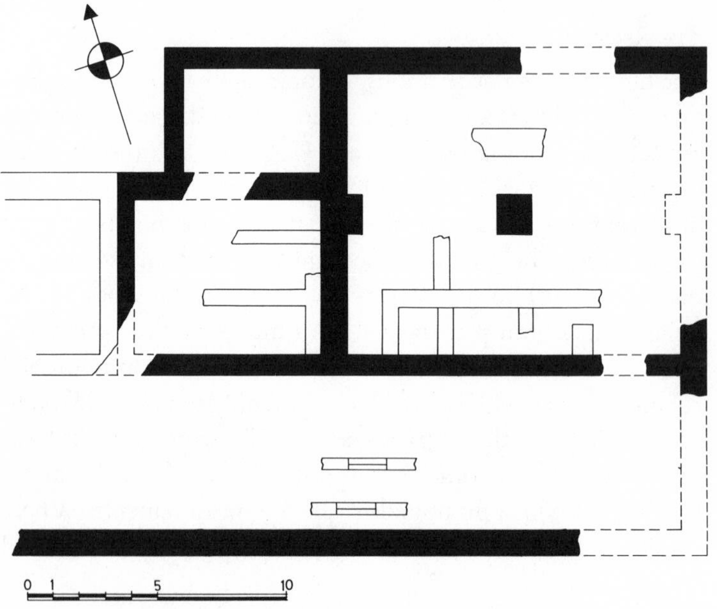

FIGURE 11. Plan of the building at Kolophon.

was encroached upon by the eastern end of the stoa, and closed off completely by the construction of our building. Earlier walls were also abundant in the area and seem to indicate another building on the same site with the same orientation.[32]

Date

Holland found six datable coins in the stoa area from *ca.* 389–*ca.* 350 B.C.[33] Although the stratigraphic context of these coins is not mentioned, the condition of the site when excavated was such that these coins were almost certainly found beneath the floor of the stoa (see above, p. 109). The coins should, therefore, provide a *terminus post quem* for the construction of the stoa. If the stoa was built, at the earliest, in the mid-fourth century B.C., our building must belong in the second half of that century. It cannot have been in use long, for it must have suffered along with the rest of the city in 299 B.C. when Lysimachos captured Kolophon and transplanted the citizen body to Ephesos.[34]

Identification

Since the building appeared to be a public or civic structure, Holland suggested that it was a prytaneion based on the discovery of three lead weights in the large room.[35] We have already seen (chapter two, p. 35 and note 26) that weights and measures are not necessarily indicative of a prytaneion. Moreover, the form of the Kolophonian structure does not fit well with our criteria: there is no courtyard and no room for

32 Holland, *op. cit.* 105–106, was not certain whether or not some of these walls might have been contemporary with the building. Although absolute certainty is not possible, there is an indication that none of these walls belonged with our building. As mentioned before, large blocks were used in the construction of the walls at the point of juncture with other walls. No such blocks are now in place in the walls of our building except at the intersections of the main walls as shown in figure 11. Proper cleaning of the junctures of the other walls should reveal whether or not they are bonded into the main walls, but present conditions at the site do not allow such an examination.

33 Holland, *op. cit.* (note 30) 107 and note 14.

34 Pausanias I, 9, 7, and VII, 3, 4.

35 Holland, *op. cit.* (note 30) 106.

dining couches, and there is only one dominant room rather than the necessary two rooms.

Although these objections might seem fatal to the identification of the building at Kolophon as a prytaneion, it retains interest for us because of its affinities with two other buildings in our discussion. These structures, at Morgantina and Priene, are like the present one in being later additions to stoas, in being less than monumental in construction, in bordering the agoras of their cities, and in dating from early Hellenistic times. The possible ramifications of these affinities will be discussed after the building at Priene has been presented.

Magnesia on the Maeander

Location

The agora of Magnesia is surrounded by a colonnade behind the southern side of which lie a series of shops—except at the southwest corner. At this point is the building which, it has been suggested, was a prytaneion.[36] The building is bounded east and west by streets (the eastern street runs into the colonnade of the agora from the south), while the area to the south is unexcavated.

The Remains

The most striking feature of the structure is the enormous courtyard (34.20 × 25.90 meters) with a peristyle colonnade.[37] The columns of this colonnade were of the Doric order with one, at the southwest corner, of Hellenistic heart-shaped plan (see fig. 12).[38] The courtyard, and the whole building, was entered from the agora through a door in the wall behind the southern colonnade of the agora. This opening had two Ionic columns in-antis and formed a propylon for the building.

36 K. Humann, *Magnesia am Maeander* (Berlin 1903) 112. For a view of the general location see plates II and III therein. See (A 348–352) for relevant *testimonia*.

37 My discussion of the remains must rely wholly upon the short description and the one photograph presented by Humann, *Magnesia* 113, 137–138, and fig. 115. This meager information cannot be supplemented by personal observations since the remains have been refilled, apparently by the annual flooding of the Maeander Valley.

38 Humann, *Magnesia* 137, fig. 147.

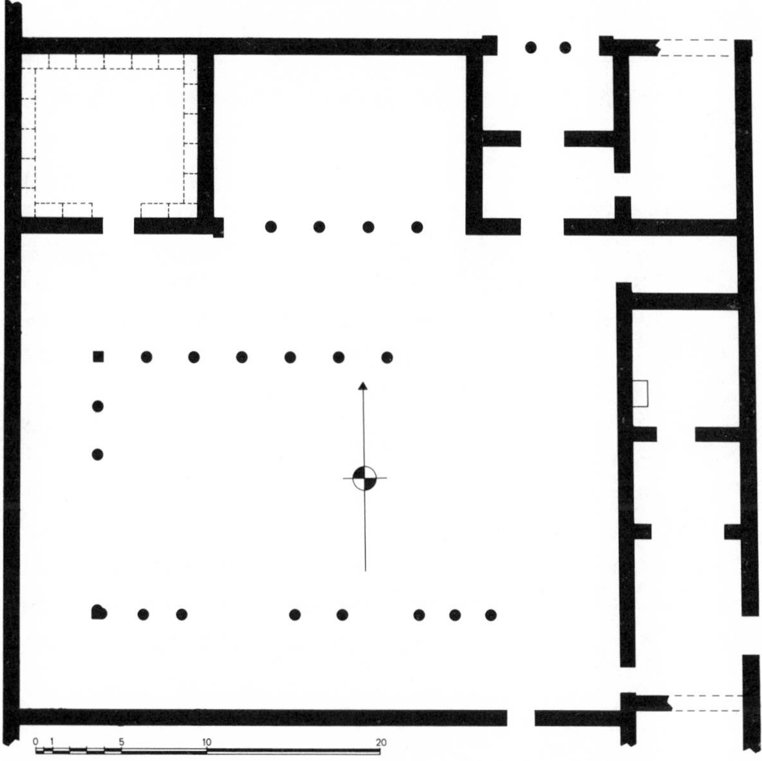

FIGURE 12. Plan of the building at Magnesia.

A series of rooms open off the courtyard on its northern and eastern sides, the largest of which is at the center on the north (14.60 × 9.20 meters). This room is an exedra with an Ionic tetrastyle in-antis façade opening out onto the peristyle court. In it was discovered the base of the statue of a certain Lucius Aphranios from the first century B.C.[39] The walls of this room were found standing to a considerable height and consisted of a course of double orthostates with a string course preserved above.

West of this room (i.e., in the northwest corner of the building) is another, smaller room. This room has an off-center door, and a border which appears to have followed the perimeter of the room.[40] These features indicate that dining couches belong in this room. The precise measurements of the room, its door,

39 *IVM* 143.

40 While the excavator made no mention of this border, it is clearly discernible in his photograph; see note 38.

and the border are not published and therefore one can only suggest approximate dimensions. However, it appears that twenty couches of the relatively small size of 0.80 × 1.65 meters would fit here.

Fragments of wall plaster, found throughout these two rooms, must have served as wall decoration. This decoration was the plastic panel relief type, in imitation of stone, known best from Pompeian wall painting as the First Style.[41]

The other room in the building which holds interest for us lies in the center of the eastern side. Accessible only indirectly from the southeast corner of the courtyard, this room was preceded by two anterooms. In the room was discovered a stone altar-hearth (1.00 meter high, 1.37 meters square, decorated with bucrania, mesomphalic phiales, and hanging garlands) which was inscribed: "Themison, son of Apollonios, and his son Nikanor, having been proedroi for the month of Zmision in [the archonship?] of Kleainos, dedicated the hearth."[42] The letter forms and the mention of Kleainos date the hearth to around 100 B.C.

Date

Although no date for the building is ever explicitly indicated by Humann, it must be contemporary with the south colonnade of the agora, for the wall common to colonnade and building is bonded with every north–south wall of the structure. The excavators date the construction of the south colonnade, along with the other buildings of the agora, in the second half of the third century B.C.[43] There is no way to verify this dating, nor to give it any more precision, but compatible with this date is the epigraphically attested existence of the prytaneion of Magnesia in the year 221/0 B.C. (A 348).

Identification

The discovery of the hearth, identified as such by its inscription, was the only evidence which the excavators used to justify their

41 Humann, *Magnesia* 138.

42 *IVM* 220: *Θεμίσων Ἀπολλωνίου καὶ ὁ υἱὸς αὐτοῦ Νικάνωρ προεδρεύσαντες / τὸν μηνὰ τὸν Ζμισιῶνα τὸν ἐπὶ Κλεάινου τὴν ἑστίαν ἀνέθηκαν.* *Tosi* 161 says: "*un altare . . . dedicato a Hestia.*"

43 Humann, *Magnesia* 22.

hesitant identification of this building as the prytaneion of Magnesia. The structure has, however, other features which strengthen its claim. Among these are its location and its quality of construction; and it is at least possible that the two principal rooms which open off the courtyard on the north were for the hearth of Hestia and for dining. Also present in the building, along its eastern side, are the requisite subsidiary rooms. It is unfortunate that we do not have a complete record of the objects found in the various parts of the building. One would like to know, for example, if any traces of burning were found in the exedra. Then too, the discovery of the small inscribed hearth in one of the eastern rooms, rather than in the exedra, is disturbing to any attempt to identify the exedra with the area sacred to Hestia (although the small hearth can scarcely have been *the* hearth of Hestia). The building at Magnesia must, therefore, rank with those which are possibly prytaneia, and which may be more clearly identified upon re-excavation of their remains in the future.

Morgantina

The building at Morgantina lies at the extreme southeast corner of the agora, and is a southern extension of the East Stoa of the agora (pl. 13d).[44] The two northernmost rooms (rooms I, II) of the building were a part of the East Stoa originally, but were turned around to become members of the later building under discussion. The dominant architectural feature of the building is the three-sided peristyle off which open a series of smaller rooms (see fig. 13). Although certain rooms have elements (basin, hearth, and bar) which set them off from one another, none can be said to be a principal room in the sense that one has come to expect for the Hestia Hall. Neither do any of the rooms properly accommodate standard-size dining couches.

Erected in the first half of the third century B.C., this building

44 See the preliminary reports by E. Sjöqvist, *AJA* 62 (1958) 161, and R. Stillwell, *AJA* 63 (1959) 167–168. A detailed presentation of this building by the present author is now in manuscript form and should appear as part of a more general publication of the civic architecture at Morgantina. I will not, therefore, discuss the building in great detail here.

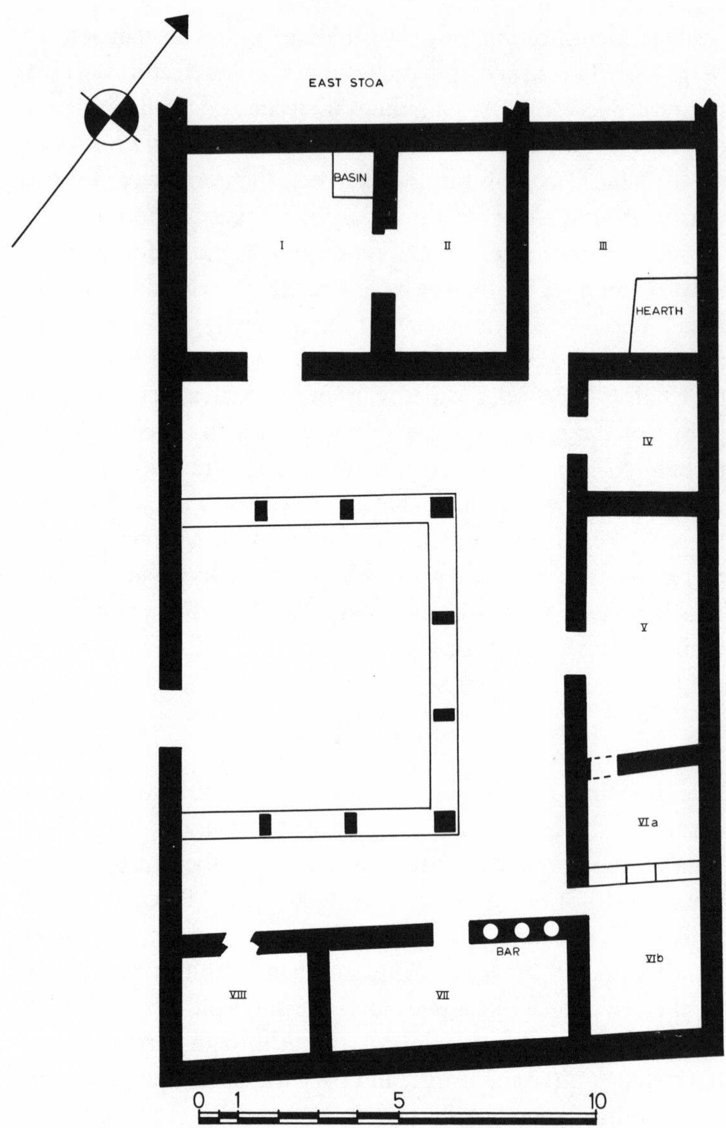

FIGURE 13. Plan of the building at Morgantina.

can be called public on the basis of its location, but its identification as a prytaneion is not so easily justified. The dominant hearth and dining rooms are lacking, and the raised hearth in Room III is placed in an apparently subsidiary area. In the following section on Priene, we will note the similarities between this building and those at Priene and Kolophon. For the moment, it is enough to say that the Morgantina building, unlike the prytaneia which we have discussed above, has a basically domestic plan, and its accoutrements (basin, bar, hearth, etc.) can be more easily understood as the outfittings for a "public house" than for a prytaneion.

Priene

Location

The building frequently identified as the prytaneion of Priene lies northeast of the agora, behind the east end of the Sacred Stoa. The structure occupies slightly less than a quarter of one of Priene's *insulae*, the northwestern quarter being taken up by the Ekklesiasterion,[45] and the southern half by the east end of the Sacred Stoa.

The Remains

As has been the case elsewhere, the building at Priene has suffered greatly during the seventy-five years since its excavation.[46] Even when first uncovered, however, the situation was confused because the building had been reconstructed in Imperial times and much of the original plan was then obscured. Yet certain aspects of the earlier plan can be recognized.

The overall dimensions of the building are 17.50 × 24.00 meters. The west and south walls of the building are, respectively, the east wall of the Ekklesiasterion and the north wall of the Sacred Stoa; the building was constructed against these earlier structures. The back wall of the stoa in this area rests on bedrock cut down to receive it, and it is the bedrock cutting for foundations on the east side of our building (actually offset 0.47 meters east of the east wall of the Stoa) which indicates the wall line of the building on that side (pl. 14c).

Only a few of the original, Greek, elements within the

45 Or the bouleuterion, as that building is more frequently, if less correctly, called; see *McDonald* 89–91 *contra* G. Kleiner, "Priene," *RE* Suppl. IX (1962) 1204. For *testimonia* relevant to Priene, see (A 392–413).

46 H. Schrader (and T. Wiegand), *Priene* (Berlin 1904) 233–234. In addition to the earth washed down from above and jumbles of displaced blocks, it is sad that the damage has included a part of the eastern wall of the Ekklesiasterion which was a full course higher in 1900 than it is today.

building can be identified (fig. 14).[47] These consist of three rooms along the northern side of the structure (Rooms I, II, and III) which are of equal depth (5.05 meters) but of varying widths (5.23, 4.40 and 5.43 meters, respectively). The height of the floors in these rooms varies considerably from one to the next. The preserved threshold block of Room I (pl. 14d) shows no significant difference in height compared to the level of the courtyard, but in Room III bedrock is visible just inside the doorway (pl. 15a) about 0.35 meters above the northern stylobate of the courtyard. Because of this difference in floor levels,

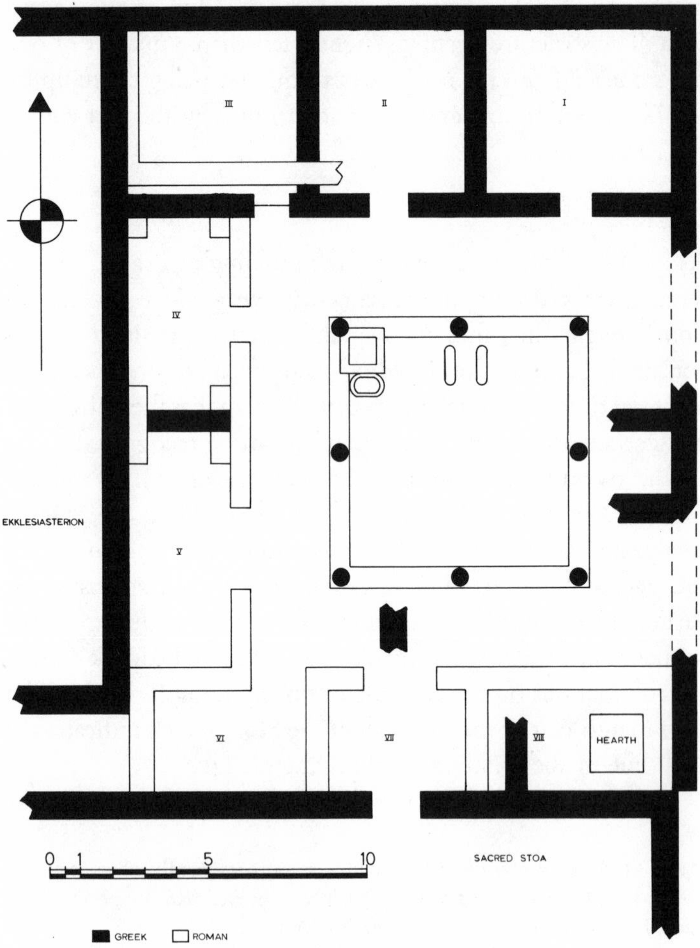

FIGURE 14. Plan of the building at Priene.

47 See Schrader, *loc. cit.*

the absence of indications of couches, and our ignorance of the objects discovered within the rooms, it is impossible to establish the original function of Rooms I–III individually or as a group.

Among the other Greek elements there was, according to the excavators, an east–west wall between Rooms IV and V which apparently continued in use even after the Roman remodeling of the building. It is not now possible to make any judgement with regard to the date of this wall. Four other wall traces from the Greek period were also defined by the excavators. Two of these are east–west walls on the eastern side of the courtyard, and two are north–south walls, one in the southern part of the courtyard, the other within Room VIII.[48] Of these, only that in Room VIII is now visible, and with such scanty remains a reconstruction of the plan of the earlier building is not possible.

There are, however, two other elements which must belong to this early period. The first of these is the threshold block which opened into Room VII from the Sacred Stoa. This is built directly into the toichobate of the northern wall of the stoa and differs from the other blocks in the same course only in its greater length and in its cuttings for door valves (pl. 14a).

The other early element, clearly a part of the original establishment, as well as of the later building, is the hearth in Room VIII. This consists of a stump of bedrock protruding about 0.30 meters above the level of the toichobate of the stoa (pl. 15c).[49] This small construction has deteriorated sadly since the excavation, but traces of burning survive on the square stone found on top of the structure at the center (pl. 15c) and confirm its function as a hearth. That the hearth was original to the earlier period is obvious from the fact that its construction involved the retention of bedrock. It was apparently much used and rebuilt at least once, from which time would come the

48 The type of rubble construction of this wall agrees with that of the southernmost of the two east–west walls which can be seen in the lower right foreground in figure 224 of Schrader, *Priene* 232.

49 Schrader, *Priene* 233, is apparently referring to this bedrock by his use of the term *Fussboden*, although his description is not clear. Certainly the mass which now remains does not consist of the rubble, stones, bone splinters, and mortar which Schrader mentions.

concrete and rubble layer on top of it (a fragment of which is visible in plate 15c, now having slipped off to the side of the hearth's bedrock base).

The building during the Imperial period is more easily defined. It consisted of a square courtyard, about 6.97 meters on each side of the peristyle, with three unfluted columns to a side. The columns have a base diameter of about 0.51 meters. The court was paved with large limestone slabs and sloped slightly downwards to the southeast where a channel drained water into the street.

Surrounding this peristyle court on three sides were several rooms. It appears that some of the rooms had vaults over them during this period. Traces of supports for vaulting are noticeable in Rooms IV and V, and the west wall of Room III, built up against the east wall of the Ekklesiasterion, still retains in its uppermost preserved course the beginnings of the spring of a brick and mortar vault (pl. 15d).

At the northwest corner of the paved court was a large square marble basin (pl. 16a) designed to catch water falling from this corner of the peristyle roof. South of this basin is a roughly chiseled trough, apparently for the overflow of water from the basin. East of these waterworks, just south of the north central column of the peristyle, were found two carved marble legs of what was an altar table.[50] Finally, just to the north and outside of the opening of Room V, there is a re-used unfluted column shaft which bears an inscription (pl. 15b, see below) and which rests on a late Doric capital turned upside down to serve as a base (pl. 14b).

The main entrance into the building was apparently through the already mentioned door in Room VII from the Sacred Stoa. The east wall of the building—the only other possible area for an entrance—shows no trace of a door in its preserved areas.

The purposes of the several rooms, except for Room VIII with its hearth, are obscure. In the later configuration there is no space which would accommodate couches in the normal

50 The original position of these legs is indicated in figure 14. There were actually two marble slabs per leg unit, and although they now lie on their sides near the basin, they appear to have been *in situ* at the time of excavation, as can be seen in the photograph reproduced by Schrader, *Priene* 232, fig. 224.

manner, and the nature of the building in the earlier period is unclear. One would like to think of the court as a part of that original plan, but the extant court cannot be placed before Imperial times.[51] Although it is reasonable to suppose that the earlier building should have some reflection in the later structure, the vividness of that reflection is impossible to measure.

Date

There is very little evidence for the precise date of either of the two periods of construction. The excavators left the question unanswered, but did indicate a *terminus post quem* for the earlier building period which involves the two neighboring structures, the Ekklesiasterion and the Sacred Stoa. The former is clearly earlier than the building under discussion since our building was constructed up against its east wall. In fact, the east face of that wall of the Ekklesiasterion was provided with a smoothly polished surface, suitable for the interior face of the west wall of our building. This surface treatment is very different from that of the west wall of the Ekklesiasterion and shows that the whole area had been carefully planned and thought out before any construction began.[52] Thus the date of our building is later, but probably only slightly, than the construction of the Ekklesiasterion.

The chronological relationship between the Sacred Stoa and our building is not so clear. Although it would appear that the stoa was built first and our building than constructed up against it, the bedrock cutting for the north wall of the stoa is some 0.50 meters further north of the line of the wall itself, and might indicate a wall here earlier than the north wall of the stoa. Then too, the Sacred Stoa was provided, at the time of its construction, with the previously mentioned door which was the only means of access to our building. Thus, if the stoa was built first, its design certainly took cognizance of the structure soon to be erected on the northeast corner of the "city block," and it is

51 Kleiner, *op. cit.* (note 45) 1204, says that "*man jedoch noch den alten Säulenhof erkennt*," but it is unclear to which period he refers. The excavator never suggested that the courtyard was original, and he characterized the columns and stylobate blocks as re-used from other buildings; see Schrader, *Priene* 232.

52 Compare the east wall of the Ekklesiasterion as visible in our plate 15d, with the heavy rustication of the west wall in Schrader, *Priene* 225, fig. 217.

not impossible that such recognition was forced by the prior existence of the building under discussion.

The widely accepted dating for construction of the Ekklesiasterion and the Sacred Stoa is the later years of the third century and the first half of the second century B.C. This must mean that the Ekklesiasterion and the prytaneion, if we so term the building, were originally elsewhere, for the existence of a prytaneion at Priene almost two centuries earlier is attested epigraphically (A 392–395). The same would hold true for the Ekklesiasterion, because it is not reasonable to assume that there was no meeting place for the assembly of Priene before *ca.* 200 B.C.[53] One would wish to be absolutely certain, therefore, of the dating of the Ekklesiasterion and the Sacred Stoa.

For the Ekklesiasterion, the excavators suggest only a date earlier than that of the Sacred Stoa since the construction technique of the former seems "older," and since the erection of the stoa blocked light through the south window of the Ekklesiastion.[54] For a date the period around 200 B.C. is offered; that is, a time shortly before the construction of the Sacred Stoa which is dated to the decade 160–150 B.C.[55] A secure *terminus ante quem* for the stoa is provided by the inscriptions on its walls which date back to about 130 B.C.[56] For the actual date of the building, two pieces of evidence are provided. One is the mixture of Doric and Ionic elements on the façade of the stoa. There are Doric columns with fillets rather than sharp arrises, Doric capitals and frieze, but an Ionic geison running above the frieze. While it is true that such a mixture is characteristic of the Hellenistic period, we have already seen at Delos a later fourth century parallel for the treatment of the columns, and the use of an Ionic geison over Doric triglyphs and metopes is known already in the fifth century B.C. on the Propylaea at Athens and the Stoa at Brauron.[57] Furthermore, the treatment of the tri-

53 Kleiner, *op. cit.* (note 45) 1204, realizes this difficulty and posits the use of the theater by the Ekklesia of Priene prior to the construction of their own meeting place.

54 Schrader, *Priene* 229.

55 *Ibid.* 214–217.

56 *IVP* 107–130.

57 Ch. Bouras, *Η ΑΝΑΣΤΗΛΩΣΙΣ ΤΗΣ ΣΤΟΑΣ ΤΗΣ ΒΡΑΥΡΩΝΟΣ* (Athens 1967) 164–166; see 61–71 with figures for both Brauron and the Propylaea. The reason for this combination of the orders may have been the

glyphs on the Sacred Stoa is almost identical to that of the triglyphs of the South Stoa at Magnesia which was built, at the very least, fifty years before the supposed date for construction of the Sacred Stoa at Priene.[58] Thus, the architectural members of the Sacred Stoa provide only the widest limits for its date.

The other dating evidence used by the excavator is an extremely fragmentary inscription which preserves the letters *ΕΩΣΑΡΙ*.[59] This has been restored to read: [*Βασιλεὺς* *'Οροφέρνης Βασιλ*]*έως Ἀρι*[*αράθου*]. Considering the obviously late date of the letter forms (e.g., the broken cross bar of the *alpha*) and the known ties between Orophernes, King of Cappodocia from 158 to 156 B.C., and Priene, the restoration is not unreasonable.[60] This block was taken to be an architrave block of the Sacred Stoa and the inscription on it as part of the dedication of the stoa. If this were so, the stoa should be dated to the years around 155 B.C. There are, however, several difficulties with such an interpretation. First, the block in question has broken ends, top, and back sides, so that even its assignment to a building, as opposed to a statue base, for example, cannot be claimed with security. Second, there is an inscription which provided that a "law be written up on the diaphragma of the north stoa."[61] Schrader accepted an early date for this inscription, but got around its implication of such an early date

---

problem of corner contraction which was even more acute in the upper reaches of the mutules than in the frieze, or it may have had to do with economics; the Ionic geison was less expensive to carve than the more complicated Doric.

58 See Humann, *Magnesia* 22. Note in particular the similar treatments on the triglyphs of the downward and inward cut of the tops of the inner glyphs; the lower level of the tops of the outer glyphs; and the outward flare of the fascia above the triglyph blocks (Schrader, figure 189, vis-à-vis Humann, figure 122). There are also similarities in the profiles of the Doric capitals both in the treatment of the annulets and in the outward flare of the abacus (Schrader, figure 188, vis-à-vis Humann, figure 125).

59 *IVP* 204, but see *addenda* therein, p. 311, for another possible restoration.

60 This relationship between Priene and Orophernes is summarized, with the sources, by C. B. Welles, *Royal Correspondence in the Hellenistic Period* (New Haven 1934) 255–260.

61 *IVP* 99: *ἀναγράψαι δὲ καὶ τὸ ψήφισμα . . . ἐν τῶι διαφράγματι τῆς στοᾶς τῆς βορέου*. Schrader, *Priene* 216, took this inscription to be of the fourth century B.C. as will be obvious from the outline of his argument given in the present text. Hiller von Gaertringen, *IVP*, provides the evidence for a date of about 100 B.C. for the inscription.

for the Sacred Stoa; he supposed there to have been another, earlier, north stoa beneath the western two-thirds of the present Sacred Stoa. We need not examine the argumentation closely since the style of the inscription is patently at least as late as the mid-second century B.C., and thus does not suggest there was any pre-existing structure on the site nor an earlier date for the Sacred Stoa. This inscription was, however, the basis for Schrader's reconstruction of an early north stoa which has been accepted by scholars ever since.[62] The evidence for this earlier stoa is very slight once the epigraphical testimony is removed from the argument.

Finally, whether or not one accepts Schrader's early stoa, there is still left a complete *insula* which had no structures on it for about 150 years after the layout of the city, for it was only after such an interval, according to the accepted chronology, that the Ekklesiasterion, the "prytaneion," and the eastern third of the Sacred Stoa were constructed. The Ekklesia and the Boule could have met, of course, in the theater or elsewhere, but is it likely that a city block, so central in the plan of the city, was left vacant for so long? One should consider the possibility, whatever date is accepted for the Sacred Stoa, that the Ekklesiasterion and the building east of it were much older. That there is a difference in the construction dates of the Ekklesiasterion and the stoa is indicated by a difference in their clamps. In the former building a simple hook clamp was employed, while the stoa utilized dove-tail clamps with a square downward-projecting peg at either end. While it is true that there is no evidence for considering these hook clamps to be older, neither is there any evidence against it. In any case, it seems improbable that there was a century and a half delay in the construction of the Ekklesiasterion and the building under discussion, so important to the civic life of the city.[63] In short, a date in the late fourth century B.C. is in no way impossible for the construction of these buildings, and such a date is eminently more suitable in terms of the political history of Priene.

62 E.g., by Kleiner, *op. cit.* (note 45) 1208; and by M. Schede, *Die Ruinen von Priene*[2] (Berlin 1964) 49.

63 The use of the arch in the Ekklesiasterion does not militate against an earlier date for the building; the arched gate of the agora is also from the fourth century B.C.; see Schrader, *Priene* 229.

Identification

In arguing for an earlier date for the Ekklesiasterion and its eastern neighbor, one might seem to be begging the question of identification since the existence of a prytaneion in Priene in the fourth century B.C. is epigraphically attested. Indeed, an archaeologically derived date for any building to be identified as the prytaneion of Priene must be at least as early as that date. We have noted a great reluctance in the ancient world to shift the position of the hearth of Hestia in the prytaneion, and in a town like Priene, laid out at one time, with foreknowledge of all the civic needs and their architectural manifestations, it is inconceivable that the prytaneion would have been moved. If the building under discussion is to be identified as the prytaneion, it must be possible to date it to the (epigraphically attested) years around 325 B.C. We have seen that such a date may be possible for our building.

There are three independent indications that the building was a prytaneion. First is the building's location. It need hardly be said that a building adjoining the Ekklesiasterion and just off the agora from which one entered the structure (i.e., through the Sacred Stoa) is precisely where one might expect to find the prytaneion. Second, there is the substantial hearth in Room VIII which is quite suitable for worship of Hestia. Finally, there has been mentioned already the inscription (pl. 15b) outside Room V which records thanks given by the city of Priene to a benefactor of the third century A.D., a certain Marcus Aurelius Tatianus.[64] That this document is an official one is obvious, since the granters of the thanks are the city, the Boule, and the Synedrion of the Gerousia, while Tatianus is described as agoranomos, panegyriarchos, prostates, archiprytanis, and boularchon. In the past, the title archiprytanis has been seized upon as proof of the building's identification. Of course, this title affords no such proof, any more than the other titles prove that the building was, for example, an agoranomeion or a bouleuterion. The inscription does show the public nature of the structure, but nothing more.

In terms of our architectural criteria the arguments for the identification of the building as the prytaneion are not strong,

64 *IVP* 246.

especially considering the obscurity of the original plan. It has been impossible to recover traces of dining facilities for any period; the hearth area of Room VIII does not qualify as a predominant part of the building; and the extant courtyard may or may not be original to the pre-Imperial building. Moreover, the quality of construction, while not particularly humble, cannot compare with that of the neighboring Ekklesiasterion and Sacred Stoa. It is unlikely, therefore, that this is a proper prytaneion.[65]

Hypothesis

We have seen three buildings, at Kolophon, Morgantina, and Priene, which are not unlike in plan. The most striking similarity among these buildings is that all are on or very near the agoras of their respective cities, and are physically attached to the principal stoas of those agoras. All have a more domestic than public plan and it is tempting to see the emergence of a building type in them. Most intriguing is the fact that all may be from the mid-fourth to the early third century B.C., which reflects a similarity in the histories of the three cities: all had been founded much earlier, and were revitalized in the fourth century B.C. All three exhibit physical manifestations of this revitalization in new layouts of the town sites where these buildings were. Is it possible that the true prytaneia of all three cities were located in some other areas, and that the buildings which we have been discussing were "prytaneion-annexes" in the new civic centers? (We have already seen that the same situation in Athens produced a prytaneion-annex in the form of the tholos.) Such "annexes" would share some of the functions of the prytaneion, but their form would not be that of a prytaneion.

There is, however, another possibility. It was noted in chapter one that, just at this time, the *testimonia* indicate a shift in emphasis and importance of the prytaneion. Perhaps the buildings at Kolophon, Morgantina, and Priene are architectural demonstrations of this change. As some of the international functions of the poleis lost importance to the Hellenistic

65 This judgement has already been anticipated by McDonald, *AJA* 52 (1948) 375, and by *Tosi* 162.

monarchies, so too some of the functions of the prytaneion would have been of less importance. Thus, new prytaneia of the early Hellenistic period might be of a different plan from earlier prytaneia. The remaining area of potential growth for the prytaneion would be religious, but such development would not be universal. Whenever and wherever the significance of Hestia increased, so the prytaneion might also grow. Thus, for example, the Ephesian building would have a new courtyard in front and an altar area added to one side. Elsewhere, there would be little impetus for expansion of the prytaneion, and the institution and its architectural form would either stagnate or move into new areas producing official structures related to, but not identical with, the traditional prytaneion type.

SUMMARY AND CONCLUSIONS

IT HAS been seen that the prytaneion probably had its roots in the Geometric period, and that by the Archaic period it was firmly established as a civic institution. It brought with it from earlier times its name, which had almost certainly been derived from the office of the prytaneis. This office had had considerable governmental authority, later increasingly diluted, like the offices of the Archon Basileus and others which emerged into late Archaic and Classical periods as remnants of once far more powerful positions in the political structure.[1]

Although the office which gave the structure its name was gradually submerged and blended into the wider political framework, the building was not. Instead, it grew and flourished as an institution in its own right. This was possible because its functions were not limited to the provision of office space for politically moribund officials. Had that been the sole purpose of the prytaneion, it would undoubtedly have suffered the same obscurity as buildings like the basileion or the boukoleion.

1 The reader will recognize that the discussion of the origins of the prytaneion and its early connection with the prytaneis is theoretical. There is no evidence concerning the prytaneis before the early Classical period, and the outline offered above is therefore necessarily inferential but, hopefully, reasonable. On the origins of the prytaneis see also F. Gschnitzer, "Prytanis," *RE*, Suppl XIII (1973) 801–809.

Rather, by whatever chance, the prytaneion had gained possession of the hearth of Hestia whose eternal flame was the symbol of the life of the city. This was best displayed through the custom of providing, in the immediate vicinity of the hearth, hospitality in the form of meals for foreign visitors and distinguished citizens. This custom, although overtly motivated by politico-religious considerations of the privileges of guests, came to be an exhibition of the vitality of the city in international politics. Thus the prytaneion assumed its own role in the life of the Classical city, independent of the office of prytanis.

As a building with political and religious roles to perform in civic life, the prytaneion as an institution spread throughout Greece. Whether or not it originated tied to any particular form of government (e.g., democracy) is difficult to say for, with the exception of Athens with its more plentiful sources, it is usually impossible to date the inception of the prytaneion in a given city vis-à-vis the then existing form of government of that city. Nonetheless, once established, the prytaneion was immune to changes in forms of government: there could be, for example, a prytaneion at Pergamon under the Attalids, while the prytaneion at Syracuse survived the numerous consititutional upheavals there.

For an institution so closely tied to the status of a city in international politics, it is not surprising that the importance of the prytaneion waned with the decline of the city, especially in the Roman period. This is not to say that either the prytaneion or the city ceased to function in a meaningful way, but rather that the roles which they played were changed and became more introverted. Invitations to Xenia in the prytaneion, for example, have practically disappeared from the sources by the late Hellenistic period. For the prytaneion this meant a shift in emphasis to either the religious (e.g., the increased importance of Hestia at Ephesos), or the antiquarian (e.g., the relics and statues of famous ancients displayed in the Athenian prytaneion in the time of Pausanias), or a combination of both. The final result was, of course, that the prytaneion, always so intimately and now so obviously connected with Hestia, could, no better than she, survive the advent of officially accepted Christianity.

The main goal of this study, however, has been the determination of what, if any, generic architectural plan existed for the prytaneion. The ancient *testimonia* have been examined both for explicit references to elements within the building, general appearance, and location, and also for implicit indications of parts of the building necessary to meet the demands imposed on the architecture by the functions of the prytaneion. Proceeding with an examination of the remains, it was possible to gain a more tangible idea of the form of the prytaneion from the situation at Athens, and from the structures at Delos, Lato, and Olympia.

In this way it was discovered that the building was well built—sometimes so as to occasion comment by ancient authors—and that it was usually located on or near the agora. It was also seen that the two major functions of the prytaneion necessitated two main areas within the building: rooms for Hestia's hearth and for dining. Not necessarily capable of accommodating all the possible diners at one time, the latter was arranged to take them in turns. Along with these larger rooms, as indicated in the *testimonia* and found in the remains, are subsidiary rooms for storage. While the sources mention the existence of a courtyard, it was observed that the prytaneion at Lato, and to a certain extent that at Delos, lacked a typical courtyard. The prodomos may be included. In the prytaneia at Delos, Lato, and Olympia, as well as in the Athenian tholos, the artifacts were of a type which had been expected both from inference and from specific ancient reference. Thus we were able to arrive at criteria by which to judge other candidates. Turning to the best qualified of these candidates (and relegating the others to Appendix C), a few were found which, on the basis of our criteria, seem very likely to have been typical prytaneia, while others may belong to a secondary type. This type—seen at Kolophon, Morgantina, and Priene—was either a generic prytaneion of later development, or else a civic building related to, but not itself, a proper prytaneion.

Emerging from all this is a usable generic prytaneion plan: a comparison of the buildings at Lato, Delos, Ephesos, and perhaps Magnesia with this plan shows them to be prytaneia. It is this plan which ought to be entered in the world of Greek civic architecture alongside the bouleuterion and the ekklesiasterion, and against which suspected prytaneia excavated in the future should be evaluated.[2]

2 Although the prytaneion is a civic building, its relationship to other civic structures like the bouleuterion is, so to speak, spiritual rather than architectural. As a generic form, the prytaneion belongs to that group of buildings where dining was done, such as the pandokeion and others, and, to a certain extent, the private home. A description of the characteristics which distinguish the prytaneion from these types is not possible without a careful study which would reveal their own architectural peculiarities. Until such a study is produced, it is important to remember that the prytaneion is, in its architectural plan, a member of the family of ancient dining establishments; it is the specific function and location of the prytaneion which place it in the sphere of ancient civic architecture.

APPENDIX A

The *Testimonia*

Foreword

In Appendix A are gathered all the ancient *testimonia* which contain an explicit reference to the prytaneion. A complete presentation of all existing passages has been sought, but oversights are not excluded. The *testimonia* have consecutive numbers for the whole series, but are grouped according to the cities, alphabetically arranged, for which they testify to the existence of a prytaneion. Within each group the entries are arranged in a chronological sequence which depends, where possible, on the date of the circumstances described, but elsewhere on the date of the author. Thus, for example, (A 13) is placed in the time of Solon since it purports to reflect a situation which existed at that time, whereas (A 211) is placed in Plutarch's own time because it describes a situation current during his visit to Athens.

The *scholia* have been dated to the period of roughly the third to the fifth centuries A.D. Certain of them may well be earlier than this, but those such as (A 241) which attempt to identify or define the prytaneion must belong to a time when this building was no longer much used or understood. Then too, some of the *scholia* contain a tradition which depends on that found in the *scholia* D and Oxon. to Aelius Aristides (A 257,

258), and they should therefore be posterior to both Aristides and his scholiasts.

The passages listed in this appendix are only those with explicit mentions of a prytaneion, or of some attribute of that building at a site where the existence of a prytaneion is otherwise attested. At sites where no evidence of the former type exists, none of the latter has been included. For example, when we hear of dedications or sacrifices to Hestia Prytaneia at Sinope (*AJA* 9, 1905, 313) and at Syros (*CIG* 2347k), but have no specific evidence of the existence of a prytaneion at either site, the *testimonia* regarding Hestia Prytaneia are not included. To present these passages would, I feel, involve an assumption which is not necessarily valid as to the presence of a prytaneion at these sites.

Since many of the entries of Appendix A are more completely discussed in the text, the notations which accompany the sources have been held to a minimum. It is hoped that the notations which do appear will serve to elucidate questions involving the passages or their chronological position in the series. Questions concerning the various passages and their relation to or importance for the prytaneion are considered in the text, particularly in chapters one through three.

The translations of the *testimonia* are my own, although I have consulted, with regard to some of the literary sources, both the *Loeb Classical Library* and R. E. Wycherley's *The Athenian Agora III: The Literary and Epigraphical Testimonia* (Princeton 1957). I would particularly thank C. Roebuck and R. Stroud for their careful readings of the *testimonia*, which have resulted in a reduction of errors. Words or phrases not included in the original text of the source as presented in the appendix, but which are essential for the comprehension of the translation and which can be derived from the larger context of the original passage, are so indicated in the translations by their placement either outside the quotation marks, or within parentheses. Orthography, as so frequently, has been a problem. Consistency has been desired but not achieved. Thus the *kappas* of Koressos and Kos, which are pronounced in English as hard consonants, are transliterated differently from the *kappas* of Cyrene and Cyzicus.

Although mine is the responsibility for errors in the texts

and translations presented here, this compilation of ancient *testimonia* is, to a large extent, based upon a collection of sources for the prytaneion which was made by W. A. McDonald some thirty years ago. For his generosity in sharing this collection I give my thanks.

Adramyttion

1 *CIG* 2349b, 13–15 *ca.* 70 B.C.

κ[λη]θῆναι δὲ αὐτοὺς κα[ὶ ἐπὶ] / ξενισμὸν ε[ἰς] τὸ [πρυταν]εῖον ἐπὶ τὴν Βουλαίαν Ἑστίαν, με[ρίσ]/αντος Ἀρχέο[υ] τοῦ ταμίου εἰς τὴν ἐγδοχὴν αὐτῶν ὅσον ἂν / τῷ δήμῳ δόξῃ. πέμψαι δὲ τὸν Ἀρχέαν καὶ ἑκάστῳ τ[ῶ]ν δι/καστῶν καὶ τῶν γραμματέων ξένια τὰ ἐκ τοῦ νόμου.

Resolved . . . "to invite them to Xenismos in the prytaneion at (the hearth of) Hestia Boulaia while Archeas the treasurer divides up their portions, as much as the Demos decides. Archeas is also to send to each of the dikasts and secretaries the customary Xenia."

Aigiale

2 *IG* XII[7], 515, 46–47 II B.C.

πομπευέτω/σαν δὲ τὸν βοῦν ἐκ τοῦ πρυτανείου [οἱ] πρυτ[άνει]ς καὶ [ὁ] γυμνασίαρχος / [κ]αὶ οἱ ἔφηβοι.

"Let the prytaneis, the gymnasiarch, and the ephebes lead the bull from the prytaneion."

Aigina

3 *Michel* 340, 45 *ca.* 150 B.C.

ὑπάρχε[ι]ν δὲ αὐ[τ]ῶι καὶ σίτη/[σ]ιν ἐν πρυτανείωι διὰ βίου.

Resolved . . . "that Sitesis in the prytaneion be his (Kleon of Pergamon, governor of Aigina) for life."

Airai

4 *Michel* 497, 4–13 III B.C.

καὶ ἢν θέλη(ι) οἰκεῖν / ἐν Αἰρῆσιν δίδοσθαι αὐτῶι / ὀκτὼ ὀβόλους ἡμέρης ἑκάστ/ης παρὰ τῆς πόλεως καὶ ἐς οἰ/κίην πεντήκοντα δραχμὰς τ/οῦ ἐνιαυτοῦ καὶ εἰς πρυτανεῖ/ον καλεῖν τὰς δημοσίας ἑορ/τάς· ταῦτα εἶναι καὶ αὐτῶι κ/αὶ ἐκγόνοις.

Resolved . . . "that, if he should wish to live in Airai, eight obols be given to him every day from the city and fifty drachmai every year for his household and to call him into the prytaneion for the public festivals. These privileges shall belong to him and to his descendants."

Akraiphiai

5 *IG* VII, 4131, 35–37 *mid*-II B.C.

καλέσαι δὲ αὐτοὺς καὶ ἐπὶ ξένια εἰς [τὸ πρυτα]νεῖον ἐπὶ τὴν / κοινὴν ἑστίαν καὶ ἀπολογίσασθαι τὸ ἄλωμα πρὸς τοὺς / κατόπτας.

Resolved ... "to invite them (ambassadors from Larissa) to Xenia in the prytaneion at the common hearth and to make an account of the things at hand for their expense."

Andania

6 *Michel* 694, 112 93 B.C.

οἱ ἱε/[ροὶ ὅσ]α κα διοικήσωντι ἐν τᾶι παναγύρει ἢ κατακρίνωντί τινας, σύνεσιν ἀνενεγκάντω εἰς τὸ πρυτανεῖον.

"Let the priests, as many as shall be directors in the festival or judges for something, call up a meeting in the prytaneion."

Andros

7 *IG* XII[5], 739, 94 Augustan

The text is exceedingly fragmentary in this area and has preserved only ...*καὶ πρυταν[εῖον*...

Apollonia

8 *IVM* 45, 45–47 *ca.* 207 B.C.

[δόμεν δ' αὐτοῖς] καὶ ξένια τὰ /[μέγιστα ἐκ] τῶν [νόμων κα]ὶ [κλ]ηθῆμεν αὐτο[ὺς/εἰς τὸ πρ]υτανεῖον [εἰς] τὰν [κ]οινὰν ἑστίαν.

Resolved ... "that we should give the greatest amount of Xenia lawful to them (proxenoi in Magnesia) and call them into the prytaneion to the common hearth."

Argos

9 Diodorus Siculus XIX, 63 *ca.* 315 B.C.

τῶν δ' ἐναντιουμένων καταλαβῶν εἰς πεντακοσίους συνηδρευκότας ἐν τῷ πρυτανείῳ τούτους μέν ἀποκλείσας τῆς ἐξόδου ζῶντας κατέκαυσε.

"Finding about 500 of his opponents gathered in the prytaneion, he (Apollonides, a general of Cassander) shut them off and burned them alive."

Astypalaea

10 *IG* XII[3], 170, 23–25 early II B.C.

ἐξέστω δὲ αὐτῶι καὶ ἀνάθημα ἀναθέμε[ν] / ὅπαι κα χρήι[ζ]ηι τᾶς ἀγορᾶς ἐ[πὶ] τᾶ[ς] στοιᾶ[ς] / τᾶς παρὰ τὸ πρυτανεῖον.

Resolved ... "that it be lawful for him (an agoranomos, Arkesilas) to set up a monument wherever he chooses in the agora near the stoa beside the prytaneion."

Athens

11 Thucydides II, 15 "time of Theseus"

ἐπὶ γὰρ Κέκροπος καὶ τῶν πρώτων βασιλεών ἡ Ἀττικὴ ἐς Θησέα ἀεὶ κατὰ πόλεις ᾠκεῖτο πρυτανεῖά τε ἐχούσας καὶ ἄρχοντας ..... ἐπειδὴ δὲ Θησεὺς ἐβασίλευσε, γενόμενος μετὰ τοῦ ξυνετοῦ καὶ δυνατὸς τά τε ἄλλα διεκόσμησε τὴν χώραν καὶ καταλύσας τῶν ἄλλων πόλεων τά τε βουλευτήρια καὶ τὰς ἀρχὰς ἐς τὴν νῦν πόλιν οὖσαν, ἓν βουλευτήριον ἀποδείξας καὶ πρυτανεῖον, ξυνῴκισε πάντας.

"From the time of Kekrops and the first kings to the time of Theseus, Attica was always inhabited in small towns, each having its own prytaneion and magistrates... But when Theseus ruled, being possessed of both intelligence and power, he reorganized other things in the country and abolished the bouleuteria and the magistracies of the other towns, and united them all into the city which now exists, establishing one bouleuterion and one prytaneion."

12 Plutarch, *Theseus* XXIV, 3 "time of Theseus"

Καταλύσας οὖν τὰ παρ' ἑκάστοις πρυτανεῖα καὶ βουλευτήρια καὶ ἀρχάς, ἓν δὲ ποιήσας ἅπασι κοινὸν ἐνταῦθα πρυτανεῖον καὶ βουλευτήριον ὅπου νῦν ἵδρυται τὸ ἄστυ, τήν τε πόλιν Ἀθήνας προσηγόρευσε καὶ Παναθήναια θυσίαν ἐποίησε κοινήν.

"(Theseus) having abolished in each (town) the prytaneia and bouleuteria and magistracies, made one prytaneion and bouleuterion common to all where the town is now situated and called the city Athens and made a common festival—the Panathenaia."

13 Plutarch, *Solon* XIX, 3 594/3? B.C.

Ἀτίμων ὅσοι ἄτιμοι ἦσαν πρὶν ἢ Σόλωνα ἄρξαι, ἐπιτίμους εἶναι πλὴν ὅσοι ἐξ Ἀρείου πάγου ἢ ὅσοι ἐκ τῶν ἐφετῶν ἢ ἐκ πρυτανείου καταδικασθέντες ὑπὸ τῶν βασιλέων ἐπὶ φόνῳ ἢ σφαγαῖσιν ἢ ἐπὶ τυραννίδι ἔφευγον ὅτε ὁ θεσμὸς ἐφάνη ὅδε.

"As many of the disenfranchised as were disenfranchised before Solon was archon are to be re-enfranchised, except for those condemned by the Areopagus, or the ephetai, or in the prytaneion by the kings on charges of homicide or manslaughter or seeking tyranny, and were in exile when this law was published."

See (A 56) for consideration of the attribution of this law to Solon.

14 Herodotus VI, 103 524? B.C.

κτείνουσι δὲ οὗτοί μιν κατὰ τὸ πρυτανήιον νυκτὸς ὑπείσαντες ἄνδρας.

"Setting men in ambush at night by the prytaneion they (the sons of Peisistratos) killed him (Kimon, father of Miltiades)."

15 Herodotus VI, 139 *ante* 501 B.C.

Ἀθηναῖοι δὲ ἐν πρυτανηίῳ κλίνην στρώσαντες ὡς εἶχον κάλλιστα καὶ τράπεζαν ἐπιπλέην ἀγαθῶν πάντων παραθέντες ἐκέλευον τοὺς Πελασγοὺς τὴν χώρην σφίσι παραδιδόναι.

"The Athenians, having spread in the prytaneion the best couch they possessed, and set beside it a table filled with all good things, bade the Pelasgians to surrender the land to them."

16 *AJA* 51 (1947) 257 484 B.C.

Χσάνθ[ιππον κατά]φεσιν ἀλειτερὸν πρ[υτ]ανεῖον
τ' ὄστρακ[ον Ἀρρί]φρονος παῖδα μά[λ]ιστ' ἀδικεῖν.

"The ostrakon agrees that Xanthippos, son of Arriphron, is a transgressor in that he has especially abused (the privilege of) the prytaneion."

This poetic ostrakon from the Athenian Agora is open to varying interpretations as Raubitschek pointed out in his original publication of it. Of interest to us is the omicron in the word prytaneion. Is it the accusative singular, or is it a genitive plural? The translation presented above is based on the assumption that an accusative is intended, as favored by Broneer, *AJA* 52 (1948) 341–343, but it is possible that we have here the genitive of prytanis as proposed by Schweigert, *AJA* 53 (1949) 266–268. If the word is the accusative of prytaneion, then the sentiment expressed is not unlike that which Aristophanes frequently directs against Kleon and other politicians (e.g., A 35, 40).

17 Athenaeus IV, 137e first quarter V B.C.

ὁ δὲ τοὺς εἰς Χιωνίδην ἀναφερομένους Πτωχοὺς ποιήσας, τοὺς Ἀθηναίους φησίν, ὅταν τοῖς Διοσκούροις ἐν πρυτανείῳ ἄριστον προτιθῶνται, ἐπὶ τῶν τραπεζῶν τιθέναι 'τυρὸν καὶ φυστὴν δρυπεπεῖς τ' ἐλάας καὶ πράσα', ὑπόμνησιν ποιουμένους τῆς ἀρχαίας ἀγωγῆς. Σόλων δὲ τοῖς ἐν πρυτανείῳ σιτουμένοις μᾶζαν παρέχειν κελεύει, ἄρτον δὲ ταῖς ἑορταῖς προσπαρατιθέναι.

"The author of *The Beggars* attributed to Chionides says that the Athenians, when they set out a brunch for the Dioskouroi in the prytaneion, place on the table 'cheese and barley puffs and ripe olives and leeks' making a remembrance of the old way of life; but Solon ordered that a barley cake be given to those eating in the prytaneion, and wheat bread to be added on festivals."

The attribution of the play to Chionides was obviously doubted even in antiquity as noted by Athenaeus, but for want of another author, we leave it assigned to this Chionides who won first prize in Athens in *ca.* 486 B.C. according to Suda Lexicon.

18 Plutarch, *Aristides* XXVII *ca.* 465 B.C.
καὶ τὰς μὲν θυγατέρας ἱστοροῦσιν ἐκ τοῦ πρυτανοίου τοῖς νυμφίοις ἐκδοθῆναι δημοσίᾳ, τῆς πόλεως τὸν γάμον ἐγγυώσης καὶ προῖκα τρισχιλίας δραχμὰς ἑκατέρᾳ ψηφισαμένης.
"They also tell how his (Aristides') daughters were given out in marriage from the prytaneion at public expense with the city providing the dowry and voting a gift of 3000 drachmas to each."

19 *IG* I², 19, 14 453 B.C.
[*καλέσαι δὲ καὶ ἐπ*]*ὶ χσένια τὲν πρεσβείαν τôν 'Ε*[*γεσταίον* / *ἐς πρυτανεῖον ἐς τὸν*] *νομιζόμενον χρόνον.*
Resolved . . . "to invite the embassy of Segesta to Xenia in the prytaneion at the customary time."

20 Plutarch, *Kimon* X, 6 first half V B.C.
ὁ δὲ τὴν μὲν οἰκίαν τοῖς πολίταις πρυτανεῖον ἀποδείξας κοινόν.
"He (Kimon) made his house a prytaneion common to the citizens."

21 Herodotus I, 146, 2 mid-V B.C.
οἱ δὲ αὐτῶν ἀπὸ τοῦ πρυτανηίου τοῦ Ἀθηναίων ὁρμηθέντες καὶ νομίζοντες γενναιότατοι εἶναι 'Ιώνων, οὗτοι δὲ οὐ γυναῖκας ἠγάγοντο ἐς τὴν ἀποικίην ἀλλὰ Καείρας ἔσχον, τῶν ἐφόνευσαν τοὺς γονέας.
"Those who set out from the prytaneion of the Athenians and considered themselves to be the most genuine of the Ionians, did not take wives with them to the colony, but got Carian women whose parents they killed."

22 Plutarch, *De Herodoti Malignitate* 858F (mid-V B.C.)
τοὺς δὲ νομίζοντας αὐτῶν γενναιοτάτους εἶναι καὶ ὁρμηθέντας ἀπὸ τοῦ πρυτανηίου τῶν Ἀθηναίων ἐκ βαρβάρων παιδοποιήσασθαι γυναικῶν.
"(Herodotus says that) those who thought themselves to be the most noble of them (the Ionians) and who had set out from the Athenian prytaneion fathered children by barbarian women."

23 *IG* I², 35c, 21 *post* 445 B.C.
[*καλέσαι δὲ* / *τὸς θεορ*]*ὸς ἐς τὸ πρ*[*υτανεῖον ἐπὶ χσένια ἐς αὔριον*]
Resolved . . . "to invite the ambassadors (from Kolophon) to Xenia in the prytaneion on the next day."

24 *IG* I^2, 49, 14–15 442/1 B.C.

[καλ]έσαι δὲ καὶ ἐπ[ὶ χσένια ../....]δὲν ἐς τὸ πρυ[τανεῖ]ο[ν] ἕος ἂν ἐ̂ι [Ἀθένεσιν]

Resolved . . . "to invite (a judge from Eretria) to Xenia in the prytaneion while he is in Athens."

The text given here is from *Hesperia* VI (1937) 323.

25 Cratinus *apud* Plutarch, *Solon* XXV, 1 *ca.* 440 B.C.

πρὸς τοῦ Σόλωνος καὶ Δράκοντος οἷσι νῦν
φρύγουσιν ἤδη τὰς κάχρυς τοῖς κύρβεσιν

"(I swear) by Solon and Draco with whose kyrbeis they now roast the barley."

Plutarch is quoting from a play of Cratinus who refers to the wooden tablets (*kyrbeis*) upon which were inscribed the laws of Solon which Plutarch had seen in the Athenian prytaneion (A 211). The passage is included here because the allusion by Cratinus to food in connection with the *kyrbeis* fits well with the location of the laws of Solon by the third quarter of the fifth century B.C. See chapter three, pp. 43–44, note 14.

26 *IG* I^2, 77, 4–18 431–421 B.C.

[ἐ̂ναι τὲν σίτεσιν τὲν ἐ]μ πρυτανείοι πρôτον μὲν τôι [h/ιεροφάντει γενομένοι κ]ατὰ τὰ π[ά]τρια· ἔπειτα τοῖσι Ἁρμ/[οδίο καὶ τοῖσι Ἀριστογέ]τονος, hὸς ἂν ἐ̂ι ἐγγυτάτο γένος / [ἀεὶ hο πρεσβύτατος, ἐ̂ναι κ]αὶ αὐτοῖσι τὲν σίτεσι[ν κ]αὶ ἐ[κ/γόνοισι hυπάρχεν δορειὰ]ν παρὰ Ἀθεναίον κατὰ τὰ [δ]εδομ/[ένα· καὶ τôν μάντεον hὸς ἂ]ν hο Ἀπόλλον ἀνhέλ[ει] ἐχ[σ]εγόμε/[νος τὰ νόμιμα λαβε̂ν πάντα]ς σίτεσιν καὶ τὸ λοιπὸν hὸς ἂν /[ἀνhέλει τὲν σίτεσιν ἐ̂ναι] αὐτοῖσι κατὰ ταὐτά. κα[ὶ hοπόσ/οι νενικέκασι 'Ολυμπίασι] ἒ Πυθοῖ ἒ hΙσθμοῖ ἒ Νεμέ[αι τὸς γ/υμνικὸς ἀγôνας, ἐ̂ναι αὐτ]οῖσι τὲν σίτεσιν ἐν πρυτανε[ίο/ι καὶ ἄλλας ἰδίαι τιμὰς π]ρὸς τε̂ι σιτέσει κατὰ τα[ὐτά], ἔ[πε/ιτα λαβε̂ν τὲν σίτεσιν ἐν] τôι πρυτανείοι hο[π]όσο[ι τεθρί/πποι τελείοι ἒ hίπποι κ]έλετι νενι[κ]έκασι 'Ολυμπί[ασι ἒ / Πυθοῖ ἒ hΙσθμôι ἒ Νεμέαι ἒ] νικέσοσι τὸ λοιπό[ν]. ἐ̂ναι [δὲ αὐτ/οῖσι τὰς τιμὰς κατὰ τὰ ἐς τ]ὲν στέλε[ν] γεγραμ[μ]ένα.

"First there shall be Sitesis in the prytaneion for him who is the Hierophantes according to custom; then for whomever is the oldest male descendant of Harmodios and Aristogeiton, to them shall be the gift according to the grants of the Athenians; and to all those of the Manteis whom Apollo the expounder of customs should choose to have Sitesis, to these shall be Sitesis in the same way. Also those who have won the gymnastic games at Olympia or Delphi or Isthmia or Nemea shall have Sitesis in the prytaneion and other honors in addition to Sitesis in the same way; then those shall have Sitesis in the prytaneion who have won a four horse chariot race or a horse race at Olympia or Delphi or Isthmia or Nemea, or shall win in the future. They shall have the honors according to the things written on the stele."

This inscription, of great importance for the information which it provides about the regular recipients of Sitesis in the Athenian prytaneion during the late fifth century B.C., is unfortunately mutilated in the important area between mention of the honors awarded to the descendants of Harmodios and Aristogeiton and to the victors in the Pan-Hellenic games. The most which can be said with certainty is that there was another type of recipient of a politico-religious nature. The text presented here is that of Ostwald, *AJPh* 72 (1951) 24–46, who restored the manteis, and earlier in the text, the hierophantes, as the now lost honorees. My agreement with Ostwald is based on the other evidence which we have for the presence of the manteis in the prytaneion and their receipt of Sitesis there (e.g., A 250, 252), but there is room for disagreement with such a restoration, and this disagreement has not been lacking. The debate has centered around the possible presence of the exegetai as honorees in the text. That the exegetai are not elsewhere attested as beneficiaries in the prytaneion has been pointed out by Oliver, *AJPh* 75 (1954) 173, but one should note the views of Bloch, *AJPh* 74 (1953) 407 ff., and *HSCP* 1957, 37 ff., as well as the connection between the prytaneion and the exegetai as revealed by (A 196–202) below.

27 *IG* I², 78, 4–6 431–421 B.C.

τôι [Ἀπό/λλονι θῦσαι, ἐπ]ειδὲ ἀνεῖλεν ἑαυτὸν ἐχσεγετὲ[ν γενό/μενον Ἀθεναίο]ις, θρόνον τε ἐχσελêν ἐν τôι πρ[υτανέο/ι στρόματα παρ]έ[χο]ντας hος κάλλιστα

Resolved . . . "to sacrifice to Apollo since he has chosen himself to be the exegete to the Athenians, and to pick out a throne in the prytaneion supplying the most lovely coverings."

As pointed out by Oliver, *AJPh* 75 (1954) 166–169, the inscription is too fragmentary to be certain that *prytaneion* is to be restored.

28 *SEG* X, 64b, 32–33 *ca.* 430 B.C.

[τὲν Βενδῖν καὶ τὸν Δελόπτεν ἀρέ]σασθαι διὰ πομ/[πêς ἀπὸ τêς ἑστίας τêς ἐκ τô πρυτανείο.]

"Bendis and Deloptes are to be propitiated by a procession from the hearth in the prytaneion."

Cf. (A 179) below.

29 *IG* I², 58, 7–9 *ca.* 428 B.C.
[*καλέσαι δὲ τὲ*]/*ν πρεσβείαν τôν Ἀφυ*[*ταίον ἐπὶ χσένια ἐς τὸ πρυ*/*τ*]*ανεῖον ἐς αὔριον.*
Resolved ... "to invite the embassy of Aphytis to Xenia in the prytaneion on the next day."

30 *IG* I², 60, 16–18 427/6 B.C.
κ[*αλέσαι τὲν πρεσβείαν τ*]/*ôν Μυτιλεναίον ἐπὶ χ*[*σένια ἐς τὸ πρυτανεῖον ἐς*] / *αὔριον*
Resolved ... "to invite the embassy of Mytilene to Xenia in the prytaneion on the next day."

31 *IG* I², 149, 5–7 429/8 or 421/0 B.C.
κα/*λέσαι μὲν* .....]*αῖον* [*τὸν* ....8..../....] *ἐπὶ χσένια ἐς τὸ πρ*[*υτανεῖο*/*ν*
Resolved ... "to invite (a proxenos) to Xenia in the prytaneion."

32 Aristophanes, *Ach.* 124–127 425 B.C.

τὸν βασιλέως ὀφθαλμὸν ἡ βουλὴ καλεῖ
εἰς τὸ πρυτανεῖον
ταῦτα δῆτ' οὐκ ἀγχόνη;
κᾄπειτ' ἐγὼ δῆτ' ἐνθαδὶ στρατεύομαι,
τοὺς δὲ ξενίζειν οὐδέποτ' ἴσχει γ' ἡ θύρα.

Herald: "The Boule invites the Eye of the King into the prytaneion." Dikaiopolis: "Don't that beat all? Here I am playing at soldiers, while the door is never closed to them for Xenia."

The "Eye" of the King is the ambassador Pseudartabus.

33 *IG* I², 67, 6–7 424? B.C.
[*καλέσαι δὲ αὐτὸς καὶ ἐπὶ χσ*]*ένια ἐς τὸ* / [*πρυτανεῖον ἐς αὔριον*]
Resolved ... "to invite them (ambassadors of Oeniadai) to Xenia in the prytaneion on the next day."

34 Aristophanes, *Equites* 167–168 424 B.C.

βουλὴν πατήσεις καὶ στρατηγοὺς κλαστάσεις
δήσεις, φυλάξεις, ἐν πρυτανείῳ λαικάσεις.

"You (the Sausage Seller) will wipe your feet on the Boule and cut the generals down to size, tie them up and throw them into jail, and consort with low women in the prytaneion."

35 Aristophanes, *Equites* 281–284 424 B.C.

ναὶ μὰ Δία κἄγωγε τοῦτον, ὅτι κενῇ τῇ κοίλιᾳ
ἐσδραμὼν ἐς τὸ πρυτανεῖον, εἶτα πάλιν ἐκθεῖ πλέᾳ.
νὴ Δί' ἐξάγων γε τἀπόρρηθ', ἅμ' ἄρτον καὶ κρέας
καὶ τέμαχος, οὗ Περικλέης οὐκ ἠξιώθη πώποτε.

Sausage Seller: "I denounce this man (Kleon) because he enters the prytaneion with an empty belly and goes out again with it full."
Demosthenes: "And he carries out forbidden exports of which Perikles was never thought worthy, wheat bread and meat and fish fillet."

36 Aristophanes, *Equites* 535 424 B.C.

ὃν χρῆν διὰ τὰς προτέρας νίκας πίνειν ἐν τῷ πρυτανείῳ

"(Cratinus) . . . who ought for his former victories to drink in the prytaneion."

In this passage Aristophanes has substituted *πίνειν* for the expected *δειπνεῖν*. Does the play on words merely reflect the inebriate qualities of Cratinus, or is there an indication that successful playwrights usually received entertainment in the prytaneion? In the latter case, the pun would have the force of disparaging the work of Aristophanes' rival; the plays of Cratinus are worthy of drink, but not of food.

37 Aristophanes, *Equites* 575–578 424 B.C.

καὶ στρατηγὸς οὐδ' ἂν εἷς
τῶν πρὸ τοῦ σίτησιν ᾔτησ' ἐρόμενος Κλεαίνετον·
νῦν δ' ἐὰν μὴ προεδρίαν φέρωσι καὶ τὰ σιτία,
οὐ μαχεῖσθαί φασιν.

"Before this not one of the generals begged Sitesis consulting Kleainetos; but now they say they will not fight if they don't get their front row seats and their meals."

38 Aristophanes, *Equites* 709 424 B.C.

ἀπονυχιῶ σου τἀν πρυτανείῳ σιτία.

Sausage Seller: "I'll scratch out your (Kleon's) meals in the prytaneion."

39 Aristophanes, *Equites* 766 424 B.C.

εὔχομαι . . . . .
ὥσπερ νυνὶ μηδὲν δράσας δειπνεῖν ἐν τῷ πρυτανείῳ·

Kleon: "I pray that, just as I now do nothing (to deserve it), I may eat in the prytaneion."

40 Aristophanes, *Equites* 1404 424 B.C.

καὶ σ' ἀντὶ τούτων ἐς τὸ πρυτανεῖον καλῶ.

Demos: "I invite you (the Sausage Seller) into the prytaneion instead of them (Kleon and his friends)."

41 Aristophanes, *Pax* 1084 421 B.C.

οὔποτε δειπνήσεις ἔτι τοῦ λοιποῦ 'ν πρυτανείῳ.

"Never again in the future will you eat in the prytaneion."

42 *IG* I^2, 95, 4 *ante* 417 B.C.

[καλέσαι δὲ -- / -- ἐπὶ δεῖπ]νον ἐς τὸ πρυτανεῖον ἐς [αὔριον]

Resolved ... "to invite [?] to Deipnon in the prytaneion on the next day."

Although the names and offices of the beneficiaries of this decree are lacking, Woodhead, *Hesperia* 18 (1949) 82, has suggested that they were state informers.

43 *SEG* X, 108, 27–29 416/5 B.C.

[καλέσαι] / δὲ αὐτὸν [καὶ ἐπὶ ξένια / ἐς τὸ πρυτ]ανεῖον ἐ[ς αὔριον]

Resolved ... "to invite him (a proxenos from Knidos) to Xenia in the prytaneion on the next day."

44 Andocides, *De mysteriis* 45 415 B.C.

τὸν δὲ τῶν κακῶν τούτων αἴτιον Διοκλείδην ὡς σωτῆρα ὄντα τῆς πόλεως ἐπὶ ζεύγους ἦγον εἰς τὸ πρυτανεῖον στεφανώσαντες, καὶ ἐδείπνει ἐκεῖ.

"The cause of these evils, Diokleides, they led as if he were the saviour of the city in a chariot to the prytaneion and put a crown on him and he ate there."

45 [Andocides], *Against Alcibiades* 31 415? B.C.

ὁπόσοι μὲν ἄρχοντες ἐν μιᾷ πόλει γεγένηται, ὑπεύθυνοί εἰσιν, ὁ δὲ πάντων τῶν συμμάχων <ἄρχων> καὶ χρήματα λαμβάνων οὐδενὸς τούτων ὑπόδικός ἐστιν, ἀλλὰ τοιαῦτα διαπεπραγμένος σίτησιν ἐν πρυτανείῳ ἔλαβε.

"As many as were leaders in a city, they are accountable for their administration, but he (Alcibiades) who is a leader of all the allies and has wealth is not subject to trial for anything, but doing such things he receives Sitesis in the prytaneion."

This speech is almost certainly not by Andocides and belongs to a much later date, but it purports to be from the early part of 415 B.C. In the absence of another date to assign to it, we leave it at its assumed time.

46 *IG* I², 106, 23–24 411–408 B.C.
[κα]λέσαι δὲ Πολ[υ]κλέα καὶ Περαιᾶ καὶ τὸς μετ' αὐτôν καὶ ἐπὶ / [χσένια ἐς] τὸ πρυτανεῖον ἐς αὔριον.
Resolved . . . "to invite Polykles and Peraies and their company to Xenia in the prytaneion on the next day."

The restoration of *χσένια ἐς* rather than *ξένια εἰς* follows McDonald, *AJA* 59 (1955) 152.

47 *SEG* XII, 37 410/09 B.C.
45: *[καλέσαι δὲ καὶ] / ἐπὶ χσένια τὴμ πρεσβείαν ἐς τὸ πρυτα-[νεῖον ἐς αὔριον]*
63: *καλέσαι δὲ καὶ ἐπὶ χ[σένια ἐς αὔριον]*
Resolved by the Boule . . . "to invite the embassy (of Thracian Neapolis) to Xenia in the prytaneion on the next day."
Resolved by the Demos . . . "to invite them to Xenia on the next day."

48 *IG* I², 116, 41–43 409/8 B.C.
τὸς δὲ πρέσβ[ες καὶ] Ἀπολ/[λόδορον κ]αλέσαι ἐς πρυτανεῖον ἐ[πὶ χσέν]ια ἐ/[ς αὔριον]
Resolved . . . "to invite the ambassadors (of Selymbrianos) and Apollodoros to Xenia in the prytaneion on the next day."

49 *IG* I², 118, 24–26 408/7 B.C.
καλέσαι δὲ αὐτὸν καὶ ἐπ/ὶ ξένια ἐς τὸ πρυτανεῖον ἐς α/ὔριον
Resolved . . . "to invite him (Oeniades, proxenos from Palaiskiathos) to Xenia in the prytaneion on the next day."

50 *SEG* X, 136, 19–20 407/6 B.C.
[καλέσαι δὲ] καὶ ἐ/[πὶ χσένια ἐς τὸ πρυτανεῖον ἐς αὔριον]
Resolved . . . "to invite (the embassy from Carthage) to Xenia in the prytaneion on the next day."

51 *IG* I², 148, 1–2 446–404 B.C.
καλέσ]αι ἐπὶ [χ]σένια Ε[. . . . . . ἐς τὸ πρυ/τανεῖον ἐς α]ὔ[ρι]ον.
Resolved . . . "to invite E[?] to Xenia in the prytaneion on the next day."

52 *IG* I², 157, 7–9 446–404 B.C.
[καλέσαι δὲ κ]αὶ ἐπὶ χσέν[ι/α αὐτὸν ἐς τὸ πρυ]τανεῖον [ἐς / αὔριον]
Resolved . . . "to invite him (a proxenos) to Xenia in the prytaneion on the next day."

53 *IG* I², 136 446–404 B.C.
[καλέσαι δὲ -- / --- ἐς] τὸ πρυ[τανεῖον ἐς αὔριον]
Resolved . . . "to invite [?] into the prytaneion on the next day."

54 *Hesperia* 7 (1938) 274, 4 446–404 B.C.
[καλέσαι δὲ α]ὐτὸγ κα[ὶ ἐς τὸ πρυτανεῖον / ἐς αὔριον]
Resolved . . . "to invite him into the prytaneion on the next day."

This whole restoration has been rejected by McDonald, *AJA* 59 (1955) 154, because of the unparalleled use of the adverbial καί before the prepositional phrase.

55 *IG* II², 1, 37–38 405 B.C.
[καλέσαι δ' Εὔμ]αχον ἐ[πὶ δ]εῖπνον ἐς τὸ πρυτανέον / [ἐς αὔριον]
Resolved . . . "to invite Eumachos to Deipnon in the prytaneion on the next day."

See (A 58) below with accompanying note.

56 Andocides, *De mysteriis* 78 405 B.C.
ἢ ἐξ Ἀρείου πάγου ἢ τῶν ἐφετῶν ἢ ἐκ πρυτανείου ἢ Δελφινίου δικασθεῖσιν ὑπὸ τῶν βασιλέων ἢ ἐπὶ φόνῳ τίς ἐστι φυγὴ ἢ θάνατος κατεγνώσθη ἢ σφαγεῦσιν ἢ τυράννοις.
"Those who either by the Areopagus or the ephetai or in the prytaneion or the Delphinion by the Kings have been condemned and are now in exile or under a death sentence for homicide or manslaughter or attempting a tyranny."

Text of MacDowell, *Andokides* (Oxford, 1962). This is the decree of Patrokleides passed after Aegospotamoi to reinstate banished citizens except those listed above. Even a casual reading of this amnesty law and the so-called eighth law on Solon's thirteenth axon quoted by Plutarch (A 13) will show that there is a relationship between them. It is not so easy, however, to define that connection. Since one might have assumed that the Solonian version had served as his model it, is surprising that Patrokleides mentions, as his precedent, only the law of 481/0 B.C. There would seem to be two possible explanations for Patrokleides' failure to mention Solon. One is that the law of 481/0 is an intermediate step between the Solonian version and this decree, and was cited as the more recent precedent. This assumption would require the existence of a system of archives in Athens extending back to the early sixth century B.C. The other explanation is that the law is not Solonian, but was only attributed to Solon after a fourth century revision of the Athenian code. See chapter three, pp. 43–44, note 14; cf. Hignett, *A History of the Athenian Constitution* (Oxford 1952) 311–313.

57 *IG* I², 106a, 10–11 *ante* 404/3 B.C.
[καλέσαι δὲ αὐ]τὼ καὶ ἐπὶ ξένια ἐς [τὸ πρυτανέον ἐ/ς αὔριον]

Resolved ... "to invite them (two proxenoi) to Xenia in the prytaneion on the next day."

58 *IG* II², 1 403/2 B.C.

50–51: καλέσαι δὲ καὶ ἐπὶ / [δεῖπνον τὴν πρεσβ]είαν τῶν Σαμίων ἐς τὸ πρυτανέον ἐς αὔριον
54–55: καλέσαι δὲ τὴν πρεσβείαν τῶν Σαμίων ἐπὶ δεῖπνον / [ἐς τὸ πρυτανέ]ον ἐς αὔριον
63: [καλέσαι δὲ ἐπὶ ξένια Σαμίος τὸ]ς ἥκοντας ἐς τὸ πρυτανέον ἐς αὔριον
74–75: καλέσαι δὲ κ[αὶ ἐπὶ ξ]ένια / [ἐς τὸ πρυτανέον καὶ Ποσῆν καὶ τὸς ὑὲς] καὶ Σαμίων τὸς ἐπ[ιδημôντα]ς
50–51: Resolved ... "to invite the embassy of the Samians to Deipnon in the prytaneion on the next day."
54–55: Resolved ... "to invite the embassy of the Samians to Deipnon in the prytaneion on the next day."
63: Resolved ... "to invite the Samians who have arrived to Xenia in the prytaneion on the next day."
74–75: Resolved ... "to invite Poses and his sons and the Samians who are in town to Xenia in the prytaneion."

These four passages and (A 55) above are all from the same stone, although (A 55) was passed into law two years before being inscribed. The first of those presented here (lines 50–51) is part of a decree reaffirming the privileges granted to the Samians for their loyalty two years before. The second (54–55) is part of a rider which reaffirms these privileges once again. The third is part of a decree commending Poses who is apparently one of the "Samians who have arrived," while the last passage is part of a rider confirming the validity of the previous passage. It is not clear why Xenia has replaced Deipnon as the honor to be granted in these last two cases, since we would expect that the rights of citizenship for the Samians evidenced in the earlier law would still be in effect, but Poses and his company might be part of another group of Samians not included in the grants of the earlier decree.

59 *Hesperia* 40 (1971) 281, 11–12 403/2 B.C.

... δὲ το/ῖς ὀρφανο[ῖς] ἀποδίδω[σι .... 10 ....]τô / πρυτανεί-[ο .....
Resolved ... "to grant to the orphans .. [?] .. the prytaneion."

The text of this decree, concerned with provisions for the orphans of citizens who had died under the Thirty, is so poorly preserved in the area where the prytaneion is mentioned that we cannot be sure even of the case of the word. Rather than the accusative, it seems more likely to have been a genitive with a preposition (ἐκ or ἀπό), but we can not be certain. For one interpretation of the significance of the prytaneion in this text, see chapter one, pp. 19–20.

60 *IG* II², 6, 17–19 *post* 403/2 B.C.
κα/λέσαι δὲ καὶ ἐπὶ ξένια Εὐ/ρύπυλον ἐς τὸ πρυτανεῖο/ν ἐς αὔριον
Resolved . . . "to invite Eurypylos (a proxenos) to Xenia in the prytaneion on the next day."

61 *IG* II², 13b, 6–8 399/8 B.C.
[καλέσαι δὲ / α]ὐτὸν καὶ τὸ[ν ὑὸν ἐπὶ ξένι]α ἐς τὸ πρυτα[νέον ἐς αὔριον]
Resolved . . . "to invite him (Aristeas of Achaea) and his son to Xenia in the prytaneion on the next day."

62 Plato, *Apology* 36d 399 B.C.
οὐκ ἔσθ' ὅ τι μᾶλλον, ὦ ἄνδρες Ἀθηναῖοι, πρέπει οὕτως, ὡς τὸν τοιοῦτον ἄνδρα ἐν πρυτανείῳ σιτεῖσθαι, πολύ γε μᾶλλον ἢ εἴ τις ὑμῶν ἵππῳ ἢ συνωρίδι ἢ ζεύγει νενίκηκεν Ὀλυμπίασιν· . . . . εἰ οὖν δεῖ με κατὰ τὸ δίκαιον τῆς ἀξίας τιμᾶσθαι, τούτου τιμῶμαι ἐν πρυτανείῳ σιτήσεως.
Socrates: "Is it not more fitting, Athenians, that such a man should be fed in the prytaneion rather than someone who has won in the horse race or the two or four horse chariot race at Olympia? . . . If I must assess justly a worthy punishment, I propose this, Sitesis in the prytaneion."

63 Cicero, *De oratore* I, 54, 232 (399 B.C.)
Quod cum interrogatus Socrates esset, respondit, sese meruisse, ut amplissimis honoribus et praemiis decoraretur, et ei victus quotidianus in prytaneo publice praeberetur; qui honos apud Graecos maximus habetur.
"When Socrates was asked this, he replied that he was worthy of being decorated with the most splendid honors and rewards, and daily sustenance should be provided for him at public expense in the prytaneion—an honor which is of the highest among the Greeks."

64 Diogenes Laertius II, 42 (399 B.C.)
ἕνεκα μέν, εἶπε, τῶν διαπεπραγμένων τιμῶμαι τὴν δίκην τῆς ἐν πρυτανείῳ σιτήσεως.
"'On account of my actions,' he (Socrates) said, 'I should be honored justly with Sitesis in the prytaneion.'"

65 *IG* II², 17 394/3 B.C.
11–12: *καλέσαι δὲ Σθόρυ[ν τὸν Θάσιον ἐπὶ ξένι/α ἐς α]ὔριον ἐς τὸ πρυτανεῖο[ν]*

34–35: *καλέσαι δὲ αὐ[τὸν ἐπὶ δειπ]/νον εἰς τ[ὸ] πρυτανεῖον εἰς αὔριον*
11–12: Resolved by the Boule ... "to invite Sthorys the Thasian to Xenia in the prytaneion on the next day."
34–35; Resolved by the Demos ... "to invite him to Deipnon in the prytaneion on the next day."

In between these two passages, the Demos has changed the recommendation of the Boule to include a grant of citizenship to Sthorys; thus he was to have received Xenia in the prytaneion, but now, as a citizen, is entitled to Deipnon there.

66 *IG* II², 19b, 10–11 394/3 B.C.
[καλέσαι] ἐπὶ δεῖπνον [ἐς τὸ πρυτανεῖον / ἐς αὔριον]
Resolved ... "to invite (a new citizen from Rhodes, Phil ... des) to Deipnon in the prytaneion on the next day."

67 *IG* II², 21, 17–18 390–89 B.C.
κα[λέσαι ἐπὶ δεῖπνον εἰς / τὸ πρυτανεῖ]ον εἰς αὔρ[ιον]
Resolved ... "to invite (the ambassador of King Seuthes) to Deipnon in the prytaneion on the next day."

68 *IG* II², 22, 11–12 390/89 B.C.
κ]αλέσαι δὲ Πα[....⁸....ον καὶ ξένι/α ἐ]ς τὸ [πρυτανεῖον ἐς αὔριον]
Resolved ... "to invite Pa[?] to Xenia in the prytaneion on the next day."

69 Plato, *Protagoras* 337d *ca.* 390 B.C.
ἡμᾶς οὖν αἰσχρὸν τὴν μὲν φύσιν τῶν πραγμάτων εἰδέναι σοφωτάτους δὲ ὄντας τῶν Ἑλλήνων, καὶ κατ' αὐτὸ τοῦτο νῦν συνεληλυθότας τῆς τε Ἑλλάδος εἰς αὐτὸ τὸ πρυτανεῖον τῆς σοφίας καὶ αὐτῆς τῆς πόλεως εἰς τὸν μέγιστον καὶ ὀλβιώτατον οἶκον τόνδε, μηδὲν τούτου τοῦ ἀξιώματος ἄξιον ἀποφήνασθαι, ἀλλ' ὥσπερ τοὺς φαυλοτάτους τῶν ἀνθρώπων διαφέρεσθαι ἀλλήλοις.
"It would be shameful if we, knowing the nature of things and being the wisest of the Greeks, and having now assembled for this very purpose in the very prytaneion of Greece and in the greatest and wealthiest house of wisdom and of this city (the house of Kallias), display nothing worthy of this reputation, but argue with one another like the poorest of men."

70 Isaeus V, 47 *ca.* 389 B.C.
ἐβουλήθης μᾶλλον Δικαιογένους καλεῖσθαι ὑὸς ἢ Ἁρμοδίου, ὑπεριδὼν μὲν τὴν ἐν πρυτανείῳ σίτησιν, καταφρονήσας δὲ προεδριῶν καὶ ἀτελειῶν, ἃ τοῖς ἐξ ἐκείνων γεγονόσι δέδοται.

"You wished to be called the son of Dikaiogenes rather than the son of Harmodios, despising the Sitesis in the prytaneion, disdaining the seats of honor, and the exemptions which were given to the descendants of these men."

71 *IG* II², 51, 15–17 *ante* 387/6 B.C.
[*καλέσαι δ/ὲ*] *καὶ ξ*[*ένια Ἀκ..⁵.. ἐς τ*]/*ὸ πρυτανέ*[*ον ἐς αὔριον*]
Resolved... "to invite Ak[?] (a proxenos) to Xenia in the prytaneion on the next day."

72 *IG* II², 53, 9–10 *ante* 387/6 B.C.
κα[*λέσ*]*αι δὲ καὶ ἐπ*/[*ὶ*] *ξέ*[*νι*]*α Φίλυτον* [*ἐ*]*ς τὸ πρυτ*[*ανέον*] *ἐς αὔριον*
Resolved... "to invite Philytos (a proxenos) to Xenia in the prytaneion on the next day."

73 *IG* II², 54, 7–8 *ante* 387/6 B.C.
[*καλέσαι δὲ αὐτὸν καὶ ἐ*]*πὶ ξένια ἐ*/[*ς τὸ πρυτανέον ἐς αὔριον*]
Resolved... "to invite him (a proxenos) to Xenia in the prytaneion on the next day."

74 *IG* II², 24, 15–17 387/6 B.C.
καλέσαι δ[*ὲ Ἄρ*]*χιππ*[*ον καὶ τὸς ἄλλο*]/*ς πρέσβες τὸς Θασί*[*ων ἐς*] *τὸ πρ*[*υτανέον ἐς αὔρ*]/*ιον ἐπὶ ξένια*
Resolved... "to invite Archippos and the other ambassadors of the Thasians to Xenia in the prytaneion on the next day."

75 *IG* II², 29 386/5 B.C.
4–5: *κ*[*αλέ*]*σαι δὲ αὐτὸν ἐπὶ ξέν*[*ι*]/*α εἰς τὸ πρυτανεῖον εἰς αὔριον*
17–18: *καλέσαι αὐτὸν ἐπὶ ξένια εἰς τ*[*ὸ π*]/*ρυτανεῖον εἰς αὔριον*
Resolved by the Boule... "to invite him (a proxenos) to Xenia in the prytaneion on the next day."
Resolved by the Demos... "to invite him to Xenia in the prytaneion on the next day."

76 *IG* II², 33, 3–5 385/4 B.C.
[*καλ/έ*]*σαι δ*[*έ κ*]*αὶ ἐ*[*πὶ ξένι' αὐ*]*τὸς ἐ*[*ς τὸ πρυ/τ*]*ανεῖον εἰς* [*αὔριον*]
Resolved... "to invite them (a group of exiled Thasians) to Xenia in the prytaneion on the next day."

77 *IG* II², 34, 32–34 378/7 B.C.
[*καλ/έσαι δὲ τὴν πρεσβίαν τὴ*]*ν τῶν Χί*[*ων ἐπὶ / ξένια ἐς τὸ πρυτανε*]*ῖον ἐς αὔρι*[*ον*]
Resolved... "to invite the embassy of the Chians to Xenia in the prytaneion on the next day."

78 *IG* II², 70, 14–17 *ante* 378/7 B.C.
[ἐπαινέ]σαι δὲ Ἀντίοχ[ον κ/αὶ Στέφαν]ον καὶ Εὐρύ[πυλον / καὶ καλέσ]αι ἐπὶ δε[ῖπνον ἐς / τὸ πρυταν]εῖον ἐς [αὔριον]
Resolved . . . "to honor Antiochos and Stephanos and Eurypylos (Athenians) and call them to Deipnon in the prytaneion on the next day."

79 *IG* II², 81, 12–14 *ante* 378/7 B.C.
[καλέσαι δὲ . . . . / . . .]ον ἐπὶ ξένια [εἰς τὸ πρυτανεῖον / εἰς] αὔριον
Resolved . . . "to invite [?] (a Megarian) to Xenia in the prytaneion on the next day."

80 *IG* II², 84 *ante* 378/7 B.C.
7–9: [κα]λέσαι δ/[ὲ κ]αὶ ἐπὶ ξένια [ε]ἰς τὸ πρυ/[τ]ανεῖον εἰς αὔ[ρ]ιον
12–15: καλέσαι δὲ καὶ ἐπ[ὶ] ξένια Πολ/υχαρτίδηγ κα[ὶ] Ἀκλιβιά-δ/ην τὸν ὑὸν αὐτο [ε]ἰς τὸ πρυταν/εῖον εἰς αὔριον
Resolved by the Boule . . . "to invite them to Xenia in the prytaneion on the next day."
Resolved by the Demos . . . "to invite Polychartides and his son Alcibiades to Xenia in the prytaneion on the next day."

81 *IG* II², 40 378/7 B.C.
2–4: [καλέσα]ι δὲ καὶ τὼ Θηβ[αίων / πρέσβη ---]ον ἐπὶ ξένια ἐς τὸ [π/ρυτανεῖον ἐς αὔριον]
7–12: καὶ Θεόπομτον κα/[ὶ . . . .⁸. . . . καὶ τὸν τρι]ήραρχον Ἀριστόμ[α]χο/[ν καὶ καλέσαι ἐπὶ δεῖ]πνον ἐς τὸ πρυτανεῖ[ον / ἐς αὔριον. ἐπαινέσαι] δὲ καὶ Ἀντίμαχον τὸγ [. / . . . . .¹². . . . . τὸν Μυ]τιληναῖον καὶ καλέσα/[ι ἐπὶ δεῖπνον ἐς τὸ πρ]υτανεῖον ἐς αὔριον
Resolved . . . "to invite the embassy of the Thebans and [?] to Xenia in the prytaneion on the next day."
Resolved . . . "to invite Theopompos and [?] and the trierarch Aristomachos to Deipnon in the prytaneion on the next day. To honor Antimachos the . . . of Mytilene and invite him to Deipnon in the prytaneion on the next day."

82 *IG* II², 41, 12–14 378/7 B.C.
[καλέσαι δὲ τοὺς πρέσ/βεις τῶν Βυζ]αντ[ίων ἐπὶ ξέν/ια] ἐς τὸ πρυτανεῖον ἐς [αὔρ]/ιον
Resolved . . . "to invite the ambassadors of the Byzantines to Xenia in the prytaneion on the next day."

83 *IG* II², 95, 9–11 377/6 B.C.
[*ἐπαινέσαι δὲ Ἀπολλων/ίδην καὶ καλ]έσαι ἐπ[ὶ ξένια εἰς τὸ πρυτανεῖον εἰ/ς αὔριον]*
Resolved . . . "to honor Apollonides (a proxenos) and invite him to Xenia in the prytaneion on the next day."

84 *SEG* XXI, 230, 4–6 *ca.* 377 B.C.
[*κ/αλ]έσαι δὲ [τὸς πρέσβες τὸ/ς ἥ]κοντα[ς ἐπὶ δεῖπνον ἐς / τὸ] πρυτ[ανεῖον ἐς αὔριον]*
Resolved . . . "to invite the ambassadors who have arrived (from Arethousa in Euboea) to Deipnon in the prytaneion on the next day."

85 *Hesperia* 10 (1941) 337, 12–13 400–375 B.C.
[*καλέσαι δὲ α]ὐτὸν καὶ [ἐπὶ ξένια ἐς τὸ / πρυτανεῖον ἐς] αὔριον*
Resolved . . . "to invite him (a foreigner) to Xenia in the prytaneion on the next day."

86 *IG* II², 102, 13–16 375–373 B.C.
κ[αὶ καλέσ]αι ἐπὶ ξένια τοὺ[ς / πρέ]σβεις [τοὺς παρ' Ἀμ]ύντο καὶ τοὺς π[ε/μφθ]έντα[ς ὑπὸ τõ δήμο] ἐπὶ δεῖπνον εἰς/[τὸ πρυτανεῖον εἰς αὔρ]ιον
Resolved . . . "to invite the ambassadors from Amyntas to Xenia and those sent by the Demos to Deipnon in the prytaneion on the next day."

87 *Michel* 91, 13–15 369/8 B.C.
ἐ[π]αινέσαι δὲ Πυθόδω/ρον τὸν Δήλιον καὶ κ[α]λέσ[α]ι ἐ[πὶ] ξένια εἰς τὸ πρυτα/νεῖον εἰς τρίτην ἡμέραν.
Resolved . . . "to honor Pythodoros the Delian (a proxenos) and invite him to Xenia in the prytaneion on the third day."

88 *IG* II², 107, 24–34 368/7 B.C.
ἐπαινέσαι δὲ τοὺς πρέσβεις τοὺς / [πεμφ]θέντας εἰς Μυτιλήνην καὶ καλέσαι ἐπὶ δεῖπνον εἰς / [τὸ πρυ]τανεῖον εἰς αὔριον. καλέσαι δὲ καὶ τοὺς συνέδρο[υ/ς τοὺς] Μυτιληναίων ἐπὶ ξένια εἰς τὸ πρυταν[ε]ῖο[ν] εἰς αὔ[ρι/ον. κ]αλέσαι δὲ καὶ τοὺς συνέδρους τῶμ Μηθυμναίων / [καὶ Ἀ]ντισσαίων καὶ Ἐρεσίων καὶ Πυρραίων ἐπὶ ξ[ένια / εἰς τ]ὸ πρυτανεῖον εἰς αὔριον. . . ἐπαινέσαι δὲ τοὺς πρέσβεις / [τοὺ]ς πεμφυέντας εἰς Λέσσβον Τ[ι]μόνοθον καὶ Αὐτόλυκ[ον κ]αὶ Ἀ[ρ]ιστοπείθην καὶ καλέσαι αὐτοὺς ἐπὶ δεῖπνον εἰ/[ς τ]ὸ πρυτανεῖον εἰς αὔριον.
Resolved . . . "to honor the ambassadors sent to Mytilene and invite them to Deipnon in the prytaneion on the next day; to invite the delegates from Mytilene to Xenia in the prytaneion on the next day; to invite the delegates of Methymna and Antissa and

Eresos and Pyrrha to Xenia in the prytaneion on the next day; ... to honor Timonothos and Autolykos and Aristopeithes, the ambassadors sent to Lesbos, and invite them to Deipnon in the prytaneion on the next day."

89 *IG* II², 141, 25–28 376–360 B.C.
καλέσα/ι δὲ ἐπὶ ξένια τὸν ἥκοντα παρὰ / τô Σιδωνίων βασιλέως ἐς τὸ πρυτα/νεῖον ἐς αὔριον.
Resolved ... "to invite the one who has come from the King of Sidon to Xenia in the prytaneion on the next day."

90 *IG* II², 109b 363/2 B.C.
5–7: *καλέσαι [δὲ Ἀστυκράτην καὶ τὸς μετ' / α]ὐτô ἐπὶ ξένια [εἰς τὸ πρυτανεῖον εἰς αὔ]/ριον*
29–31: *καλέσ/αι δὲ Ἀστ[υ]κράτη κ[αὶ τὸς] μ[ε]τὰ Ἀστυκράτο/ς ἐπὶ ξένια ἐς τὸ πρυτανέον ἐς αὔριον*
Resolved by the Boule ... "to invite Astykrates and those with him (fugitives condemned by the Amphictyonic Council) to Xenia in the prytaneion on the next day."
Resolved by the Demos ... "to invite Astykrates and those with him to Xenia in the prytaneion on the next day."

91 *IG* II², 110, 18–19 363/2 B.C.
καλέσαι δὲ [καὶ / Με]νέλαον ἐπὶ ξένια εἰς τὸ πρυτανεῖον εἰς [αὔριον]
Resolved ... "to invite Menelaos (who had helped the Athenians in the wars in Chalcidice) to Xenia in the prytaneion on the next day."

92 *IG* II², 111, 55–56 362/1 B.C.
καλέσαι αὐτὸς ἐπὶ [ξ]έ[νια εἰς τ]ὸ πρυτανεῖον ἐς / αὔριον
Resolved ... "to invite them (ambassadors from Kea) to Xenia in the prytaneion on the next day."

93 *IG* II², 146, 3–5 *ante* 361 B.C.
[καλέσαι δὲ / α]ὐτὸν ἐπὶ ξένι[α εἰς τὸ πρυτανεῖον εἰς / αὔρι]ον
Resolved ... "to invite him to Xenia in the prytaneion on the next day."

94 *IG* II², 116, 38 361/0 B.C.
κ/[αλέ]σαι αὐτὸς [ἐπὶ ξ]ένια [ε]ἰς [τὸ πρ]υτα[νε]ῖον [εἰς] αὔρι/[ον]
Resolved ... "to invite them (ambassadors of the Thessalian League) to Xenia in the prytaneion on the next day."

95 *IG* II², 124 357/6 B.C.
9: *καλέσ[αι α]ὐτὸς ἐ[π]ὶ ξένια εἰς τὸ πρυ[ταν/εῖον] εἰς αὔριον*
12: *καλ[έσα/ι] ἐπὶ δεῖπνον εἰς τὸ πρυτ[α]νεῖον ἐς [α]ὔριον*

Resolved . . . "to invite them (ambassadors from Karystos) to Xenia in the prytaneion on the next day."
Resolved . . . "to invite (the Athenian ambassadors to Karystos) to Deipnon in the prytaneion on the next day."

96 *IG* II², 127, 30–34 356/5 B.C.
κα[λέσ]αι ἐπὶ ξένια ἐς / [τὸ πρυτανεῖον εἰς] α[ὔριον· ἐπαινέσ]αι δὲ καὶ Πεισιάνα[κ/τα καὶ καλέσαι ἐπὶ δεῖπνον ἐς τὸ πρυταν]εῖον εἰς αὔριο/[ν· καλέσαι δὲ ἐπὶ ξένια τοὺς πρέσβες τὸς ἥ]κοντας παρὰ τ/[ῶν ἄλλων βασιλέων εἰ]ς τ[ὸ] π[ρ]υ[τ]ανεῖον [ε]ὶς αὔριον.
Resolved . . . "to invite them (the brother and ambassador of King Ketriporis) to Xenia in the prytaneion on the next day; to honor Peisianax (the Athenian ambassador to Ketriporis) and invite him to Deipnon in the prytaneion on the next day; to invite the ambassadors who have come from the other kings to Xenia in the prytaneion on the next day."

97 *IG* II², 149, 11–14 *ante* 355 B.C.
ἐπαινέσαι / [δὲ τοὺς πρέσβεις τ]ῶν Ἀθηναίων τὸς πεμφθέντας / [καὶ τὸς πρέσβεις τὸ]ς ἐκ τῶν συμμάχων καὶ καλέ/[σαι ἐπὶ δεῖπνον ἐς τ]ὸ πρυτανεῖον εἰς αὔριον.
Resolved . . . "to honor the ambassadors of the Athenians who were sent and the ambassadors from the allies (Euboean cities) and invite them to Deipnon in the prytaneion on the next day."

98 *Michel* 1458, 20–22 355/4 B.C.
[ἐπαινέσαι δὲ Φι]/λίσκον καὶ καλέσα[ι ἐπὶ ξένια εἰς τὸ π]/ρυτανεῖο[ν] εἰς αὔ[ρ]ι[ον]
Resolved . . . "to honor Philiskos (a proxenos) and invite him to Xenia in the prytaneion on the next day."

99 *IG* II², 132, 16–17 355/4 B.C.
[καλέσαι δ]ὲ αὐτὸν [ἐπὶ ξέν/ια εἰς τὸ πρυτανεῖ]ο[ν] εἰς [αὔριον]
Resolved . . . "to invite him (a proxenos) to Xenia in the prytaneion on the next day."

100 *IG* II², 151, 8–9 *ante* 353/2 B.C.
καλ[έσαι δὲ καὶ ἐπὶ ξένια ἐ/ς τὸ] πρυ[τανεῖον εἰς αὔριον]
Resolved . . . "to invite [?] to Xenia in the prytaneion on the next day."

101 *IG* II², 161, 4–6 *ante* 353/2 B.C.
καλέσα[ι α/ὐτοὺς ἐπὶ ξένια ἐς τὸ] πρυτανεῖο[ν / ἐς αὔριον]
Resolved . . . "to invite them (proxenoi) to Xenia in the prytaneion on the next day."

102 *IG* II², 182, 9–10 *ante* 353/2 B.C.
καλέσαι δὲ αὐτοὺς ἐπὶ ξένι[α ἐς τὸ πρυτ]/ανεῖον εἰς αὔριον
Resolved . . . "to invite them (proxenoi) to Xenia in the prytaneion on the next day."

103 *IG* II², 188, 12–13 *ante* 353/2 B.C.
[καλ]έσαι δὲ καὶ [. . . . 14 . . . .] ἐς τὸ πρυτα[ν/εῖον εἰς αὔριον]
Resolved . . . "to invite [?] (a proxenos) to the prytaneion on the next day."

The text presented here is that of McDonald, *AJA* 59 (1955).

104 *IG* II², 193, 2–3 *ante* 353/2 B.C.
κα[λέσαι δὲ] Πρ[ῶτιν τὸν Θασίον / κ]αὶ ἐπὶ ξ[έν]ια ε[ἰς τὸ π]ρυτ[ανεῖον εἰς αὔρ/ι]ον
Resolved . . . "to invite Protis of Thasos to Xenia in the prytaneion on the next day."

105 *IG* II², 197, 5–7 *ante* 353/2 B.C.
[καλέσαι δὲ κ]/αὶ ἐπὶ ξένια ἐς [τὸ πρυτανεῖον ἐς α]/ὔριον
Resolved . . . "to invite [?] to Xenia in the prytaneion on the next day."

106 Demosthenes, *Against Aristokrates* 645 352 B.C.
Τέταρτον τοίνυν ἄλλο πρὸς τούτοις τοὐπὶ πρυτανείῳ· τοῦτο δ' ἐστίν, ἐὰν λίθος ἢ ξύλον ἢ σίδηρος ἤ τι τοιοῦτον ἐμπεσὸν πατάξῃ, καὶ τὸν μὲν βαλόντ' ἀγνοῇ τις, αὐτὸ δ' εἰδῇ καὶ ἔχῃ τὸ τὸν φόνον εἰργασμένον, τούτοις ἐνταῦθα λαγχάνεται.
"In addition to these there is a fourth court, that in the prytaneion. Its function is that, if a stone or piece of wood or iron or any such thing should fall and strike someone, and one is ignorant of the person who threw it, but knows and has the instrument of the murder, he takes action against these things there."

107 Demosthenes, *Against Aristokrates* 663b 352 B.C.
ἴστε δήπου τοῦτ', ὦ ἄνδρες Ἀθηναῖοι, ὅτι χαλκῆς εἰκόνος οὔσης παρ' ὑμῖν Ἰφικράτει καὶ σιτήσεως ἐν πρυτανείῳ καὶ δωρειῶν καὶ τιμῶν ἄλλων.
"I suppose you know, Athenians, that Iphikrates had a bronze statue and Sitesis in the prytaneion and gifts and other honors from you."

108 Demosthenes, *Against Polykles* 13 *ca.* 350? B.C.
καὶ ὁ δῆμος ἀκούσας ταῦτα ἐπῄνεσέ τέ με, καὶ ἐπὶ δεῖπνον εἰς τὸ πρυτανεῖον ἐκάλεσεν.
"And the Demos, hearing these things, praised me (Apollodoros, a trierarch) and invited me to Deipnon in the prytaneion."

109 *IG* II², 245, 11–12 mid-IV B.C.
[καλέ]σαι δὲ καὶ ἐπὶ ξένια [τὸς μετὰ / . . .¹¹. . .]ος ἐς αὔριον
Resolved . . . "to invite them (Boeotian refugees) to Xenia on the next day."

110 *IG* II², 206, 35–36 349/8 B.C.
ἐπα[ινέσαι δὲ Θεογένη/ν κ]αὶ [κα]λέ[σ]α[ι] ἐ[πὶ ξένια εἰς τὸ πρυτ/ανεῖον εἰς αὔριον]
Resolved . . . "to honor Theogenes (a proxenos) and invite him to Xenia in the prytaneion on the next day."

111 *IG* II², 210, 14–15 349/8 B.C.
[τοὺς πρέσβεις τ/ῶν] Ἀκανθίων καὶ Δ[ιέων καὶ καλέσαι ἐπὶ ξένια / ἐς] τὸ πρυτανεῖον [εἰς αὔριον]
Resolved . . . "to invite the ambassadors of Akanthos and Dion to Xenia in the prytaneion on the next day."

112 *IG* II², 212, 52–53 347/6 B.C.
καλέσαι αὐτοὺς ἐπὶ ξένια εἰς τὸ πρυτα[νε]/ῖον εἰς αὔριον
Resolved . . . "to invite them (ambassadors of Spartokos and Paerisades) to Xenia in the prytaneion on the next day."

113 Demosthenes, *De falsa legatione* 234 346 B.C.
τῆς πρώτης ἐκείνης πρεσβείας γράφων τὸ προβούλευμ' ἐγὼ καὶ πάλιν ἐν τῷ δήμῳ ταῖς ἐκκλησίαις, ἐν αἷς ἐμέλλετε βουλεύεσθαι περὶ τῆς εἰρήνης, οὐδενὸς οὔτε λόγου πω παρὰ τούτων οὔτ' ἀδικήματος ὄντος φανεροῦ, τὸ νόμιμον ἔθος ποιῶν καὶ ἐπῄνεσα τούτους καὶ εἰς πρυτανεῖον ἐκάλεσα.
"When I wrote the probouleuma about that first embassy and again before the people in the assemblies in which you were concerned in discussing the peace, since neither unjust word nor deed of theirs was exposed, I made the usual proposal and praised them and invited them to the prytaneion."

114 Demosthenes, *De falsa legatione* 31 346 B.C.
ἡ βουλὴ δ' ἡ μὴ κωλυθεῖσ' ἀκοῦσαι τἀληθῆ παρ' ἐμοῦ οὔτ' ἐπῄνεσε τούτους οὔτ' εἰς τὸ πρυτανεῖον ἠξίωσε καλέσαι.
"The Boule, not being prevented from hearing the truth from me, did not praise them nor think it right to invite them to the prytaneion."

115 Aeschines, *De falsa legatione* 46 346 B.C.
ἔγραψε γὰρ ἡμᾶς στεφανῶσαι θαλλοῦ στεφάνῳ ἕκαστον εὐνοίας ἕνεκα τῆς εἰς τὸν δῆμον, καὶ καλέσαι ἐπὶ δεῖπνον εἰς τὸ πρυτανεῖον εἰς αὔριον.

"He (Demosthenes) wrote that each of us should be crowned with an olive crown on account of our kindness to the Demos and be invited to Deipnon in the prytaneion on the next day."

116 *IG* II², 218, 21–22 346/5 B.C.
ἐπαινέ/σαι δὲ Διοσκουρίδην καὶ καλέσαι ἐπὶ ξένι[α] / εἰς τὸ πρυτανεῖον εἰς [α]ὔριον.
Resolved . . . "to praise Dioskourides (an exile from Abdera) and invite him to Xenia in the prytaneion on the next day."

117 *IG* II², 220, 20–22 344/3 B.C.
ἐπ[αινέσαι δὲ καὶ τοὺς π/ρέσ]βεις τῶ[ν Πελλανέων καὶ καλέ/σαι] ἐπὶ ξέν[ια εἰς τὸ πρυτανεῖον / εἰς] αὔριον
Resolved . . . "to praise the ambassadors of Pellania and invite them to Xenia in the prytaneion on the next day."

118 *IG* II², 226, 26–31 343/2 B.C.
καλέσαι δὲ Ἀρύββαν / ἐπὶ δεῖπνον εἰς τὸ πρυταν/εῖον ἐς αὔριον, καλέσαι δὲ / καὶ τοὺς μετ' Ἀρύββου ἥκον/τας ἐπὶ ξένια εἰς τὸ πρυτανεῖον ἐς αὔριον.
Resolved . . . "to invite Arybbas to Deipnon in the prytaneion on the next day, but to invite those with Arybbas to Xenia in the prytaneion on the next day."

This Arybbas had been the King of Molossia until expelled by Philip of Macedon. Arybbas then came to Athens where he was received and, in the terms of a part of this same inscription, confirmed in the citizenship which had been granted to his ancestors. Thus he is invited to Deipnon in the prytaneion while those of his company are to receive Xenia.

119 Aeschines, *De falsa legatione* 80 343 B.C.
καὶ γὰρ τὰς εἰκόνας ἵστατε, καὶ τὰς προεδρίας καὶ τοὺς στεφάνους καὶ τὰς ἐν πρυτανείῳ σιτήσεις δίδοτε, οὐ τοῖς τὴν εἰρήνην ἀπαγγείλασιν, ἀλλὰ τοῖς τὴν μάχην νικήσασιν.
"You set up statues and award seats of honor and crowns and Siteseis in the prytaneion not to those who announce peace, but to those who are victorious in battle."

120 *IG* II², 228, 16–18 341/0 B.C.
καλέσαι το[ὺς Ἐλα]/ιουσίους ἐπὶ δεῖπνον εἰς [τὸ πρυ]/τανεῖον εἰς αὔριον
Resolved . . . "to invite the Elaiousians (who have been awarded the same privileges as the Athenian colonists in the Chersonesos) to Deipnon in the prytaneion on the next day."

121 Theopompos, *apud* Athenaeus VI, 254b *ca.* 340? B.C.
ἣν ὁ μὲν Πύθιος ἑστίαν τῆς Ἑλλάδος ἀνεκήρυξε, πρυτανεῖον δὲ Ἑλλάδος ὁ δυσμενέστατος Θεόπομπος ὁ φήσας ἐν ἄλλοις πλήρεις εἶναι τὰς Ἀθήνας Διονυσοκολάκων καὶ ναυτῶν καὶ λωποδυτῶν, ἔτι δὲ ψευδομαρτύρων καὶ συκοφαντῶν καὶ ψευδοκλητήρων.
". . . (Athens) which the Pythian proclaimed as the hearth of Greece, but the most hostile Theopompos said in other places that the prytaneion of Greece was the Athens of Dionysos-flatterers and sailors and thieves, even of perjurers and sycophants and false witnesses."

Theopompos has taken the symbolic equation of Athens and the prytaneion (cf. A 69, 227) and given it a savage twist, for if the equation is valid, and Athens is full of crooks, Greece must be even worse since the best people would be in her prytaneion, Athens.

122 *IG* II², 232, 15–18 340/39 B.C.
ἐπαινέσαι [δὲ καὶ τὸν ἥκοντ]/α ἐκ Τενέδου κα[ὶ καλέσαι αὐτὸν] / ἐπὶ ξένια εἰς τ[ὸ πρυτανεῖον εἰ]/ς αὔριον
Resolved . . . "to praise the one who has come from Tenedos and invite him to Xenia in the prytaneion on the next day."

123 *IG* II², 238, 20–22 338/7 B.C.
καλέ/[σαι δὲ αὐτοὺς] ἐπὶ ξένια εἰς τὸ / [πρυτανεῖον] εἰς αὔριον
Resolved . . . "to invite them (ambassadors from Andros) to Xenia in the prytaneion on the next day."

124 *IG* II², 251, 10–12 *ante* 336/5 B.C.
[καλέσαι δὲ καὶ αὐτὸ]/ν ἐ[πὶ ξένια ἐς αὔριον ἐς τ]/ὸ [πρυτανεῖον]
Resolved . . . "to invite him (a new citizen) to Xenia in the prytaneion on the next day."

There are serious doubts about the text as presented above. First, the new citizen should receive Deipnon, not Xenia. Second, the sequence of the phrases *ἐς αὔριον* and *ἐς τὸ πρυτανεῖον* is the reverse of the normal order. Finally, the inscription is so fragmentary in this area that restoring entertainment in the prytaneion, although it was normal, is not certain here at all.

125 *IG* II², 254, 6–8 *ante* 336/5 B.C.
καλέ[σαι δὲ . . ¹³ . . / . . . καὶ τὸς ἄλλο]ς φεύγ[οντας ἐπὶ ξένια ἐς τὸ / πρυτανεῖον ἐς α]ὔρι[ον
Resolved . . . "to invite [?] and the other fugitives to Xenia in the prytaneion on the next day."

126 *IG* II², 264, 15–17 *ante* 336/5 B.C.
[καλέσ]αι δὲ τὸν ἥκοντα παρὰ / [Ἰατροκλέους ἐ]πὶ ξένια εἰς τὸ πρυτα/[νεῖον εἰς αὔριο]ν
Resolved . . . "to invite the one who has come from Iatrokles to Xenia in the prytaneion on the next day."

127 *IG* II², 265, 9–11 *ante* 336/5 B.C.
[κα]/λέσα[ι δὲ καὶ ἐπὶ ξένια ἐς τὸ π]/ρυτα[νεῖον εἰς αὔριον]
Resolved . . . "to invite (a proxenos) to Xenia in the prytaneion on the next day."

128 *IG* II², 274, 8–9 *ante* 336/5 B.C.
[καλέσαι ἐπὶ δεῖπν]ον εἰς τὸ πρυτανεῖ/[ον εἰς αὔριον]
Resolved . . . "to invite (the ambassadors from Sestos) to Deipnon in the prytaneion on the next day."

129 *IG* II², 276, 11–12 *ante* 336/5 B.C.
καλέσαι ἐ[π/ὶ ξένι]α εἰς τὸ πρυτανεῖον εἰς αὔριον
Resolved . . . "to invite (Asklepiodoros) to Xenia in the prytaneion on the next day."

130 *IG* II², 279, 7–8 *ante* 336/5 B.C.
κ[αλέσαι δὲ Βίω]να τὸν [Τήνιον ἐπὶ / ξένια εἰς τὸ πρυτανεῖον ε]ἰς αὔρ[ιον]
Resolved . . . "to invite Bion of Tenos to Xenia in the prytaneion on the next day."

131 *IG* II², 282, 9–11 *ante* 336/5 B.C.
καλέ[σαι δὲ / αὐτὸν καὶ ἐπὶ] δεῖπνον εἰς τὸ πρ[υτ/ανεῖον εἰς αὔ]ριον
Resolved . . . "to invite him (a new citizen) to Deipnon in the prytaneion on the next day."

132 *IG* II², 288, 17–18 *ante* 336/5 B.C.
κα[λέσαι ἐπὶ ξένια εἰς τὸ πρ]/υταν[εῖον εἰς αὔριον]
Resolved . . . "to invite (proxenoi) to Xenia in the prytaneion on the next day."

133 *IG* II², 302, 5–6 *ante* 336/5 B.C.
κ]/αλέσαι δὲ Ἡγέλ[οχον ἐπὶ ξένια εἰς τὸ πρυτανεῖον ε]/ἰς αὔριον
Resolved . . . "to invite Hegelochos to Xenia in the prytaneion on the next day."

134 *IG* II², 426, 19–20 *post* 336/5 B.C.
καλέσ/[αι δὲ . . ⁸. . ἐπὶ] ξένια εἰς τὸ / [πρυτανεῖον εἰς αὔ]ριον
Resolved . . . "to invite [?] (a proxenos) to Xenia in the prytaneion on the next day."

135 *IG* II², 434, 5–7 *post* 336/5 B.C.
[καλέσ/αι ἐπ]ὶ ξένια εἰς τὸ πρ[υτανεῖον εἰς / αὔριο]ν
Resolved . . . "to invite (a proxenos) to Xenia in the prytaneion on the next day."

136 *IG* II², 435, 11–12 *post* 336/5 B.C.
κα[λέσαι δὲ . .¹². ./. .¹². . κ]αὶ ἐπὶ ξένια εἰς τ[ὸ πρυτανεῖον εἰς αὔρι/ον]
Resolved . . . "to invite (foreign exiles) to Xenia in the prytaneion on the next day."

137 *IG* II², 336b, 2–3 334/3 B.C.
[καλέσαι] δὲ Ἄρχι[ππον ἐπὶ δεῖπνον εἰς / τὸ πρυτα]νεῖον εἰς [αὔριον]
Resolved . . . "to invite Archippos (a new citizen) to Deipnon in the prytaneion on the next day."

138 *IG* II², 346, 3–5 332/1 B.C.
[κα]λέσαι δ[ὲ καὶ α/ὐτὸν ἐπὶ ξένια] ε[ἰ]ς το πρυ[τανεῖ/ον εἰς αὔριον]
Resolved . . . "to invite him (the son of one Aristides) to Xenia in the prytaneion on the next day."

139 Lykourgos, *Against Leokrates* 87 *ca.* 332 B.C.
τῷ δὲ Κλεομάντει τῷ Δελφῷ ἡ πόλις αὐτῷ τε καὶ ἐκγόνοις ἐν πρυτανείῳ ἀίδιον σίτησιν ἔδοσαν
"The city gave to Kleomantes of Delphi and to his descendants perpetual Sitesis in the prytaneion."

140 Aeschines, *Against Ktesiphon* 178 330 B.C.
τότε μὲν διαφέροντες, νυνὶ δὲ πολλῷ καταδεέστεροι. δωρεαὶ δὲ καὶ στέφανοι καὶ κηρύγματα καὶ σιτήσεις ἐν πρυτανείῳ πότερα τότε ἦσαν πλείους ἢ νυνί;
"Then (in the days of our fathers) men were better, but now worse by far. And regarding gifts and crowns and proclamations and Sitesis in the prytaneion—were these more plentiful then or now?"

141 Aeschines, *Against Ktesiphon* 196 330 B.C.
οἱ γὰρ ἀγαθοὶ στρατηγοὶ ὑμῖν καὶ τῶν τὰς σιτήσεις τινὲς εὑρημένων ἐν τῷ πρυτανείῳ ἐξαιτοῦνται τὰς γραφὰς τῶν παρανόμων.
"Your good generals and some of those who have got Siteseis in the prytaneion beg off their unconstitutional proposals."

142 *IG* II², 418, 1–3 *post* 330 B.C.
καλέσαι / [δὲ καὶ τοὺς πρ]έσβεις εἰς τὸ πρυταν/[εῖον ἐπ]ὶ ξένια εἰς αὔριον

Resolved . . . "to invite the ambassadors (of Carthage) to Xenia in the prytaneion on the next day."

143 Aristotle, *Ath. Pol.* III, 5 329/8 B.C.
ἦσαν δ' οὐχ ἅμα πάντες οἱ ἐννέα ἄρχοντες, ἀλλ' ὁ μὲν βασιλεὺς εἶχε τὸ νῦν καλούμενον Βουκόλιον, πλησίον τοῦ πρυτανείου . . . . . ὁ δὲ ἄρχων τὸ πρυτανεῖον, ὁ δὲ πολέμαρχος τὸ Ἐπιλύκειον . . . . . θεσμοθέται δ' εἶχον τὸ θεσμοθετεῖον. ἐπὶ δὲ Σόλωνος [ἅπ]αντες εἰς τὸ θεσμοθετεῖον συνῆλθον.
"The nine archons were not all together, but the King had what now is called the Boukolion, near the prytaneion . . . the Archon had the prytaneion, the Polemarch the Epilykeion . . . the Thesmothetai had the Thesmotheteion. In the time of Solon they all moved into the Thesmotheteion together."

144 Suda, *s.v.* *ἄρχων* (329? B.C.)
τὸ δὲ ἦν πλησίον τοῦ πρυτανείου
"It (the Boukolion) was near the prytaneion."

145 Bekker, *Anecdota Graeca* I, 449, 17 (329? B.C.)
τὸ δὲ ἦν πλησίον τοῦ πρυτανείου
"It (the Boukolion) was near the prytaneion."

146 Aristotle, *Ath. Pol.* XXIV, 3 329/8 B.C.
ἔτι δὲ πρυτανεῖον καὶ ὀρφανοὶ καὶ δεσμωτῶν φύλακες· ἅπασι γὰρ τούτοις ἀπὸ τῶν κοινῶν ἡ διοίκησις ἦν.
"And also the prytaneion, and orphans, and jailers; for the maintenance for all these was from public funds."

147 Aristotle, *Ath. Pol.* LXII, 2 329/8 B.C.
ἀθλοθέται δ' ἐν πρυτανείῳ δειπνοῦσι τὸν Ἑκ[ατ]ομβαιῶνα μῆνα, ὅ[τ]αν ᾖ τὰ Παναθήναια, ἀρξάμενοι ἀπὸ τῆς τετράδος ἱσταμένου.
"The games directors dine in the prytaneion during the month of Hekatombaion, when the Panathenaia occurs, beginning from the fourth of the month."

148 *Hesperia* 43 (1974) 323, 26–28 *ante* 325/4 B.C.
καλέσαι δὲ καὶ ἐπὶ ξέ/[ν]ια Σώπατρον εἰς τὸ πρυτα[ν/ε]ῖον εἰς αὔριον
Resolved . . . "to invite Sopatros (a proxenos from Akragas) to Xenia in the prytaneion on the next day."

149 Dinarchus, *Against Demosthenes* 43 *ca.* 324 B.C.
εἴπατέ μοι πρὸς Διός, ὦ ἄνδρες, προῖκα τοῦτον οἴεσθε γράψαι Διφίλῳ τὴν ἐν πρυτανείῳ σίτησιν, καὶ τὴν εἰς τὴν ἀγορὰν ἀνατεθησομένην εἰκόνα;

"By Zeus, tell me, gentlemen, do you think that he (Demosthenes) proposed unbribed that Diphilos should have Sitesis in the prytaneion and have his statue erected in the agora?"

150 Dinarchus, *Against Demosthenes* 101 *ca.* 324 B.C.
ἀλλὰ περιεῖδες αὐτὸν ἐν τῇ ἀγορᾷ χαλκοῦν σταθέντα καὶ τῆς ἐν τῷ πρυτανείῳ σιτήσεως κεκοινωνηκότα τοῖς Ἁρμοδίου καὶ Ἀριστογείτονος ἀπογόνοις.
"You allowed his (Demades') bronze statue to stand in the agora and him to share Sitesis in the prytaneion with the descendants of Harmodios and Aristogeiton."

151 *IG* II², 365b, 10–11 323/2 B.C.
καλέσαι [αὐτὸν ἐπὶ δ]/εῖπνον εἰς τὸ πρυτανεῖον εἰς [αὔριον]
Resolved ... "to invite him (Lapyris, a proxenos from Kleonai) to Deipnon in the prytaneion on the next day."

152 *IG* II², 366, 12–14 323/2 B.C.
καλ[έσαι / ἐπὶ] δεῖπνον εἰς / [τὸ π]ρυτανεῖον
Resolved ... "to invite [?] to Deipnon in the prytaneion."

153 Timokles *apud* Athenaeus VI, 237 f *ca.* 320? B.C.
γέρα γὰρ αὐτοῖς ταὐτὰ τοῖς τὠλύμπια
νικῶσι δίδοται χρηστότητος εἵνεκα
σίτησις. οὗ γὰρ μὴ τίθενται συμβολαί,
πρυτανεῖα ταῦτα πάντα προσαγορεύεται.
"These same honors are given to them (parasites) as to those who win at Olympia on account of their goodness, that is Sitesis. Where payments are not established, all these are to be called prytaneia."

154 *IG* II², 385b, 16–17 319/8 B.C.
[εἶνα]ι δὲ αὐ[τῶι καὶ σίτησιν ἐμ πρυτανείωι καὶ ἐκ/γ]ό[νω]ν ἀεὶ τῶ[ι πρεσβυτάτωι]
Resolved ... "that he (Aristonikos of Karystos) and the oldest of his descendants shall have Sitesis in the prytaneion forever."

155 *IG* II², 450b, 3–4 314/3 B.C.
δοῦναι δὲ αὐτῶι καὶ [σίτ/η]σιν ἐμ πρυτανείωι
Resolved ... "to give him (Asandros of Macedon) Sitesis in the prytaneion."

156 *IG* II², 456, 26–27 307/6 B.C.
[καλέ]/σαι αὐτοὺς ἐπὶ δεῖπνον [ε]ἰ[ς τ]ὸ πρυτ[ανεῖον εἰς αὔριο]/ν
Resolved ... "to invite them (ambassadors of Kolophon) to Deipnon in the prytaneion on the next day."

157 *IG* II², 466, 45–46 307/6 B.C.
καλέσαι δὲ [α]ὐτο[ὺ/ς καὶ ἐπὶ ξ]έ[νια] εἰς τὸ πρυτανεῖον εἰς αὔριον
Resolved . . . "to invite them (ambassadors of Tenos) to Xenia in the prytaneion on the next day."

158 [Plutarch], *Vitae decem Oratorum* 843c 307/6 B.C.
ἐπ' Ἀναξικράτους ἄρχοντος· ἐφ' οὗ ἔλαβε καὶ σίτησιν ἐν πρυτανείῳ αὐτός τε ὁ Λυκοῦργος καὶ ὁ πρεσβύτατος αὐτοῦ τῶν ἐκγόνων κατὰ τὸ αὐτὸ ψήφισμα.
". . . in the archonship of Anaxikrates, in which year Lykourgos himself and the oldest of his descendants got Sitesis in the prytaneion by the same decree."

159 [Plutarch], *Vitae decem Oratorum* 852a, e 307/6 B.C.
852a: Λυκόφρων Λυκούργου Βουτάδης ἀπεγράψατο αὐτῷ εἶναι σίτησιν ἐν πρυτανεῴ κατὰ τὴν δοθεῖσαν δωρέαν ὑπὸ τοῦ δήμου Λυκούργῳ Βουτάδῃ.
852e: δοῦναι δὲ σίτησιν ἐν πρυτανείῳ τῶν ἐκγόνων ἀεὶ τῶν Λυκούργου τῷ πρεσβυτάτῳ εἰς ἅπαντα τὸν χρόνον.
852a: "Lykophron, son of Lykourgos, of Boutadai proposed that he should get Sitesis in the prytaneion in accordance with the grant made by the Demos to Lykourgos of Boutadai."
852e: The Demos resolved . . . "to give Sitesis in the prytaneion to the oldest of the descendants of Lykourgos for all time."

160 *IG* II², 510, 1–3 *post* 307/6 B.C.
[εἶναι δὲ αὐτῶι καὶ σίτησιν ἐ]ν πρυ[τα/νείωι αὐτῶι καὶ τῶν ἐκγόνων ἀεὶ] τῶι πρεσ/[βυτατῶι]
Resolved . . . "that he and the oldest of his descendants will have Sitesis in the prytaneion forever."

161 *IG* II², 542, 10–11 *ante* 303 B.C.
[καλέσαι δὲ τοὺς τῶν . . ⁹ . . π/ρέ]σβεις καὶ ἐπὶ ξ[ένια εἰς τὸ πρυτανεῖον εἰς αὔρι/ον]
Resolved . . . "to invite the ambassadors of [?] to Xenia in the prytaneion on the next day."

162 *Hesperia* 8 (1939) 37, 40–41 303/2 B.C.
[καλέσαι αὐτοὺς ἐπὶ ξέν]ια εἰ[ς τὸ πρυτανεῖον εἰς αὔριον]
Resolved . . . "to invite them (ambassadors of Sikyon) to Xenia in the prytaneion on the next day."

163 *IG* II², 513, 6–8 late IV B.C.
εἶ/[ναι δὲ αὐτῶι καὶ σίτησιν ἐν πρυταν]είωι καὶ αὐτῶι / [καὶ ἐκγόνων τῶι πρεσβυτάτωι]

Resolved ... "that he and the oldest of his descendants shall have Sitesis in the prytaneion."

164 *IG* II², 528, 4–5 late IV B.C.
[κα]λέσαι [δὲ ..¹¹.. ἐπὶ ξένια εἰς / τ]ὸ πρυτα[νεῖον εἰς αὔριον]
Resolved ... "to invite [?] to Xenia in the prytaneion on the next day."

165 *SEG* XXIV, 112, 10–11 307/6–302/1 B.C.
[καλέσαι το]ὺ[ς] πρέσβε[ις τῶν Πρ]ιη/[νέων ἐπὶ ξένια εἰς τὸ πρ]υτανεῖον ε[ἰς αὔρι]ον
Resolved ... "to invite the ambassadors of Priene to Xenia in the prytaneion on the next day."

166 *IG* II², 567, 21–22 late IV B.C.
καλέ[σαι δὲ τοὺς πρέσβεις τῶν Πριηνέων ἐπὶ ξένια] / εἰς τὸ πρυτανεῖ[ον εἰς αὔριον]
Resolved ... "to invite the ambassadors of Priene to Xenia in the prytaneion on the next day."

167 *IG* II², 572, 10–11 late IV B.C.
καλέσαι ἐ[πὶ ξένια εἰς τὸ / πρυτανε]ῖον εἰς αὔρ[ιον
Resolved ... "to invite (the ambassadors of Opuntia) to Xenia in the prytaneion on the next day."

168 *IG* II², 594, 4–6 late IV B.C.
κ]αλέσα/[ι δ' αὐτὸν ἐπὶ ξένια εἰς τὸ πρυ]τανεῖ/[ον εἰς αὔριον]
Resolved ... "to invite him to Xenia in the prytaneion on the next day."

169 *IG* II², 646, 34–35 295/4 B.C.
[εἶναι δ' αὐτ]ῶι καὶ σίτησιν ἐμ πρυτ/[ανείωι καὶ ἐκγ]όνων ἀεὶ τῶι πρεσβυτ[ά/τωι]
Resolved ... "that he (Herodoros) and the oldest of his descendants shall have Sitesis in the prytaneion forever."

170 *IG* II², 657, 64–65 288/7 B.C.
εἶναι αὐτῶι σίτησιν ἐν πρυτανείωι καὶ ἐκ/γόνων ἀεὶ τῶι πρεσβυτάτωι
Resolved ... "that he (Philippides) and the oldest of his descendants shall have Sitesis in the prytaneion forever."

171 *IG* II², 660, 42–43 285/4 B.C.
καλέ[σαι δὲ αὐτὸν καὶ ἐπὶ ξένια εἰς τὸ] / πρυτανεῖον εἰς αὔριον
Resolved ... "to invite him (an ambassador from Tenos) to Xenia in the prytaneion on the next day."

172 Plutarch, *Demosthenes* XXX, 5 280/79 B.C.
Τούτῳ μὲν ὀλίγον ὕστερον ὁ τῶν Ἀθηναίων δῆμος ἀξίαν ἀποδιδοὺς τιμὴν εἰκόνα τε χαλκῆν ἀνέστησε καὶ τὸν πρεσβύτατον ἐψηφίσατο τῶν ἀπὸ γένους ἐν πρυτανείῳ σίτησιν ἔχειν.
"A little later the Demos of the Athenians gave a fitting honor and erected a bronze statue and voted that the oldest of his descendants should have Sitesis in the prytaneion."

173 [Plutarch], *Vitae decem Oratorum* 847d 280/79 B.C.
ἔστι δ' αὐτοῦ εἰκὼν ἐν τῷ πρυτανείῳ εἰσιόντων πρὸς τὴν ἑστίαν ἐν δεξιᾷ ὁ πρῶτος ..... χρόνῳ δ' ὕστερον Ἀθηναῖοι σίτησιν τ' ἐν πρυτανείῳ τοῖς συγγενέσι τοῦ Δημοσθένους ἔδοσαν καὶ αὐτῷ τετελευτηκότι τὴν εἰκόνα ἀνέθεσαν ἐν ἀγορᾷ ἐπὶ Γοργίου ἄρχοντος, αἰτησαμένου αὐτῷ τὰς δωρεὰς τοῦ ἀδελφιδοῦ Δημοχάρους· ᾧ καὶ αὐτῷ πάλιν ὁ υἱὸς Λάχης Δημοχάρους Λευκονοεὺς ᾐτήσατο δωρεὰς ἐπὶ Πυθαράτου ἄρχοντος, δεκάτῳ ὕστερον ἔτει, εἰς τὴν τῆς εἰκόνος στάσιν ἐν ἀγορᾷ καὶ σίτησιν ἐν πρυτανείῳ αὐτῷ τε καὶ ἐκγόνων ἀεὶ τῷ πρεσβυτάτῳ καὶ προεδρίαν ἐν ἅπασι τοῖς ἀγῶσι. καὶ ἔστι τὰ ψηφίσματα ὑπὲρ ἀμφοτέρων ἀναγεγραμμένα, ἡ δ' εἰκὼν τοῦ Δημοχάρους εἰς τὸ πρυτανεῖον μετεκομίσθη.
"There is a statue of him (Demosthenes) in the prytaneion, the first on the right going toward the hearth ... At a later time the Athenians gave Sitesis in the prytaneion to his relatives and erected a statue of him, although he was dead, in the agora in the archonship of Gorgias when his nephew Demochares requested the gifts for him. Again for him (Demochares), Laches the son of Demochares of Leukonoe requested gifts in the archonship of Pytharatos, the tenth year after, involving the erection of a statue in the agora and Sitesis in the prytaneion for him and the eldest of his descendants forever and a seat of honor at all the games. The decrees on behalf of both are inscribed, but the statue of Demochares was transferred to the prytaneion."

174 [Plutarch], *Vitae decem Oratorum* 850 f 280/79 B.C.
Δημοχάρης Λάχητος Λευκονοεὺς αἰτεῖ Δημοσθένει τῷ Δημοσθένους Παιανιεῖ δωρεὰν εἰκόνα χαλκῆν ἐν ἀγορᾷ καὶ σίτησιν ἐν πρυτανείῳ καὶ προεδρίαν αὐτῷ καὶ ἐκγόνων ἀεὶ τῷ πρεσβυτάτῳ.
"Demochares son of Laches of Leukonoe proposes for Demosthenes son of Demosthenes of Paiania gifts of a bronze statue in the agora and Sitesis in the prytaneion and a seat of honor for him and his oldest descendant forever."

175 *IG* II^2, 672, 34 279/8 B.C.
[εἶναι δὲ αὐτ]ῶι σίτησιν ἐν πρυτανείωι
Resolved ... "that he (Komeas) shall have Sitesis in the prytaneion."

176 *IG* II², 682, 81–82 276/5 B.C.

εἶναι αὐτῶι σίτ/ησιν ἐμ πρυτανείωι καὶ ἐκγόνων τῶι πρεσβυτ/άτωι ἀεὶ

Resolved . . . "that he (Phaidros) and the oldest of his descendants shall have Sitesis in the prytaneion forever."

A stele recently discovered in the Athenian agora records honors to the brother of this Phaidros, one Kallias. Although Kallias is given many honors, including a bronze statue in the agora, he is not awarded Sitesis. Is it possible that there was a restriction on the award of Sitesis in the prytaneion so that only one member of a family was eligible for the grant?

177 [Plutarch], *Vitae decem Oratorum* 851d 271/0 B.C.

Ἄρχων Πυθάρατος· Λάχης Δημοχάρους Λευκονοεὺς αἰτεῖ δωρεὰν τὴν βουλὴν καὶ τὸν δῆμον τὸν Ἀθηναίων Δημοχάρει Λάχητος Λευκονοεῖ εἰκόνα χαλκῆν ἐν ἀγορᾷ καὶ σίτησιν ἐν πρυτανείῳ <*αὐτῷ*> *καὶ τῶν ἐκγόνων ἀεὶ τῷ πρεσβυτάτῳ καὶ προεδρίαν ἐν πᾶσι τοῖς ἀγῶσιν.*

"In the archonship of Pytharatos; Laches son of Demochares of Leukonoe proposes that the Boule and the Demos of the Athenians make a gift to Demochares son of Laches of Leukonoe of a bronze statue in the agora and Sitesis in the prytaneion for him and the oldest of his descendants forever and a seat of honor at all the games."

178 *IG* II², 686, 17–18 266/5 B.C.

καλέσαι δὲ αὐτ[οὺς ἐπὶ ξένια εἰς τὸ πρυτανεῖ]/ον εἰς αὔριον

Resolved . . . "to invite them (ambassadors of King Areas) to Xenia in the prytaneion on the next day."

179 *IG* II², 1283 261/0? B.C.

6–7: *τὴν πονπὴν π/ένπειν ἀπὸ τῆς ἑστίας τῆς ἐκκ τοῦ πρυτανείου*

14–16: *ὡ]ς ἂν [ἕ]λωνται οἱ ἐν τῶι ἄστει συνκαθι[στάνα]/ι τὴν πομπὴν καὶ τήνδε οὖν ἐκ τοῦ πρυτανείου εἰς Πει[ραιᾶ] / πορεύεσθαι*

Resolved by the Orgeones of Bendis . . . "that (Thracians) are to conduct the procession from the hearth out of the prytaneion . . . the procession is to be set up as those in the city choose and it is to pass from the prytaneion to the Peiraeus."

180 *IG* II², 831, 4–5 mid-III B.C.

[-- κ]αλέσα/[ι ---- εἰς τὸ πρυ]τανεῖ/[ον --]

Resolved . . . "to invite [?] to the prytaneion."

181 *IG* II², 832, 15–16 229/8 B.C.

εὐε[ρ]γέ[τ]α[ς] καὶ [συμ]βούλους ἀγαθοὺς γενομένους / ἐτίμησ[εν σ]ίτ[ωι ἐμ πρ]υτανείωι

Resolved . . . "to honor those having been benefactors and good advisors with food in the prytaneion."

182 *Hesperia* 4 (1935) 526, 44–45 226/5 B.C.
καλέσαι δὲ αὐτὸν καὶ ἐπὶ δεῖπνον εἰς τὸ πρυτα/νεῖον εἰς αὔριον
Resolved . . . "to invite him (Prytanis of Karystos) to Deipnon in the prytaneion on the next day."

183 *Hesperia* 13 (1944) 253, 17 *ca.* 220 B.C.
[καλέ]σαι δὲ αὐτοὺς καὶ ἐπὶ δεῖπνον εἰς τὸ πρυτανεῖον εἰς αὔριον
Resolved . . . "to invite them (ambassadors from Ephesos) to Deipnon in the prytaneion on the next day."

184 Agora I 7182, 16–17 late III B.C.
καλέσαι δὲ αὐτοὺ[ς] / καὶ ἐπ[ὶ δεῖ]πνον εἰς τὸ πρ[υτα]νεῖον εἰς αὔριον
Resolved . . . "to invite them (Pausimachos and Aristophanes) to Deipnon in the prytaneion on the next day."

185 *IG* II², 861, 23–25 late III B.C.
καλέ/[σαι δὲ καὶ αὐτοὺς ἐπὶ ξένια εἰς τὸ πρυτανεῖον εἰς] αὔριον
Resolved . . . "to invite them (judges from Lamia) to Xenia in the prytaneion on the next day."

186 *IG* II², 884, 15–17 *ca.* 200 B.C.
[καλέσαι δὲ Ἧριν] / καὶ Μηνοφάνην καὶ Ἑκαταῖ[ο]ν κ[αὶ τὸν ταμί]α[ν ἐπὶ / δ]εῖπνον εἰς πρυτανεῖον ἐπὶ ξέν[ια εἰς αὔρ]ιο[ν
Resolved . . . "to invite Heris (commander of the Byzantine fleet) and Menophanes and Hekataios and the treasurer to Deipnon (and) to Xenia in the prytaneion on the next day."

> The use and intent of both Deipnon and Xenia in this decree are puzzling. We might suppose that Deipnon was voted to those citizens among the four men mentioned, while Xenia was voted to Menophanes and Hekataios who were proxenoi. That there has been a compression of the text is shown, for example, by the omission of the normal article preceding prytaneion.

187 *IVM* 37, 36–37 *ca.* 200 B.C.
καλέσαι δὲ αὐτοὺς καὶ / ἐπὶ ξένια εἰς τὸ πρυτανεῖον εἰς αὔριον
Resolved . . . "to invite them (ambassadors from Magnesia) to Xenia in the prytaneion on the next day."

188 *SEG* XXI, 418, 11 early II B.C.
. . . *εἰς τὸ πρυτανεῖον] εἰς αὔρ/[ιον*
Resolved . . . "to invite [?] (a new citizen) to the prytaneion on the next day."

189 *Hesperia* 5 (1936) 423 196/5 B.C.
32–35: *αἰτεῖ/[ται νῦν δοῦν]αι ἑαυτοῦ τὸν δῆμον ...... καὶ σίτησιν ἑαυτῶι ἐν πρυ/[τανείωι καὶ ἐγγόνων ἀ]εὶ τῶι πρεσβυτάτωι*
53–54: *εἶναι δὲ αὐτῶ[ι καὶ σίτησιν / ἐν πρυτανείωι κα]ὶ ἐγ[γόνων ἀ]εὶ τῶι πρεσβυτάτωι*
"(Kephisodoros, a citizen) proposes that the Demos give him ... (other honors) ... and Sitesis in the prytaneion for himself and the oldest of his descendants forever."
The Demos resolves ... "that there shall be Sitesis in the prytaneion for him and the oldest of his descendants forever."

190 Polemon *apud* Harpokration, *s.v.* *ἄξονες* *ca.* 190 B.C.
Οἱ Σόλωνος νόμοι ἐν ξυλίνοις ἦσαν ἄξοσι γεγραμμένοι .... ἦσαν δὲ, ὥς φησι Πολέμων ἐν τοῖς Πρὸς Ἐρατοσθένην, τετράγωνοι τὸ σχῆμα διασώζονται δὲ ἐν τῷ πρυτανείῳ, γεγραμμένοι κατὰ πάντα τὰ μέρη.
"The laws of Solon were written on wooden axones ... they were, as Polemon says in the speech Against Eratosthenes, quadrangular in shape and were preserved in the prytaneion being inscribed on all sides."

Cf. (A 25, 211, 231).

191 *SEG* XXIV, 135, 51–52 *ca.* 170 B.C.
[εἶναι δὲ αὐτ]ῶι καὶ σίτησ[ιν ἐμ πρ]υτανείωι αἰτησαμένωι κ[α/τὰ τοὺς νό]μους
Resolved ... "that he (Menodoros, a citizen) having requested it shall have Sitesis in the prytaneion according to custom."

192 *IG* II², 1236, 11 first half II B.C.
καλέσαι αὐτοὺς εἰς τὸ πρυτανεῖον ἐπὶ τὴν κοινὴν ἑστία[ν τοῦ δήμου]
Resolved ... "to invite them (Philonides and Dikaiarchos) into the prytaneion to the common hearth of the Demos."

193 *Michel* 1510, 12–13 167–146 B.C.
εἶναι δὲ αὐτῶ[ι καὶ σίτησιν] ἐμ / πρυτανείωι
Resolved ... "that there shall be to him (Epikles, an Athenian cleruch in Lemnos) Sitesis in the prytaneion."

194 *IG* II², 985, 10–11 *ca.* 150 B.C.
[καλέσαι δὲ αὐτὸν ἐπὶ ξένια εἰς / τ]ὸ πρυτανεῖον εἰς α[ὔριον]
Resolved ... "to invite him (a Milesian) to Xenia in the prytaneion on the next day."

195 *SEG* XV, 104, 5–7 127/6 B.C.

[ἐπειδὴ οἱ ἔφηβοι οἱ ἐφηβεύσ]αντες ἐπὶ / Διονυσίου ἄρχοντος θ[ύσαντες ταῖς ἐγγραφαῖς τὰ εἰσιτήρια] ἐν τῶι πρυ/τανείωι ἐπὶ τῆς κοινῆ[ς ἑστίας μετά τε τοῦ κοσμητοῦ καὶ τοῦ ἱε]ρέως τοῦ / Δήμου καὶ τῶν Χα[ρίτων ἐκολούθουν τοῖς τε νόμοις καὶ τοῖς ψηφίσμ]ασιν.

"Since the Ephebes who came of age in the archonship of Dionysios, having sacrificed the initiation sacrifices for their registration in the prytaneion at the common hearth in company with the Kosmetes and the priest of Demos and the Charites, followed the laws and the decrees . . ."

196 *IG* II², 1006, 6–8 122/1 B.C.

ἐπειδὴ οἱ ἔφηβοι οἱ ἐπὶ Δημητρίου ἄρχοντος θύσαντες ταῖς ἐγγραφαῖς ἐν τῶι πρυτανείωι ἐπὶ / τῆς κοινῆς ἑστίας τοῦ δήμου μετά τε τοῦ κοσμ[η]τοῦ καὶ τοῦ ἱερέως τοῦ δήμου καὶ τῶν Χαρίτων καὶ / τῶν ἐξηγητῶν κατὰ τοὺς νόμους καὶ τὰ ψηφίσματα τοῦ δήμου ἐπόμπευσαν τῆι Ἀρτέμιδι / τῆι Ἀγροτέραι

"Since the Ephebes in the archonship of Demetrios, having sacrificed for their registration in the prytaneion on the common hearth in company with the Kosmetes and the priest of Demos and the Charites and the exegetai according to the laws and the decrees of the Demos, proceeded to the shrine of Artemis Agrotera . . ."

197 *SEG* XXI, 476, 3–4 *ca.* 120 B.C.

[ἐπειδὴ οἱ ἔφηβοι οἱ ἐπὶ --- ἄρχοντος θύσαντες τα]ῖς ἐγγραφαῖς ἐ[ν τῶι πρυτανείωι ἐπὶ τῆς / κοινῆς ἑστίας τοῦ δήμου καὶ καλλιερήσαντες μετά τε τοῦ κοσμητοῦ καὶ τοῦ ἱερέως τοῦ δήμου καὶ τῶν Χαρίτων] καὶ τῶν ἐ[ξηγητῶν ἐπόμπευσαν τῆι Ἀρτέμιδι / τῆι Ἀγροτέραι]

"Since the Ephebes in the archonship of [?] having sacrificed for their registration in the prytaneion at the common hearth of the Demos, and having received favorable omens in company with the Kosmetes and the priest of Demos and the Charites and the exegetai, proceeded to the shrine of Artemis Agrotera . . ."

198 *IG* II², 1008, 4–7 118/7 B.C.

ἐ]πειδὴ οἱ ἔφηβοι οἱ ἐπὶ Ἱ/[ππάρχου ἄρχοντος θύσαντες ταῖς ἐγγραφ]αῖς ἐν τῶι πρυτανείωι ἐπὶ τ[ῆς κ]οινῆς ἑστίας τοῦ δήμου / [κ]αὶ καλλιερ[ήσαντες μετά τε τ]οῦ κοσμητοῦ καὶ τοῦ ἱε[ρέω]ς τοῦ δήμου κα[ὶ τ]ῶν Χ[αρ/ί]των καὶ τῶν ἐξ[ηγητῶν ἐπόμπευσαν τῆ]ι Ἀρτέμιδι τῆι Ἀγροτέραι . . .

"Since the Ephebes in the archonship of Hipparchos, having sacrificed for their registration in the prytaneion at the common hearth of the Demos and having received favorable omens in company with the Kosmetes and the priest of the Demos and the Charites and the exegetai, proceeded to the shrine of Artemis Agrotera . . ."

199 *Hesperia* 16 (1947) 170, 7–10 116/5 B.C.

ἐπειδὴ οἱ ἐφηβεύσαντες ἐπὶ Μενοίτου ἄρχοντος θύσαντες ταῖς ἐγ/γραφαῖς ἐν τῶι πρυτανείωι ἐπὶ τῆς κοινῆς ἑστίας μετά τε τοῦ κοσμητοῦ καὶ / τοῦ ἱερέως τοῦ δήμου καὶ τῶν Χαρίτων καὶ τῶν ἐξηγητῶν κατὰ τὴν δή/μου προαίρεσιν

"Since those coming of age in the archonship of Menoitos, having sacrificed for their registration in the prytaneion at the common hearth in company with the Kosmetes and the priest of Demos and the Charites and the exegetai according to the precepts of the demos . . ."

200 *IG* II², 1011 106/5 B.C.

5–7: *ἐπειδὴ οἱ ἔφηβοι οἱ ἐπὶ Ἀριστάρχου ἄρχοντος θύσαντες ταῖς ἐγγραφαῖ[ς τ]ὰ εἰ[σιτ]ητήρια ἐν [τῶι] / πρυτανείωι ἐπὶ τῆς κοινῆς ἑστίας τοῦ δήμου μετά τε τοῦ κοσμητ[ο]ῦ καὶ τῶν ἐξηγητῶν καὶ τοῦ ἱερέως [τ]οῦ τε δήμου καὶ Χαρ[ί]/των κατὰ τὰ ψηφίσματα ἐπόμπευσάν τε τῆι Ἀρτέμ[ιδ]ι τῆι Ἀγροτέρ[αι*

33–35: *ἐπ[ει]δὴ Εὔδοξος Εὐδόξου Ἀχερδούσιος χει[ροτονηθεὶ]ς κοσμη/[τὴ]ς ἐπὶ τοὺς ἐφήβους εἰς τὸν ἐπὶ Ἀριστάρχου ἄρχοντος ἐνιαυτὸν ἔθυσεν ἐν τῶι πρυτανε[ί]ωι τὰ εἰσιτητήρια ἐπὶ τῆς κοινῆς ἑστ[ίας τ]οῦ δήμου μετά τε τῶν / παιδευτῶν καὶ τῶν ἐξηγητῶν ποιησάμενος τὴν εἰς τὰς θυσίας δαπάνην ἐκ τῶν ἰδίων.*

5–7: "Since the ephebes in the archonship of Aristarchos, having sacrificed the initiation sacrifices for their registration in the prytaneion at the common hearth of the Demos in company with the Kosmetes and the exegetai and the priest of Demos and the Charites according to the decrees, proceeded to the shrine of Artemis Agrotera . . ."

33–35: "Since Eudoxos son of Eudoxos of Acherdous having been elected Kosmetes for the ephebes in the year of the archonship of Aristarchos, made the initiation sacrifices in the prytaneion at the common hearth of the Demos in company with the instructors and the exegetai paying for the sacrifices from his personal wealth . . ."

201 *IG* II², 1028 101/0 B.C.

5–8: *ἐπειδὴ οἱ ἔφηβοι οἱ ἐπὶ Ἐχεκράτου ἄρχοντος θύσαν/τες ἐν ταῖς ἐγγραφαῖς ἐν τῶι πρυτανείωι ἐπὶ τῆς κοινῆς ἑστίας τοῦ δήμου / καὶ καλλιερήσαντες μετὰ τοῦ κοσμητοῦ καὶ τοῦ ἱερέως τοῦ δήμου καὶ τῶν Χα/ρίτων καὶ τῶν ἐξηγητῶν ἐπόμπευσάν τε τῆι Ἀρτέμιδι τῆι Ἀγροτέραι ἐν ὅπλοις*

70–73: *ἐπειδὴ Τίμ[ω]ν Τιμαρχίδου Βουτάδης χειρ[ο]/τονηθεις κοσμητὴς ἐπὶ τοὺς ἐφήβους εἰς τὸν [ἐνι]αυτὸν τὸν ἐπὶ Ἔχεκρατου ἄρχον/τος παραλαβὼν τὴν ἐ[γ]χειρισθεῖσαν ἑαυτ[ῶι πί]στιν ὑπὸ τοῦ δήμου καὶ θύσας ἐν τῶι πρυτανείωι ἐκ τῶν ἰδίω[ν] μετὰ τῶν ἐφήβων [ἐπὶ] τῆς κοινῆς ἑστίας κατὰ τὰ ἐψηφισ[μέ]/να τῶι δήμωι*

5–8: "Since the Ephebes in the archonship of Echekrates, having sacrificed for their registration in the prytaneion at the common hearth of the Demos and having received favorable omens in company with the Kosmetes and the priest of demos and the Charites and the exegetai, proceeded to the shrine of Artemis Agrotera under arms . . ."

70–73: "Since Timon son of Timarchides of Boutadai, having been elected Kosmetes for the ephebes in the year of the archonship of Echekrates and having assumed the responsibility entrusted to him by the Demos and having sacrificed in the prytaneion from his own wealth in company with the ephebes at the common hearth according to the decrees of the Demos . . ."

202 *SEG* XXIV, 189, 3–4 late II B.C.

[ἐπειδὴ οἱ ἔφηβοι οἱ ἐπὶ . . . . . ἄρχοντος θύσαντες ταῖς ἐγγραφαῖς ἐν τῶι πρυτ]ανείωι ἐ[πὶ τῆς / κοινῆς ἑστίας τοῦ δήμου, καὶ καλλιερήσαντες μετά τε τοῦ κοσμητοῦ καὶ τοῦ ἱερέως τοῦ δήμου καὶ τῶν Χαρίτων καὶ τῶν ἐξηγητῶν ἐπόμ]πευσαν τ[ε̃ι Ἀρτέ/μιδι τε̃ι Ἀγροτέραι]

"Since the ephebes in the archonship of [?], having sacrificed for their registration in the prytaneion at the common hearth of the demos and having received favorable omens in company with the Kosmetes and the priest of demos and the Charites and the exegetai, proceeded to the shrine of Artemis Agrotera . . ."

203 *AAA* 4 (1971) 441, 4–5 late II B.C.

καλέσαι δὲ αὐτοὺς ἐπὶ ξένια τὸν κεχειροτονημέν/ον ἐπὶ τὴν ἀποδοχὴν τῶν φίλων καὶ συμμάχων Ἡράκωντα Ῥαμνούσιον

Resolved . . . "that Herakon of Rhamnous, having been elected for the reception of friends and allies, invite them (men from Stiris) to Xenia."

Although the prytaneion is not specifically mentioned in this text, the formulaic invitation makes it almost certain that the Xenia was to be offered in the prytaneion.

204 *IG* II², 1024, 34–36 late II B.C.

[καλέ]σαι δὲ [καὶ] αὐ/[τοὺς ἐπὶ ξένια εἰς τὸ πρυτα]νεῖον εἰς / [αὔριον]

Resolved . . . "to invite them (two proxenoi) to Xenia in the prytaneion on the next day."

205 *Kerameikos* III, A38a late II B.C.
νίκησας / ἐμ πρυτα/νείωι
"(Demarchos?) was victorious in the prytaneion."

This brief note was found inscribed on the tombstone of one Demarchos. If he is to be understood as the subject, Demarchos apparently was afforded entertainment in the prytaneion, presumably because of a victory at some game.

206 Plutarch, *Numa* IX, 6 88/7 B.C.
ἐὰν δὲ ὑπὸ τύχης τινὸς ἐκλίπῃ, καθάπερ Ἀθήνησι μὲν ἐπὶ τῆς Ἀριστίωνος λέγεται τυραννίδος ἀποσβεσθῆναι τὸν ἱερὸν λύχνον . . . . . οὔ φασι δεῖν ἀπὸ ἑτέρου πυρὸς ἐναύεσθαι, καινὸν δὲ ποιεῖν καὶ νέον, ἀνάπτοντας ἀπὸ τοῦ ἡλίου φλόγα καθαρὰν καὶ ἀμίαντον.
"If by some misfortune it should cease, as it is said that the sacred lamp was extinguished at Athens in the time of Aristion the tyrant . . . they say it must not be rekindled from another fire, but made fresh and new, lighting a pure and unpolluted flame from the sun."

207 *IG* II², 1053, 9–10 third quarter I B.C.
κα]λέσαι δὲ αὐτοὺς ἐπὶ τὴν κοινὴν τῆς πό/[λεως ἑστίαν]
Resolved . . . "to invite them (cleruchs in Lemnos) to the common hearth of the city."

208 *IG* II², 1051c, 22–23 *post* 38/7 B.C.
[καλέ/σαι δὲ αὐτοὺς ἐπὶ τὴν κοινὴν τῆ]ς πόλεως ἑστίαν
Resolved . . . "to invite them (cleruchs from Lemnos) to the common hearth of the city."

209 *IG* II², 2877 early Augustan
Θεόφιλος Διοδώρου / Ἁλαιεὺς ἐπιμε[λη]τὴ[ς] / γενόμενος πρυτανείο[υ]
"Theophilos son of Diodoros of Halais as the custodian of the prytaneion (dedicated it)."

210 *IG* II², 1990, 9 A.D. 61/2
σείτησιν ἐν πρυ[τα]νείωι διὰ βίου
Resolved . . . "that (Epiktetes, a kosmetes of the ephebes) is to have Sitesis in the prytaneion for life."

211 Plutarch, *Solon* XXV, 1 I–II A.D.
κατεγράφησαν εἰς ξυλίνους ἄξονας ἐν πλαισίοις περιέχουσι στρεφομένους, ὧν ἔτι καθ' ἡμᾶς ἐν πρυτανείῳ λείψαντα μικρὰ διεσώζετο·

"They (the laws of Solon) were set down on wooden axones which revolved in their frames, of which slight traces were still preserved in the prytaneion in my time."

212 Plutarch, *Numa* IX, 6 I–II A.D.

ἐπεί τοι τῆς Ἑλλάδος ὅπου πῦρ ἄσβεστόν ἐστιν, ὡς Πυθοῖ καὶ Ἀθήνησιν, οὐ παρθένοι, γυναῖκες δὲ πεπαυμέναι γάμων ἔχουσι τὴν ἐπιμέλειαν.

". . . since in Greece wherever there is an undying fire, as at Delphi and Athens, not virgins, but women being done with marriage are in charge of them."

213 Plutarch, *Quaestiones Convivales* 714b I–II A.D.

τὰ γὰρ παρὰ Κρησὶν Ἀνδρεῖα καλούμενα, παρὰ δὲ Σπαρτιάταις Φιδίτια, βουλευτηρίων ἀπορρήτων καὶ συνεδρίων ἀριστοκρατικῶν τάξιν εἶχεν, ὥσπερ οἶμαι καὶ τὸ ἐνθάδε πρυτανεῖον καὶ θεσμοθετεῖον.

"The so-called andreia among the Cretans and the phiditia among the Spartans, had the disposition of secret bouleuteria and aristocratic councils, as here, I believe, did the prytaneion and the thesmotheteion."

214 Plutarch, *Moralia* 657c I–II A.D.

τέσσαρα δ', εἰς ἕνα τριῶν ὕδατος ἐπιχεομένων, οὗτος ἐστιν ἐπίτριτος λόγος, ἀρχόντων τινῶν ἐν πρυτανείῳ νοῦν ἐχόντων.

"But the four (-part mixture), being one part of wine mixed with three of water—this is the 1:3 ratio—is for certain magistrates pondering in the prytaneion."

215 Plutarch, *De sollertia animalium* 970b I–II A.D.

διὸ θαυμάσας αὐτοῦ τὴν φιλοτιμίαν ὁ δῆμος ἐκέλευσε δημοσίᾳ τρέφεσθαι, καθάπερ ἀθλητῇ σίτησιν ὑπὸ γήρως ἀπειρηκότι ψηφισάμενος.

"The Demos, admiring his (a mule's) enterprise, ordered him to be fed at public expense, voting it as they would Sitesis to an athlete who was exhausted by old age."

216 Aelian, *De natura animalium* VI, 49 from I–II? A.D.

ταῦτα οὖν μαθόντες ὁ δῆμος τῷ κήρυκι ἀνειπεῖν προσέταξαν, εἴτε ἀφίκοιτο ἐς τὰ ἄλφιτα, εἴτε ἐς τὰς κριθὰς παραβάλοι, μὴ ἀνείργειν, ἀλλ' ἐᾶν σιτεῖσθαι ἐς κόρον, καὶ τὸν δῆμον ἐκτίνειν ἐν πρυτανείῳ τὸ ἀργύριον, τρόπον τινὰ ἀθλητῇ σιτήσεως δοθείσης ἤδη γέροντι.

"The Demos, having learned this, ordered the herald to proclaim that if he (a mule) came for barley, or turned to barley corn, he should not be driven off, but allowed to eat his fill, and the Demos should pay the money to the prytaneion giving it in the same way as Sitesis to an old athlete."

217 Dio Chrysostomos L, 1 I–II A.D.
τὸ δὲ ὑμῶν ἄλλους προτιμᾶν ὅμοιον ὥσπερ εἴ τις φιλόπολις εἶναι λέγων ταῖς οἰκίαις μὲν ἥδοιτο καὶ τοῖς ἐργαστηρίοις τοῖς ἐν τῇ πόλει, τὴν δὲ ἀγορὰν καὶ τὸ πρυτανεῖον καὶ τὸ βουλευτήριον καὶ τἆλλα ἱερὰ ἀμελέστερον ὁρῴη.
"Others of you prefer it the same as if some patriot said that he was delighted with the houses and the workshops in the city, but saw the agora and the prytaneion and the bouleuterion and the other sacred buildings in great disrepair."

218 Soranus, *Hippokrates* 451 (ed. Westermann) first half II A.D.
τὴν ἐν πρυτανείῳ σίτησιν ἔδοσαν εἰς ἐκγόνους
"(The Athenians) gave Sitesis in the prytaneion to the descendants (of Hippokrates)."

219 Zenobios IV, 93 first half II A.D.
Λιμοῦ πεδίον . . . τόπος γάρ ἐστιν οὕτω καλούμενος. καὶ λέγουσιν ὅτι λιμοῦ ποτε κατασχόντος, ἔχρησεν ὁ θεὸς ἱκέτειαν θεῶν, καὶ τὸν λιμὸν ἐξιλειόσασθαι. οἱ δὲ Ἀθηναῖοι ἀνῆκαν αὐτῷ τὸ ὄπισθεν τοῦ πρυτανείου πεδίον.
"Field of Famine . . . there is a place so named. They say that when a famine came there, the god gave an oracle prescribing a supplication of the gods, and the famine was appeased. But the Athenians consecrated to it the field behind the prytaneion."

220 Harpokration, *s.v.* *ἐφέται* early II? A.D.
οἱ δικάζοντες τὰς ἐφ' αἵματι κρίσεις ἐπὶ Παλλαδίῳ καὶ ἐπὶ πρυτανείῳ καὶ ἐπὶ Δελφινίῳ καὶ ἐν Φρεαττοῖ ἐφέται ἐκαλοῦντο.
"Those who judged homicide cases in the Palladion and the prytaneion and in the Delphinion and in Phreatto were called ephetai."

221 Pausanias I, 18, 2–4 mid-II A.D.
ὑπὲρ δὲ τῶν Διοσκούρων τὸ ἱερὸν Ἀγλαύρου τέμενός ἐστιν . . . . κατὰ τοῦτο ἐπαναβάντες Μῆδοι κατεφόνευσαν Ἀθηναίων . . . . πλησίον δὲ πρυτανεῖόν ἐστιν, ἐν ᾧ νόμοι τε οἱ Σόλωνος εἰσι γεγραμμένοι καὶ θεῶν Εἰρήνης ἀγάλματα κεῖται καὶ Ἑστίας, ἀνδριάντες δὲ ἄλλοι τε καὶ Αὐτόλυκος ὁ παγκρατιαστής· τὰς γὰρ Μιλτιάδου καὶ Θεμιστοκλέους εἰκόνας ἐς Ῥωμαῖόν τε ἄνδρα καὶ Θρᾷκα μετέγραψαν. ἐντεῦθεν ἰοῦσιν ἐς τὰ κάτω τῆς πόλεως Σαράπιδός ἐστιν ἱερόν.
"Above the shrine of the Dioskouroi is the temenos of Aglauros . . . . Here the Persians climbed up and killed the Athenians (on the

Acropolis) . . . . Nearby is the prytaneion, in which the laws of Solon are inscribed and there are placed the figures of Eirene and Hestia. There are other statues, among which is that of Autolykos the pancratiast. The statues of Miltiades and Themistokles have their labels changed to those of a Roman and Thracian. For one going into the lower city from here there is the sanctuary of Sarapis."

222 Pausanias I, 20, 1 mid-II A.D.
Ἔστι δὲ ὁδὸς ἀπὸ τοῦ πρυτανείου καλουμένη Τρίποδες.
"From the prytaneion there is a street named Tripods."

223 Pausanias I, 26, 3 mid-II A.D.
Ὀλυμπιοδώρῳ δὲ τοῦτο μὲν ἐν Ἀθήναις εἰσιν ἔν τε ἀκροπόλει καὶ ἐν πρυτανείῳ τιμαί.
"Olympiodoros has honors in Athens, both on the Acropolis and in the prytaneion."

224 Pausanias I, 28, 10 mid-II A.D.
τὸ δὲ ἐν πρυτανείῳ καλούμενον ἔνθα τῷ σιδήρῳ καὶ πᾶσιν ὁμοίως τοῖς ἀψύχοις δικάζουσιν.
"The (court) in the prytaneion, as it is called, where they pass judgement on iron and all such lifeless things."

225 Pausanias IX, 32, 8 mid-II A.D.
Αὐτολύκῳ τῷ παγκρατιάσαντι, οὗ δὴ καὶ εἰκόνα ἰδὼν οἶδα ἐν πρυτανείῳ τῷ Ἀθηναίων.
". . . to Autolykos the pancratiast whose statue I saw and recognized in the prytaneion of the Athenians."

226 Aelius Aristides 103, 16 second half II A.D.
κομιδῇ γὲ ἐν ὀλίγαις ἑστίαν ἀκίνητον πρυτανείου δικαίως νέμει.
"Actually in a few (cities) the unmoved hearth of the prytaneion is properly tended."

227 Aelius Aristides 179, 11 second half II A.D.
ἀνθ' ὧν εἰ χρῆν ὥσπερ ἰδιώτου πόλεως εἰκόνα ποιήσασθαι, τῆς Ἀθηναίων προσῆκε μόνης καὶ τιμᾶν ὥσπερ ἄγαλμα κοινὸν τῆς Ἑλλάδος. ὅπερ γὰρ τῇ πόλει τὸ πρυτανεῖον. τοῦθ' ἡ πόλις πᾶσι κοινῇ γέγονε τοῖς Ἕλλησιν.
"Were it necessary to make instead of these a statue of, as it were, an individual city, Athens alone it would be fitting to honor as the common image of Greece. That which the prytaneion is to the city, this city has been to all the Greeks in common."

Cf. (A 69, 121, 233).

228 Aelius Aristides 196, 18 second half II A.D.

πρότερον μὲν οὖν ἠγάμεν ἀκούων τὸ τῆς σοφίας πρυτανεῖον καὶ τὴν τῆς Ἑλλάδος ἑστίαν καὶ τὸ ἔρεισμα καὶ ὅσα τοιαύτα εἰς τὴν πόλιν ᾔδετο.

Formerly, I heard and wondered that the prytaneion of wisdom and hearth of Greece and the mainstay and so many like things were known in the city (Athens)."

229 Aelius Aristides 372, 6 second half II A.D.

οὐ γὰρ οἱ πρὸς τῷ πρυτανείῳ κάλλιστα τὰς Ἀθήνας φυλάξουσιν.

"Those near the prytaneion will not best guard Athens."

230 Pollux VIII, 120 last quarter II A.D.

τὸ ἐπὶ πρυτανείῳ δικάζει δὲ περὶ τῶν ἀποκτεινάντων, κἂν ὦσιν ἀφανεῖς· καὶ περὶ τῶν ἀψύχων τῶν ἐμπεσόντων καὶ ἀποκτεινάντων. Προειστήκεσαν δὲ τούτου τοῦ δικαστηρίου φυλοβασιλεῖς, οὓς ἔδει τὸ ἐμπεσὸν ἄψυχον ὑπερορίσαι.

"The (court) in the prytaneion passes judgement on murderers, even if they are not known, and on inanimate objects which have fallen and killed someone. The Phylobasileis presided over this court and it was their duty to remove beyond the borders the inanimate object which had fallen."

231 Pollux VIII, 128 last quarter II A.D.

ἄξονες δὲ τετράγωνοι χαλκοῖ ἦσαν, ἔχοντες τοὺς νόμους. ἀπέκειντο δὲ οἵ τε κύρβεις καὶ οἱ ἄξονες ἐν ἀκροπόλει πάλαι· αὖθις δ' ἵνα πᾶσιν ἐξῇ ἐντυγχάνειν, εἰς τὸ πρυτανεῖον καὶ τὴν ἀγορὰν μετεκομίσθησαν.

"Axones were quadrangular and of bronze and they held the laws. In early time the kyrbeis and the axones were deposited on the Acropolis; later, in order that it would be possible for all to read them, they were transferred to the prytaneion and the agora."

232 Pollux VIII, 138 last quarter II A.D.

τὸ δὲ κηρύκειον, φόρημα ἦν τῶν πρέσβεων, καὶ εἰς τὸ πρυτανεῖον ἐπὶ ξένια ἐκαλοῦντο. Εἴποι δ' ἂν τις τοὺς πρέσβεις ὑπαλλάττων τὴν πρεσβείαν.

"The herald's staff, the burden of ambassadors, they also invited to Xenia in the prytaneion, exchanging, so to speak, the ambassadors for the embassy."

233 Athenaeus V, 187d late II A.D.

τὴν Ἀθηναίων πόλιν, τὸ τῆς Ἑλλάδος μουσεῖον, ἣν ὁ μὲν Πίνδαρος Ἑλλάδος ἔρεισμα ἔφη, Θουκυδίδης δ' ἐν τῷ εἰς Εὐριπίδην ἐπιγράμματι Ἑλλάδος Ἑλλάδα, ὁ δὲ Πύθιος ἑστίαν καὶ πρυτανεῖον τῶν Ἑλλήνων.

"Athens, the museum of Greece, which Pindar called the mainstay of Greece, Thucydides the Greece of Greece in the epigram against Euripides, and the Pythian the hearth and prytaneion of the Greeks."

Cf. (A 69, 121, 227).

234 Moeris 322P late II? A.D.
παρασίτους τοὺς δημοσίᾳ σιτουμένους ἐν τῷ πρυτανείῳ Ἀττικῶς
"Parasites were fed at public expense in the prytaneion of Attica."

235 *Hesperia* 10 (1941) 87, 20 A.D. 203
.... δ]ὲ σίτησιν ἔχειν / [....
Resolved ... "that (C. Fulvius Plautianus) shall have Sitesis."

236 *Hesperia*, Suppl. VI, no. 31 A.D. 229–231
13–15: *[καὶ ἀνδριάντα αὐτ]ῶν χαλκοῦν προῖκα στήναι ἐν τῷ συνεδρίῳ τῆς ἱερᾶς γερουσίας καὶ τῷ πρυτανείῳ ..... ὑπαρχεῖν δὲ αὐτῷ τε κ[αὶ τοῖς / παισὶν αὐτοῦ τοῖς κρ] Οὐλ› Τεισαμενῷ καὶ Πουπηνίῳ Μαξίμῳ καὶ σείτησιν τὴν ἐν τῇ θόλῳ καὶ πρυτανείῳ ἐπὶ διμοιρίᾳ.*
38–41: *[στῆναι δὲ ἀνδριάντας ἐν τῷ συνεδρίῳ καὶ] / τῷ πρυτ[ανείῳ καὶ σ]τήλας ἱδρῦσθαι καὶ παρεστάναι τοῖς ἀνδριάσιν αὐτοῦ το[ῖς ἐν τῷ συνεδρίῳ καὶ πρυτανείῳ]..... τετειμῆσθαι [δ]ὲ αὐτόν τε καὶ τοὺς κρ παῖδα[ς αὐτοῦ Μᾶρ› Οὐλ› Φλ› Τεισαμενον καὶ Πουπήνι]/ον Μάξιμο[ν σειτήσε]ι τῇ τε ἐν θόλῳ καὶ τῇ ἐν τῷ πρυτανείῳ ἐπὶ διμοιρίᾳ.*
13–15: Resolved by the Boule ... "and to erect as a gift a bronze statue of them in the council chamber of the Sacred Gerousia and in the prytaneion ... and to grant him and his sons, the most illustrious Ulpius Tisamenus and Pupienus Maximus, a double portion of Sitesis in the tholos and the prytaneion."
38–41: Resolved by the Boule ... "to erect statues in the council chamber and in the prytaneion and to set up steles and place them beside his statues in the council chamber and the prytaneion ... and that he and his sons, the most illustrious Marcus Ulpius Flavius Tisamenus and Pupienus Maximus be honored with a double portion of Sitesis in the tholos and the prytaneion."

237 *Hesperia* 32 (1962) 26 A.D. 229–231
2–4: *[καὶ ἀνδριάντα αὐτῶν χαλκοῦν προῖκα] στήναι ἐν [τῷ συνεδρίῳ τῆς ἱερᾶς γερουσίας καὶ τῷ πρυτανείῳ ..... ὑπάρχειν δὲ καὶ αὐτῷ τε καὶ τοῖς / παισὶν αὐτοῦ τοῖς] κρ Οὐλ› Τει[σαμενῷ καὶ] Πουπηνίῳ Μα[ξίμῳ καὶ σείτησιν τὴν ἐν τῇ θόλῳ καὶ πρυτανείῳ ἐπὶ διμοιρίᾳ]*

27–29: [στῆναι δὲ ἀνδριάντας ἐν τῷ συνεδρίῳ καὶ τὸ πρυ/τανείῳ καὶ στήλας ἱ]δρ[ῦ]σθαι κ[αὶ παρεστάναι τοῖς ἀνδριάσιν τοῖς αὐτοῦ τοῖς ἐν τῷ συνεδρίῳ καὶ πρυτανείῳ]
2–4: Resolved by the Boule . . . "and to erect as a gift a bronze statue of them in the council chamber of the Sacred Gerousia and in the prytaneion . . . and to grant to him (Ulpius Eubrotos) and to his sons, the most illustrious Ulpius Tisamenus and Pupienus Maximus, a double portion of Sitesis in the tholos and the prytaneion."
27–29: Resolved by the Demos . . . "to erect statues in the council chamber and in the prytaneion and to set up steles and place them beside his statues in the council chamber and the prytaneion."

238 Aelian, *Varia historia* IX, 39 — II A.D.
νεανίσκος δὲ Ἀθήνησι τῶν εὖ γεγονότων πρὸς τῷ πρυτανείῳ ἀνδριάντος ἑστῶτος τῆς Ἀγαθῆς Τύχης θερμότατα ἠράσθη.
"A young Athenian of good birth fell passionately in love with the statue of Agathe Tyche which stood near the prytaneion."

239 *IG* II², 2773, 12 — *ca.* A.D. 240
ἔτους ν νε[άτ]ου μῆνα ἐν πρυταν[είῳ σείτησιν ? --- ἕκαστ/ο]ς ⋆ Ħ
Flavius Asklepiades, by the terms of his will, gives to the council of the Areopagus . . . "a month of Sitesis in the prytaneion for the new year."

240 Libanios? *apud* Bekker, *Anecdota Graeca* — IV A.D.
Ἐπάλξεις: ἐξοχαὶ τειχῶν προμαχῶνες, ἄψις. ἔστι δὲ καὶ δικαστήριον τῶν φονικῶν, ᾠκοδόμηται δὲ πρὸς τῷ πρυτανείῳ.
"Epalxeis: projecting ramparts of the walls, a bastion. It is also a homicide court, built near the prytaneion."

241 *Scholion* Herodotus I, 146, 2 (A 21)
πρυτανεῖον, θεσμοθέσιον, θόλος καὶ ἡ τοῦ σίτου θήκη.
"Prytaneion, thesmothesion, tholos and the storage place of grain."

242 *Scholion* Thucydides II, 15, 2 (A 11)
'πρυτανεῖά τε': πρυτανεῖον ἐστιν οἶκος μέγας, ἔνθα αἱ σιτήσεις ἐδίδοντο τοῖς πολιτευομένοις. οὕτως δὲ ἐκαλεῖτο, ἐπειδὴ ἐκεῖ ἐκάθηντο οἱ πρυτάνεις, οἱ τῶν ὅλων πραγμάτων διοικηταί. ἄλλοι δὲ φασιν ὅτι τὸ πρυτανεῖον πυρὸς ἦν ταμεῖον, ἔνθα καὶ ἦν ἄσβεστον πῦρ καὶ ηὔχοντο.
"'and prytaneia': a prytaneion is a large building where Siteseis were given to those in political life. It was so called since there sat the prytaneis who arranged all the affairs (of state). Others say that the prytaneion was the treasury of fire where was the undying fire and prayers were offered."

243 *Scholion* Aristophanes, *Ach.* 124 (A 32)
'εἰς τὸ πρυτανεῖον' : ὥστε ἐκεῖ εἶναι τοὺς πρέσβεις παρὰ Ἀθηναίοις
"'into the prytaneion': because that is where the ambassadors go in Athens."

244 *Scholion* Aristophanes, *Equites* 167 (A 34)
'ἐν πρυτανείῳ': πρυτανεῖον οἰκίσκος παρὰ τοῖς Ἀθηναίοις, ἔνθα σιτοῦνται δημοσίᾳ οἱ τῆς τοιαύτης τιμῆς παρ' αὐτοῖς τυχόντες. περισπούδαστον δὲ ἦν τῆς τοιαύτης δωρεᾶς τυχεῖν. ἐπὶ γὰρ μεγάλοις κατορθώμασι τὴν τοιαύτην ἀπεδίδουν χάριν.
"'in the prytaneion': the prytaneion was a building at Athens where those among the Athenians who had received such an honor were fed at public expense. There was much eagerness to receive such a grant, for they bestowed such a favor on great successes."

245 *Scholion* Aristophanes, *Equites* 281 (A 35)
πρυτανεῖον δὲ τόπος Ἀθήνησιν οὗ τὰς δημοσίας σιτήσεις ἐποιοῦντο. τιμὴ δὲ οὐκ ἐλαχίστη τοῖς δημοσίᾳ σιτουμένοις ἦν. ταῦτα δ' εἶπεν ὅτι πένης ὢν ἐκ τῶν κοινῶν πεπλούτηκε, καὶ ὅτι ἀναξίως ἔχει τῆς ἐν πρυτανείῳ σιτήσεως.
"The prytaneion was a place at Athens where there were Siteseis at public expense. Those who dined at public expense did not have the worst of honors. This (the passage from Aristophanes) says that being poor he (Kleon) enriched himself from the common wealth, and that he had Sitesis in the prytaneion unworthily."

246 *Scholion* Aristophanes, *Equites* 407
τοῦτον δὲ ὁ Κρατῖνος 'πυρροπίπην' λέγει .... τουτέστι τὸν φύλακα τοῦ σίτου, ὡς εἰς τὸ πρυτανεῖον παρέχοντα ἄρτους.
"This person Cratinus calls a 'red-head eyer' . . . that is, the guard of the grain as providing bread for the prytaneion."

The scholiast is explaining the word *πυροπίπης* (a synonym for *σιτοφύλαξ*) which Cratinus corrupted to form the pun.

247 *Scholion* Aristophanes, *Equites* 535 (A 36)
Ἔχεται καὶ τοῦτο τῆς ἐννοίας τῆς προκειμένης, σιτεῖσθαι γὰρ ἔλεγον ἐν τῷ πρυτανείῳ οὐχι πίνειν.
"This comes from the preceding thought for they spoke of eating in the prytaneion, not drinking."

The scholiast is explaining Aristophanes' use of the word *πίνειν* as dependent upon the context, but he has missed the pun of substitution for the expected *δειπνεῖν*.

248 *Scholion* Aristophanes, *Equites* 575 (A 37)
'καὶ τὰ σιτία': σιτία γοῦν εἶκε τὴν ἐν τῷ πρυτανείῳ σίτησιν.
"'and the foods': foods surely refers to the Sitesis in the prytaneion."

249 *Scholion* Aristophanes, *Equites* 766 (A 39)
φησὶ γὰρ ὅτι ἐπὶ μεγάλοις κατορθώμασι τὴν τιμὴν ταύτην Ἀθηναῖοι παρεῖχον τοῖς ἀγαθόν τι εὐεργετήσασιν αὐτοῖς. νῦν οὖν σκώπτει τὸν Κλέωνα, δι' ὧν αὐτὸν ὁμολογοῦντα ποιεῖ, ὅτι μηδὲν διαπραξάμενος τοιοῦτον ἔργον, τῆς ἐν πρυτανείῳ σιτήσεως μετέσχεν.
"They say that the Athenians granted this honor for great successes to those who had done some good thing for them. Now he mocks Kleon in that he makes him (Kleon) acknowledge that, having accomplished no such work, he shared in the Sitesis in the prytaneion."

250 *Scholion* Aristophanes, *Pax* 1084 (A 41)
ὅτι καὶ οἱ χρησμολόγοι μετεῖχον τῆς ἐν πρυτανείῳ σιτήσεως, δῆλον ἐκ τοῦ Λάμπωνος, ὃς τούτου ἠξίωτο. φησὶν οὖν οὐκέτι ἔσται πόλεμος· τούτου γὰρ μὴ ὄντος οὐδὲν ἐλάμβανεν οὗτος ἐκ τοῦ δημοσίου. ἐπὶ γὰρ τοῦ πολέμου χρεία τῶν μάντεων.
"That Chresmologoi had a share of Sitesis in the prytaneion is clear from the case of Lampon who was worthy of this. They say there will no longer be war, for when there is no war he did not get this at public expense. The need for manteis exists in war."

251 *Scholion* Aristophanes, *Pax* 1183
'πρὸς τὸν ἀνδριάντα': .... Ἄλλως. τόπος Ἀθήνησιν παρὰ πρυτανεῖον, ἐν ᾧ ἑστήκασιν ἀνδριάντες, οὓς ἐπωνύμους καλοῦσιν.
"'by the statues': ... Otherwise, a place in Athens by the prytaneion where statues stood which they call Eponymoi."

252 *Scholion* Aristophanes, *Aves* 521
ἔτυχε δὲ καὶ τῆς ἐν πρυτανείῳ σιτήσεως
"He (Lampon) gained Sitesis in the prytaneion."

253 *Scholion* Aristophanes, *Ranae* 944
ἕτερος δὲ ἐστι Κηφισοφῶν ὁ καὶ τὸ ψήφισμα εἰσενεγκὼν ὑπὲρ τοῦ εἰρχθῆναι τῆς ἐν πρυτανείῳ σιτήσεως.
"Another Kephisophon is the one who introduced the law about restrictions of Sitesis in the prytaneion."

Is this a reference to the law embodied in *IG* I², 77 (A 26)?

254 *Scholion* Patmos, Demosthenes, *Against Aristokrates* 645 (A 106)
'ἐπὶ πρυτανείῳ' ἐν τούτῳ τῷ δικαστηρίῳ δικαζόνται φόνου, ὅταν ὁ μὲν ἀνῃρημένος δῆλος ᾖ, ζητεῖται δὲ ὁ τὸν φόνον δράσας.

καὶ ἀποφέρει τὴν γραφὴν πρὸς τὸν βασιλέα, καὶ ὁ βασιλεὺς διὰ τοῦ κήρυκος κηρύττει καὶ ἀπαγορεύει τόνδε τὸν ἀνελόντα τὸν δεῖνα μὴ ἐπιβαίνειν ἱερῶν καὶ χώρας Ἀττικῆς. ἐν τῷ αὐτῷ δὲ τούτῳ δικαστηρίῳ κἄν τε ἐμπεσὸν πατάξῃ τινα καὶ ἀνέλῃ τῶν ἀψύχων, δικάζεται τούτῳ καὶ ὑπερορίζεται.
"'in the prytaneion': In this court are tried homicide cases whenever a person clearly was killed but the murderer is missing. One submits the charge to the Basileus, and the Basileus announces, by means of the herald, and forbids the murderer to enter sacred areas and the land of Attica. Also in this court an inanimate object, if having fallen and struck someone has killed him, is judged and thrown beyond the borders."

255 *Scholion* D, Aelius Aristides 103, 14
τὸ πρυτανεῖον σύμβολόν ἐστι τῆς πόλεως· οὐδὲ γὰρ αἱ κῶμαι τοῦτο ἔχουσιν. ἀκίνητον οὖν αὐτὸ ἔχουσιν Ἀθῆναι, οὐ παρ' ἄλλου λαβοῦσαι, τουτέστιν οὐ δεξάμεναι παρ' ἄλλης πόλεως.
"The prytaneion is the symbol of the city; villages do not have it. Athens has this unmoved, they did not take it from another; that is, she did not receive it (as a colony) from another city."

256 *Scholion* A, Aelius Aristides 103, 16 (A 226)
καὶ μόνη πόλεων νέμει καὶ παρέχει τοῖς πολίταις ἑστίαν καὶ οἴκησιν πρυτανείου +καὶ κοινοῦ+ ἀκίνητον καὶ ἀμετάβλητον.
"(Athens) alone of the cities cares for and grants to the citizens the hearth and the dwelling of the prytaneion unmoved and unchanged."

Something is wrong with the text of this *scholion*, for the phrase *καὶ κοινοῦ* is unintelligible. We might simply excise these two words, or rather drastically emend the text to read *κοινὴν ἑστίαν καὶ οἴκησιν πρυτανείου*. The latter proposal has the advantage of frequent mentions of the common hearth upon which to draw for parallels (A 5, 8, 195, etc.) but it is difficult to explain how the present text resulted from the suggested reading.

257 *Scholion* D, Aelius Aristides 103, 16 (A 226)
ἐπειδὴ οὐκ ἄποικοι τινῶν, ἀλλ' αὐτόχθονες Ἀθηναῖοι καὶ μόνη πόλις, φησὶν, Ἀττικὴ πλὴν Ἀρχαδίας τοῖς ἀποίκοις ἑαυτῆς ἑστίαν, ὅ ἐστι πῦρ ἀκίνητον, μένει, ἀλλὰ ἀπὸ τῶν θεῶν κομισαμένους ἐκ τοῦ πρυτανείου δικαίως νέμει. τὸ δὲ πρυτανεῖον ἦν τόπος τῆς Ἀθηνᾶς. ἢ οὕτως· ὅτι ἐφύλαττε τὸ πῦρ, ἐξ οὗ καὶ ἄποικοι μετελάμβανον, τὸ πρυτανεῖον διπλῆν ἔχει σημασίαν. ἢ γὰρ τὸ τοῦ πυρὸς ταμεῖον ἢ τὸ τῶν πυρῶν, ὅ ἐστι τοῦ σίτου, ταμεῖον.
". . . since the Athenians were not colonists from some other cities,

but were autochthonous and Attica the only polis, they say, except Arcadia, which keeps for its own colonists the hearth, the unmoved fire, but tends justly the things given by the gods from the prytaneion. The prytaneion was a place of Athena. Or thus: that it guarded the fire from which colonists took a share. The prytaneion has a double meaning. It was either the treasury of the fire, or the treasury of grains, that is, of sitos."

258 *Scholion* Oxon., Aelius Aristides 103, 16 (A 226)

τὸ δὲ πρυτανεῖον τόπον εἶναι λέγουσι τῆς Παλλάδος ἱερὸν, ἐν ᾧ ἐφυλάττετο τὸ πῦρ, ἐξ οὗ καὶ οἱ ἄποικοι Ἀθηναίων μετελάμβανον. Διττὴν δὲ ἔχει τὴν σημσίαν· ἢ γὰρ τὸ τοῦ πυρὸς ταμεῖον ἢ τῶν πυρῶν ἤτοι τοῦ σίτου λέγει.

"They say that the prytaneion is a place sacred to Pallas in which the fire was guarded from which the Athenian colonists took a share. It has a double meaning, for it was either the treasury of the fire or the treasury of grain, of sitos, that is to say."

259 Timaeus, *Lexicon Platonicum* 402 IV A.D.

θόλος οἶκος περιφερής, ἐν ᾧ οἱ πρυτάνεις συνεισιτῶντο. πρυτανεῖον δὲ ὠνόμασται, ἐπεὶ πυρῶν ἦν ταμιεῖον.

"The tholos was a round building in which the prytaneis ate together. It was called the prytaneion since it was the treasury of grain."

260 Hesychios, *s.v. πρυτανεῖον* V A.D.

πρυτανεῖον: τρία Ἀθήνησι συσσίτια, πρυτανεῖα, θεσμοφορεῖον, πρυτανεῖον

"prytaneion: there were three common dining halls in Athens, prytaneia, thesmophoreion, prytaneion."

261 Hesychios, *s.v. σκίας* V A.D.

σκίας: .... καὶ τὸ πρυτανεῖον

"skias: ... also the prytaneion."

262 Photios 495A5 (ed. Bekker) IX A.D.

ἔστι δὲ αὐτῷ εἰκὼν ἐν τῷ πρυτανείῳ περιεζωσμένη ξίφος.

"He (Demosthenes) has a sword-girt statue in the prytaneion."

263 Photios, *s.v. προδικασία* IX A.D.

οἱ τὰς ἐπὶ φόνῳ δίκας ἐγκαλούμενοι ἐν πρυτανείῳ πρὸ τῆς δίκης διατελοῦσιν ἐπὶ τρεῖς μῆνας ἐν οἷς ἐξ ἑκατέρου μέρους λόγοι προάγονται· τοῦτό φασι προδικασίαν.

"Those indicted for homicide in the prytaneion complete three months before the trial in which speeches are introduced on each side. They call this prodikasia."

The translation of this passage by D. M. MacDowell, *Athenian Homicide Law* (Manchester 1963) 36, is misleading. He renders it as "persons accused on charges of homicide live at the prytaneion for three months before the trial . . ." This gives *διατελοῦσιν* the sense of 'inhabit' which seems wrong in this context. Furthermore, it seems to me that the participle *ἐγκαλούμενοι* exerts more force on the phrase *ἐν πρυτανείῳ* than does the main verb of the sentence and thus I have translated it.

264 Suda, *s.v.* *πρυτανεῖον* X A.D.

πρυτανεῖον· θεσμοθέτιον, θόλος. παρὰ δὲ τοῖς Ἀθηναίοις οἰκίσκος δημόσιος, ἔνθα ἐσιτοῦντο δημοσίᾳ τῆς τοιαύτης τιμῆς παρ' αὐτοῖς τυχόντες. περισπούδαστον δὲ ἦν τῆς τοιαύτης δωρεᾶς τυχεῖν· ἐπὶ γὰρ μεγάλοις κατορθώμασι τὴν τοιαύτην ἀπεδίδοντο χάριν. ἢ πυρὸς ταμεῖον, ἔνθα ἦν ἄσβεστον πῦρ, καὶ ηὔχοντο.

"prytaneion: thesmothetion, tholos. A public building at Athens where those among the Athenians who had received such an honor were fed at public expense. There was much eagerness to receive such a grant, for they bestowed such a favor on great successes. Or the treasury of fire where was the undying fire and prayers were offered."

This passage is a collection of other late sources which have already been listed. The first comes from the same tradition as (A 241) and perhaps (A 260). The second part is nearly a word-for-word copy of (A 244), while the third can be found at the end of (A 242).

265 Suda, *s.v.* *θόλος* X A.D.

οἶκος περιφερής, ἐν ᾧ οἱ πρυτάνεις εἱστιῶντο. πρυτανεῖον δέ τι ἰδίως ὠνόμασται, ἐπεὶ πυρῶν ἦν ταμιεῖον.

"A round building in which the prytaneis ate. It was called the prytaneion in particular since it was the treasury of grain."

Cf. (A 259).

266 *Etymologicum Magnum* 693 XII A.D.

πρυτανεῖον. τόπος ἦν παρ' Ἀθηναίοις, ἐν ᾧ κοιναὶ σιτήσεις τοῖς δημοσίοις εὐεργέταις ἐδίδοντο· ὅθεν καὶ πρυτανεῖον ἐκαλεῖτο, οἱονεὶ πυροταμεῖον (πυρὸς γὰρ ὁ σῖτος) τουτέστι τοῦ δημοσίου σίτου ταμεῖον.

"Prytaneion: it was a place in Athens where common Siteseis were given to public benefactors. It was prytaneion from pyrotameion (for pyros is grain) and it is the treasury of grain."

267 *Etymologicum Magnum* 694 XII A.D.
καὶ πρυτανεῖον λέγεται παρὰ τὸ ἐκεῖ φυλάττεσθαι τὸν πυρὸν, ἤγουν τὸν σῖτον οἱονεὶ πυροταμεῖον καὶ πρυτανεῖον.
"It is called a prytaneion where the pyros is guarded, or rather, the grain; a pyrotameion and a prytaneion as it were."

Bargylia

268 *Michel* 457, 32–33 *ca.* 262 B.C.
καλέσαι δὲ αὐτὸν καὶ ἐπὶ ξένια ἐ[ν τῶι / π]ρυτανείωι
Resolved . . . "to invite him (Tyron, ambassador from Teos) to Xenia in the prytaneion."

Biannos

269 *ICr* I, vi, 2, 36–37 III–II B.C.
ἐκαλέσα[μεν δ' αὐτοὺς ἐπὶ ξενισ]/μὸν ἐς τὸ πρυτανεῖον ἐπὶ τὰν κοινὰν ἑ[στίαν].
"We invited them (ambassadors from Teos) to Xenismos in the prytaneion at the common hearth."

Cyrene

270 *SEG* IX, 1, 44–46 322–307 B.C.
Ὅστις ἐκ τοῦ πολιτ[εύ]ματος δημοσίαι ἰατρεύηι ἢ παιδοτριβῆι ἢ διδάσκ[ηι] / τοξεύειν ἢ ἱππεύειν ἢ ὁπλομαχεῖν ἢ κηρύσσηι ἐν βρυτανείωι μὴ συνπορε[υέσ]/θω μυριακὰς ἀρχράς.
"Whoever of the citizen body is paid at public expense as a doctor or training master for boys, or a teacher of archers or horsemen or hoplites or a herald in the prytaneion is not to be a member of the Ten Thousand (i.e., the Ekklesia)."

For other parts of this text one should refer to P. M. Frazer, *Berytus* 12 (1958) 120–128. The readings elsewhere on the stone are not necessarily correct as presented in *SEG*.

271 *SEG* XX, 719B, 4–7 II B.C.
. . . *τοῖς δὲ ἐν τᾶι ἀ/γορᾶι καὶ τοῖς ἐ[ν] / τῶι πρυτανείω[ι*
Sacrifice a [?] "to those (gods) in the agora and to those in the prytaneion."

272 *SEG* IX, 5, 20–21 II–I B.C.
Οἱ δὲ δαμιεργοὶ καὶ ἱαροθύται τὸ πρυτανεῖον / καὶ τὰς στωιὰς κοσμησάντων
"The damiergoi and the priests are to decorate the prytaneion and the stoas."

273 *SEG* IX, 73, 7–8 II–I B.C.
ὅταν ἡ πό[λις / σ]υνάγηι στοὰν ἢ περίλυσιν, ἢ [ἐν τ]ῶι πρυταν[είωι αἱ / σ]υναρχίαι ἑστιῶνται.

"When the city assembles at the stoa or the perilysis, or when the magistrates are eating in the prytaneion . . ."

274 *SEG* IX, 4, 2 16/15 B.C.

παρακα[λέ]σαι [ἐς τὰν κοινὰν ἑστίαν ἐς τὸ πρυτανεῖον]

Resolved . . . "to invite (Barcaeus, priest of Augustus) to the common hearth in the prytaneion."

Cyzicus

275 *Michel* 532, 6–7 VI B.C.

πόλις [Μανῇ τῷ] Μηδίκεω καὶ τοῖσιν παισὶν / καὶ τοῖσιν ἐκγόνοισιν ἀτελείην καὶ πρυ/τανεῖον δέδοται.

"The city gives to Manes son of Medikeus and to his sons and to his descendants, exemption (from taxes) and (entertainment in the) prytaneion."

276 Livy XLI, 20, 7 *ca.* 170 B.C.

Cyzici (in) prytaneo—id est penetrale urbis, ubi publice, quibus is honos datus est, vescuntur—vasa aurea mensae unius posuit.

"In the prytaneion in Cyzicus—this is the center of the city where those men dine at public expense to whom this honor is given—he (Antiochos Epiphanes) set golden dishes for one table."

277 Pliny, *Naturalis historia* XXXVI, 99 *ca.* A.D. 77

Eodem in oppido est lapis fugitivus appellatus; Argonautae eum pro ancora usi reliquerant ibi. Hunc e prytanea—ita vocatur locus—saepe profugum vinxere plumbo.

"In this same city is a stone called the Fugitive; the Argonauts used it for an anchor and left it there. This often has wandered away from the prytaneion—so the place is called—and is fixed in place with lead."

Delos

278 *IG* XI², 144A *ante* 301 B.C.

98: *[τὸν τοῖχον] τ[ὸ]μ πρὸς τῶι πρυτανείωι καὶ τὰ ἄλλα τείχα δι[. . . .*

101: *[κομί/σα]σι[ν]* ΓΗΗ *ἑστιατορίου καὶ πρυταν[εί]ου τὸ κ[ατὰ] νότον ἐπισκευάσαντι Ὀλύμπωι*

98: "the wall near the prytaneion and the other walls . . ."

101: "a provision of seven drachmai for Olympos who restored the (wall?) on the south of the hestiatorion and the prytaneion."

279 *CIG* 2266, 24 III B.C.

τῆς ὀργυιᾶς τῆς ἐν τῶι πρυτανείωι [ἐπὶ] τὸ στρῶμα τοῦ νεὼ τοῦ Ἀπόλλωνος

". . . of the orgyia (a measure slightly more than six feet long) in the prytaneion for the pavement of the temple of Apollo."

280 *Michel* 852B, 18 late III B.C.

ἐπαινέσαι δὲ τοὺς θεωροὺς κ[αὶ καλέσαι ἐπὶ] / ξένια εἰς τὸ πρυτανεῖον [εἰς αὔριον]

Resolved . . . "to honor the ambassadors (of Cyzicus) and invite them to Xenia in the prytaneion on the next day."

281 *ID* 442B, 96 179 B.C.

ἄλλα ξύσματα παντοδαπά, τὰ περιγενόμενα ἀπὸ τῶν ἀργυρωμάτων τῶν ἐκ πρυτανείου

(part of an inventory) "sundry other scraps: those left over from the silver plate of the prytaneion"

282 *ID* 460F, 18 171 B.C.

--] τὸ πρυτανεῖον ⊢ [--

(part of an inventory) ". . . the prytaneion, one drachma . . ."

283 *ID* 460L', 7 171 B.C.

εἰ]ς τὸ πρυ[τανεῖον

(part of an inventory) "in the prytaneion"

284 *ID* 461Aa, 49 169 B.C.

--]ν εἰς ἀλεξανδρείου λόγον, ἀπὸ τοῦ πρυτανεῖου

(part of an inventory) "a [?] in Alexandrine reckoning, from the prytaneion."

285 *ID* 1497, 33–34 165/4 B.C.

ἀποστεῖλαι δ' αὐτῶι καὶ / ξένιον· καλέσαι δὲ αὐτὸν καὶ εἰς τὸ / πρυτανεῖον ἐπὶ τὴν κοινὴν ἑστίαν

Resolved . . . "to send Xenion to him (Amphikles, a poet) and to invite him to the common hearth in the prytaneion."

286 *ID* 1416A, I, 83–95 156/5 B.C.

ΕΝ ΤΩΙ ΠΡΥΤΑΝΕΙΩΙ· χαλκᾶ· Ἑστία[ν . . . . . ἐπὶ βω/μίσ]κου λιθίνου καθήμενον καὶ ἐπὶ βάσεως λιθίνης· ἀπολλων[ίσκον ἀρχαικὸν ὡς / ποδι]αῖον καὶ θυμιατήριον πομπικὸν ὡς τριημιποδιαῖον· Ἑρμ[ᾶς ἐπὶ βάσεων λιθί/νων] πέντε· σατυρίσκον ὡς τριπάλαστον φέροντα κρα[τηρίσκον ἐπὶ βά/σεω]ς λιθίνης· ὀμφαλὸν καὶ φύλακα <φύλακα> περὶ αὐτ[ὸν --- / ἀπο]λλωνίσκον ἐν θυρίδι καθήμενον ἐπ' ὀμφαλοῦ ὡς δί[πουν· ἄλλον --- / ἐν θ]υρίδι ἐπιβεβηκότα ἐπ' ὀμφαλαῦ λιθίνου· στέφαν[ον ---- ΕΝ ΤΩΙ / ΠΡΟ]ΔΟΜΩΙ· Ἑρμῆν ὡς δίπουν ἐπὶ βάσεως λιθίνης ἔχ[οντα ---- καὶ πρ]οσανακεκλιμένον πρὸς δενδρυφίωι [--- περιραντήριον ἔ/χο]ν ὦτα δύο, ἐφ' οὗ ἐπιγραφή ἱερὸν Ἀπόλλωνος· [ΕΝ ΤΕΙ ΑΥΛΕΙ· Ἑρμᾶς τέτ/τ]αρας ἐπὶ βάσεων λιθίνων. ΕΝ ΤΩΙ

ΑΡΧΕΙΩΙ· Ἑστίαν [ὡ]ς [δίπουν ἐπ' ὀμφα]/λοῦ καθημένην καὶ βάσεως λιθίνης. ΕΝ ΤΩΙ [ΠΡΟΔΟΜΩΙ· Ἑρμᾶς δύο ἐπὶ βάσεων] / λιθίνων.

"IN THE PRYTANEION: bronze statue; Hestia . . . seated on a little stone altar and on a stone base; an archaic statuette of Apollo about a foot high and a processional censer about a foot and a half long; five Herms on stone bases; a statuette of a satyr about three hands long holding a little crater on a stone base; an omphalos and a chain about it; a statuette of Apollo in a frame on an omphalos about two feet long; another [?] in a window standing on a stone omphalos; a garland . . . IN THE PRODOMOS: a Hermes on a stone base about two feet long holding . . . [?] . . . and leaning against a little tree; . . . a perirrhanterion having two handles on which is an inscription, sacred to Apollo. IN THE COURT: four Herms on stone bases. IN THE ARCHEION: a Hestia about two feet long seated on an omphalos and stone base. IN THE PRODOMOS: two Herms on stone bases."

287 *ID* 1417B, I, 89–102 155/4 B.C.

[ΕΝ Τ]ΩΙ ΠΡΥΤΑΝΕΙΩΙ· χαλκᾶ· Ἑστίαν ὡς δί[πουν / ἐ]πὶ βωμίσκο[υ λιθίνου καθη]μένην καὶ ἐπὶ βάσεως λιθίνης· ἀπ[ολλωνίσκ]ον / ἀρχαικὸν ὡς π[οδιαῖον καὶ] θυμιατήριον πομπικὸν ὡς τριημιποδι[αῖον· Ἑρ]/μᾶς ἐπὶ βάσ[εων λιθίν]ων πέντε· σατυρίσκον ὡς τριπάλ[ασ]τον [φέρον]/τα κρατηρί[σκον ἐπὶ] βάσεως λιθίνης· ὀμφαλὸν καὶ φύλακα περὶ αὐτόν· / τραχηλ[ὸν ἀπολ]λωνίσκον ἐν θυρίδι καθήμενον ἐπ' ὀμφαλοῦ / ὡς δίπου[ν· ἄλλον ----] ἐν θυρίδ(ι) ἐπιβεβηκότα ἐπ' ὀμφαλοῦ λιθίνου· στέφα/νο[ν ----] ΕΝ ΤΩΙ ΠΡΟΔΟΜΩΙ· Ἑρμῆν ὡς δίπουν ἐπὶ βάσεως λιθίνης / ἔχ[οντα ......]ιον καὶ προσανακεκλιμένον πρὸς δενδρυφίω[ι ...../..... περι]ραντήριον ἔχον ὦς ἓν ἐφ' οὗ ἐπιγραφή· [ἱε]ρὸν Ἀπ[όλλω/νος ΕΝ ΤΕΙ ΑΥ]ΛΕΙ· Ἑρμᾶς ὡς τέτταρας ἐπὶ βάσεως λιθίνων. [ΕΝ ΤΩΙ ΑΡΧΕΙΩΙ·]/ Ἑστ[ίαν] ὡς διποῦν ἐπ' ὀμφαλοῦ καθημένην καὶ ἐπὶ β[άσεως λιθίνης· ΕΝ ΤΩΙ] ΠΡΟΔΟΜΩΙ· Ἑρμᾶς δύο ἐπὶ βάσεων λιθίνων· ἄλλον ὡς / π[οδιαῖ]ον βάσιν οὐκ ἔχον· λεπίδ(α)ς ἀσπίδων· λημνίσκους.

"IN THE PRYTANEION: bronze statue; Hestia about two feet high seated on a little stone altar and on a stone base; archaic statuette of Apollo about a foot high and a processional censer about a foot and a half long; five Herms on stone bases; a statuette of a satyr about three hands high holding a little crater on a stone base; omphalos and a chain around it; a necklace; statuette of Apollo in a frame about two feet long on an omphalos; another [?] in a window standing on a stone omphalos; a garland. IN THE PRODOMOS:

Hermes on a stone base about two feet high holding [?] and leaning against a little tree; . . . perirrhanterion having one handle on which is an inscription, sacred to Apollo. IN THE COURT: four Herms on stone bases. IN THE ARCHEION: a Hestia about two feet high seated on an omphalos and a stone base. IN THE PRODOMOS: two Herms on stone bases; another about a foot high with no base; metal plates from shields; wool fillets."

Delphi

288 Plutarch, *Aristides* XX, 4 479 B.C.
ἀνεῖλεν ὁ Πύθιος Διὸς ἐλευθερίου βωμὸν ἱδρύσασθαι, θῦσαι δὲ μὴ πρότερον ἢ τὸ κατὰ τὴν χώραν πῦρ ἀποσβέσαντας ὡς ὑπὸ τῶν βαρβάρων μεμιασμένον ἐναύσασθαι καθαρὸν ἐκ Δελφῶν ἀπὸ τῆς κοινῆς ἑστίας.
"The Pythian replied that an altar to Zeus Eleutherios was to be constructed, but it was not to be sacrificed upon before the fire throughout the land was extinguished as having been polluted by the barbarians and relit pure from the common hearth at Delphi."

289 *FD* III^5, 62, 13–21 *ca.* 334/3 B.C.
Παγκ[ρ]άτει Ἀργείωι τοῦ περιβόλου / [τοῦ ἄνωθεν] κατὰ [τὴ]ν συγγραφὴν μναῖ εἴκοσι / [δύο .... Ἀγ]άθωνι Δ[ε]λφῶι τοῦ περιβόλου τοῦ / [παρὰ τὸ π]ρυτανεῖ[ο]ν ἀνελομένωι τὸ πλέθρον / [μνῶν εἴκο]σι ὀκτώ, τ[ού]του κατὰ τὴν συγγραφὴν / [τὸ ἥμισον] μνᾶς δέκα [τ]έσσαρας .... Εὐαινέτωι / [Δελφῶι τοῦ] κάτωθεν [ἔργ]ου κ[α]τὰ ταὐτὰ ἀνε[λο/μένωι τὸ πλ]έθρον μν[ῶν εἴκοσ]ι ὀκτώ. τούτο[υ / τὸ ἥμισον μν]ᾶς δέκα [τέσσαρας].
"To Pankrates the Argive for the upper peribolos wall according to the contract, twenty-two minai; to Agathon the Delphian for the peribolos wall by the prytaneion having contracted for one hundred feet at twenty-eight minai, of this sum one-half according to the contract, fourteen minai; to Euainetos the Delphian for the work below having contracted in the same way for one hundred feet at twenty-eight minai, half of this, fourteen minai."

290 *FD* III^1, 308, 15–16 early II B.C.
[κ]αλέσαι δὲ αὐτοὺς / καὶ ἐπὶ ξ[ένια τοὺς ἄρχοντας ἐπὶ τὰν κοινὰν ἑστίαν ἐν τὸ πρυτανεῖον]
Resolved . . . "that the archons invite them (ambassadors from Knidos) to Xenia at the common hearth in the prytaneion."

291 *FD* III^2, 20, 15 178 B.C.
καλέσαι δὲ αὐτοὺς καὶ ἐπὶ ξένια ἐν τὸ πρυτανεῖον
Resolved . . . "to invite them (ambassadors from Tetrapolis) to Xenia in the prytaneion."

292 *SGDI* II, 2646A first half II B.C.
καλέσαι δὲ αὐτὸν καὶ ἐν τὸ πρυτανεῖον ἐπὶ [τὰν] κοινὰν ἑστίαν
Resolved . . . "to invite him (Sardianus, a proxenos) to the common hearth in the prytaneion."

293 *SGDI* II, 2680, 8–12 second quarter II B.C.
ἔδωκαν δὲ καὶ / πορεύεσθαι ἐν / τὸ πρυτανεῖ/ον ἐν τὰν θυσί/αν τῶν Ῥωμα[ί]ων
"They granted it to him to go into the prytaneion for the sacrifice of the Romans."

294 *FD* III^{1}, 48, 9 165–160 B.C.
καλέσαι δὲ αὐτὸν καὶ τοὺς μετ' αὐτοῦ τοὺς ἄρχοντας καὶ ἐν τὸ πρυτανεῖον
Resolved . . . "that the archons invite him (Nikon of Megalopolis, a proxenos) and his group to the prytaneion."

295 *FD* III^{2}, 94, 17–18 150–140 B.C.
ἐκαλέσαμεν δὲ τοὺς πρεσ/βευτὰς καὶ ἐπὶ ξένια ἐν τὸ πρυτα[νεῖον ἐπὶ τὰν] κοινὰν τᾶς πόλιος ἑστίαν
"We invited the ambassadors (of Athens) to Xenia in the prytaneion at the common hearth of the city."

296 *FD* III^{1}, 152, 13–14 150–140 B.C.
ὑπάρχειν δὲ αὐτῶι πορεύεσχαι / καὶ ἐν τὸ πρυτανεῖον ἐν τὰν θυσίαν τῶν Ῥωμαίων
Resolved . . . "that it is to be permissible for him (Biaios, a proxenos) to go in the prytaneion to the sacrifice of the Romans."

297 *FD* III^{1}, 260, 8–9 146 B.C.
καλέσαι δὲ αὐτοὺς καὶ τοὺς ἄρχοντας ἐν τὸ πρυτανεῖον ἐπὶ τὰν κοινὰν ἑστίαν
Resolved . . . "to invite these leaders (of Hypataea) to the common hearth in the prytaneion."

298 *FD* III^{1}, 454, 12–14 second half II B.C.
[καλέσαι δὲ] αὐτὸν καὶ ἐ[ν τὸ / πρυτανεῖον] ἐπὶ τὰν κ[ο]ιν[ὰν / ἑστίαν]
Resolved . . . "to invite him (a Lycian) to the common hearth in the prytaneion."

299 *FD* III^{4}, 77, 38 *ca.* 94 B.C.
παρ]ακαλέ[σαι] δὲ κ[αὶ τ]ὸν πρε[σβευτὰν Βίαντα ἐπὶ ξένια ἐν τὸ] / πρυτανεῖον
Resolved . . . "to invite Bias the ambassador to Xenia in the prytaneion."

300 *FD* III⁴, 56, 19–22 91–68 B.C.
καλέσαι δὲ αὐτὸν καὶ ἐπὶ ξέ/νια ἐν τὸ βρυτανεῖον ἐπὶ τὰν κοινὰν τᾶς πόλιος ἑστίαν.
Resolved . . . "to invite him (Ariston) to Xenia in the prytaneion at the common hearth of the city."

301 *FD* III⁴, 57, 26–28 91–68 B.C.
καλέσαι [δὲ / αὐτὸν καὶ ἐπὶ ξένια ἐν τὸ πρυτανεῖον ἐπὶ τὰν κοινὰν] / τᾶς πόλιος ἑστίαν.
Resolved . . . "to invite him (the same Ariston as in A 300) to Xenia in the prytaneion at the common hearth of the city."

302 *FD* III³, 249, 16–17 100–60 B.C.
καλέσαι δὲ αὐτὰν καὶ ἐν τὸ π[ρυτα]/νεῖον ἐπὶ τὰν κοινὰν ἑστίαν
Resolved . . . "to invite her (Polygnota of Thebes) to the common hearth in the prytaneion."

303 Plutarch, *Numa* IX, 6 I–II A.D.
See (A 212) above.

304 Plutarch, *De E apud Delphos* 391 I–II A.D.
τῇ γὰρ ἕκτῃ τοῦ νέου μηνὸς ὅταν κατάγῃ τις τὴν Πυθίαν εἰς τὸ πρυτανεῖον, ὁ πρῶτος ὑμῖν γίγνεται τῶν τριῶν κλήρων εἰς τὰ πέντε, πρὸς ἀλλήλους ἐκείνης τὰ τρία, σοῦ δὲ τὰ δύο βάλλοντος.
"On the sixth day of the new month when someone leads the Pythia down into the prytaneion, the first of your three sortitions is for five, she casting three with reference to one another, you casting two."

305 *SEG* XXIII, 319, 7–9 A.D. 125–150
ἔδοξεν τῇ πόλει τειμάς τ[ε αὐτῷ] / ἡρωικας ψηφίσασθα[ι, καὶ] κατεύχεσθαι α[ὐτῷ ὡς / ἥ]ρωϊ ἐν πρυτανείῳ
"The city resolved to decree heroic honors to him (Memmius Nikandros) and to pray to him in the prytaneion as to a hero."

Dodona?

306 *SEG* XIII, 397 IV B.C.
'Επερωτῶντι τοὶ δίατοι τὸν Δία τὸν Νάϊον καὶ [τὰν Διώναν ἦ ἀναλισκόντοις τὰ ---- χρήμα]/τα ἰς τὸ πρυτανῆον τά, πὰρ τᾶς πόλιος ἔλαβε διαίους [ἐσσεῖται αὐτοῖς λώϊον καὶ ἄμεινον.] / Διάτοις· ἀναλῶσαι ἰς τὸ πρυτανῆον δικαίως ταῦτα.
"The judges ask Zeus Naios and Dione how it would be more desirable and better for those spending the wealth received from the city in the prytaneion. (The Oracle responds) To the judges: Spend this wealth in the prytaneion justly."

Dreros

307 *Michel* 23a, 16–19 late III B.C.

῾Ομνύνω / τὰν ῾Εστίαν τὰν / ἐμ πρυτανείωι / καὶ τὸν Δῆνα τὸν / Ἀγοραῖον, κτλ.

"I swear by Hestia in the prytaneion, and by Zeus Agoraios, etc."

Since this inscription, which records a treaty between Dreros and Knossos, was found at Dreros, it is listed here, but it might also imply the existence of a prytaneion at Knossos.

Elaea

308 *Michel* 515, 15–16 *ca.* 135 B.C

ἐπιτελεῖσθαι κατ᾽ ἐνι/αυτὸν ὑπὸ τοῦ ἱερέως τοῦ Ἀσκληπιοῦ πομπὴν ὡς καλλίστην ἐκ τοῦ πρυτανε[ί]/ου εἰς τὸ τέμενος τοῦ Ἀσκληπιοῦ

"Every year a procession as beautiful as possible is to be made by the priest of Asklepios from the prytaneion to the temenos of Asklepios."

309 *Michel* 515, 50–51 *ca.* 135 B.C.

κα[λ]είτωσαν αὐτὸν εἰς τὸ πρυ/τανεῖο[ν ἐπὶ] τ[ὴν κοινὴν ἑστίαν]

"(The generals) are to invite him (Attalos III) to the common hearth in the prytaneion."

Ephesos

310 *Ephesus* III, 71, 22 II–III A.D.

τὴν ἀπὸ τοῦ πρυτανείου κάθοδον ἕως τῆς ἐμβάσεως τῆς πλατείας

". . . the road down from the prytaneion to the entrance of the open square."

311 *Jahreshefte* 44 (1959) 295 II–III A.D.

. . . κ]αὶ τὸν πρὸ τοῦ πρυτανείου πυλῶν[α . . .

". . . And the gate in front of the prytaneion . . ."

312 Sokolowski, *Lois sacrées* 121, 25–30 III A.D.

εἰ δέ τι ἐνλιπὲς ὑπὸ τοῦ πρυτανεύοντος / τῶν προειρημένων καθ᾽ ἓν ἕκαστον γένηται, / ὀφείλειν τὸν πρύτανιν εἰς προκόμημα τῆς / ἐν τῷ πρυτανείῳ ἑστώσης Δήμητρος Καρ/ποφόρου ἧς ἐστι ὁ νεὼς καὶ εἰς ἐπισκευὴν / τοῦ πρυτανείου στατῆρας Δαρικοὺς ι′.

"If anything of those items listed in order publicly by the one who is prytanizing is omitted, the prytanis is to pay ten Daric staters for the ornamentation of the statue of Demeter Karpophoros which stands in the prytaneion her shrine and for the repair of the prytaneion."

Epidamnos

313 *Ditt*³, 560, 42–44 *ca.* 207 B.C.

καλέ/σα(ντα) δ' α[ὐτοὺς εἰς τὸ πρυταν]εῖο[ν ἐ]πὶ τὰν κοινὰν ἑστ[ίαν,] ἱερεῖον θῦσαι ἐφέστι/ον καὶ δίδοσ[θαι αὐτοῖς] τὰ [σ]κέλη καὶ τὸ νάκος κ[αὶ καταλιπ]έσ[θαι] α[ὐτοῖς] σκέλ[ος] καὶ τὸ νάκος καὶ ἐ[νεκέχηρον] ἀργυρίου Κορινθίου / [ἡμιμναῖον.]

Resolved . . . "to invite them (ambassadors of Magnesia) to the common hearth in the prytaneion, sacrifice an animal on the hearth and give to them the hams and the fleece and let them keep the hams and the fleece and a traveling allowance of a half-mina of Corinthian silver."

Eresos

314 *IG* XII, suppl. 139, 15–17 early II? B.C.

ὁ δὲ πρύτανις καὶ ὁ βασιλεὺς καλεσσάτω/σαν τοίς τε δικάσταις καὶ τὸν ἀγώγεα εἰς τὸ πρυτανήϊον ἐπὶ τὰν κο[ι]/νὰν ἑστίαν τᾶς πόλιος.

"The prytanis and the king are to invite the judges (from Miletus) and the guide into the prytaneion to the common hearth of the city."

315 *IG* XII², 527, 37 early II B.C.

καλέ]σαι δὲ [ν]ιν εἰς τὸ προτανήιον ἐπὶ ταῖς θυσία[ις

Resolved . . . "to invite him to the sacrifices in the prytaneion."

316 *IG* XII², 528, 7 II B.C.

. . . . ε]ἰς τὸ πρυταν[ήιον . . . .

". . . into the prytaneion . . ."

317 *IG* XII², 529, 14–16 II B.C.

κα/λέντον αὐτὸν καὶ ἐκγόνοις εἰς τὸ προτανήιον / ὄτα κε τὰν θυσίαν ταύταν ποιέωσι

Resolved . . . "that he (Agemortos) and his descendants be called into the prytaneion whenever they (the citizens) make this sacrifice."

Eretria

318 *IVM* 48, 31 *ca.* 207 B.C.

καλέσαι δὲ αὐτοὺς καὶ ἐπὶ ξένια εἰς τὸ πρυ[τα]νεῖον

Resolved . . . "to invite them (ambassadors of Magnesia) to Xenia in the prytaneion."

319 *SEG* XI, 468, 13–14 III–II B.C.

[καλέσαι δὲ / καὶ] αὐτοὺς καὶ ἐ[πὶ τὴν] κοινὴν τῆς πόλεως ἑστίαν ἐ[πὶ ξένια]

Resolved . . . "to invite them (judges from Sparta) to Xenia at the common hearth of the city."

Erythrae

320 *Michel* 505, 16–17 III B.C.

δεδόσθαι δὲ αὐτ/ῶι καὶ ἐμ πρυτανείωι σίτησιν

Resolved . . . "to give to him (Phanes) Sitesis in the prytaneion."

Gortyn

321 *ICr* I, xvi, 1, 40–41 III B.C.

ἀναγρ[α]ψάντων δὲ βε/κάτεροι ἐν βρυταν[είωι

"Let both cities (Gortyn and Lato) write it (an alliance) up in the prytaneion."

322 *Michel* 438, 10–11 *ca.* 200 B.C.

ὑπάρχειν Μάγνησιν πᾶσιν οἰκειότατα / καὶ φιλίαν ἀγήρατον καὶ ἐμ πρυτανείωι σίτησιν

Resolved . . . "that there shall be to all the Magnesians a relationship and ageless friendship and Sitesis in the prytaneion."

This decree of a Cretan confederacy regarding the sending of a colony to Magnesia is listed under Gortyn because, according to another part of the decree, Gortyn was exercising hegemony over the confederacy at that time. It is possible that the prytaneion of the confederacy was located elsewhere, or that the several prytaneia of the individual members are to be understood.

Halikarnassos

323 *Michel* 452, 10–11 late IV B.C.

καλέσαι δὲ αὐτ[ὸν] / καὶ εἰς πρυτανεῖον ἐπὶ δεῖπνον

Resolved . . . "to invite him (Zenodotos of Troizen) to Deipnon in the prytaneion."

Halos

324 Herodotus VII, 197 480 B.C.

ὃς ἂν ᾖ τοῦ γένεος τούτου πρεσβύτατος, τούτῳ ἐπιτάξαντες ἔργεσθαι τοῦ ληίτου αὐτοὶ φύλακας ἔχουσι. Λήιτον δὲ καλέουσι τὸ πρυτανήιον οἱ Ἀχαιοί. ἢν δὲ ἐσέλθῃ, οὐκ ἔστι ὅκως ἔξεισι πρὶν ἢ θύσεσθαι μέλλῃ· ὥς τ' ἔτι πρὸς τούτοισι πολλοὶ ἤδη τούτων τῶν μελλόντων θύσεσθαι δείσαντες οἴχοντο ἀποδράντες ἐς ἄλλην χώρην. χρόνου δὲ προϊόντος ὀπίσω κατελθόντες ἢν ἁλίσκωνται ἐστέλλοντο ἐς τὸ πρυτανήιον.

(A guide is telling Xerxes of the ban on the family of Phrixos in Halos.) "Whoever is the oldest of his (Phrixos') descendants, they forbid to enter the Leiton and they stand guard themselves. The

Achaeans call the prytaneion the Leiton. Should he enter, he may not come out except to be sacrificed. Moreover, many of them who were about to be sacrificed were afraid and fled to another country, but if they returned at a later date and were seized, they were put into the prytaneion."

The opening clause of this quotation is very curious since the ban would appear in the text below to apply to all of the descendants of Phrixos, not only to the oldest. The phraseology of this oldest descendant clause is quite similar to that used in decrees which provide an entertainment rather different from that offered to the descendants of Phrixos (e.g., A 26, 154). Could Herodotus have been influenced by the normal wording used to offer entertainment in the prytaneion (in which case a certain humor may be detected here), or did the phrase come into the text at a later date?

325 *Schol.* Apollonios Rhodios II, 652 from 480? B.C.

ὃς Φρίξου τὸν Ἀθάμαντος ἐξένισεν ἐπὶ τοῦ κριοῦ ὅτε ἐξέφυγε τὸν θάνατον, μέλλων σφαγιάζεσχαι. φασὶ δὲ ἐκεῖνον σφαγιασθῆναι τῷ Λαφυσίῳ Διί, καὶ μέχρι τοῦ νῦν <μὴ ἐξεῖναι> ἕνα τῶν Φρίξου ἀπογόνων εἰσιέναι εἰς τὸ πρυτανεῖον, εἰσελθόντα <δὲ> τινα ἀκουσίως <θύεσθαι> τῷ προειρημένῳ Διί.

". . . He who carried off Phrixos the son of Athamas on a ram so that he escaped death, being about to be slaughtered. They say that he was to be slaughtered to Zeus Laphysios, and that even until now a descendant of Phrixos who enters the prytaneion may not come out, but one having entered willy-nilly is to be sacrificed to the aforementioned Zeus."

This rather confused passage would seem to depend upon Herodotus (A 324).

Hierapytna

326 *Michel* 30, 15–16 II B.C.

καλέσαι τε τὸς πρεσβευτὰς [ἐς πρυ]/τανήϊον καὶ δόμεν αὐτοῖς ξένια ἀργυρίω μνᾶν

Resolved . . . "to invite the ambassadors (from Magnesia) to the prytaneion and give them Xenia of a silver mina."

Iasos

327 *Michel* 462, 27–28 late IV B.C.

[καλ]έσαι δὲ καὶ τοὺς δικ[αστ]ὰς τοὺς ἀποσταλέντας / [εἰς] τὸ πρυτανεῖον

Resolved . . . "to invite the judges being sent (to Kalymnos) into the prytaneion."

Ilion

328 *Michel* 524a, 25–26 early III B.C.

εἶναι δὲ / αὐτῶι σίτη[σ]ιν [ἐ]μ πρυ[τα]νείωι [ἕ]ως [ἂν] ζῆ[ι]

Resolved . . . "that there shall be to him (any one who kills the leader of an attempted oligarchy) Sitesis in the prytaneion as long as he shall live."

329 *Michel* 527, 20 III B.C.

εἶναι δὲ αὐτοῖς καὶ ἐν πρυτανείωι σίτη/σιν

Resolved . . . "that they (four brothers from Tenedos) shall have Sitesis in the prytaneion."

330 *CIG* 3598, 16–18 *ante* 187 B.C.

καλέσα/[ι δὲ καὶ εἰς πρυτανεῖον τὸν σύνδικο]ν

Resolved . . . "to invite the public advocate into the prytaneion."

Imbros

331 *IG* XII^{8}, 50, 4–6 *ca.* 200 B.C.

ἀ]ναγράψαι δὲ τόδε ψήφισμ[α τὸν γραμ]/ματέα τοῦ δήμου ἐν στήλῃ λιθί[ῃ καὶ] / στῆσαι ἐν τῇ αὐλῇ τοῦ πρυτανείου

Resolved . . . "that the Secretary of the Demos is to write down the decree on a stone stele and set it in the court of the prytaneion."

Iulis

332 *Michel* 401B, 34 mid-IV B.C.

καλέσαι δὲ τοὺ[ς Ἀθηναίους ἐπὶ ξένια εἰς τὸ πρυτανεῖ]/ον

Resolved . . . "to invite the Athenians to Xenia in the prytaneion."

333 *IG* XII^{5}, 1082 II B.C.

[ἐπὶ ἄρχοντος ––] τοῦ Ἰσάρχου οἵδε ἐπέδωδαν / [εἰς τὴν ἐπισκευὴν τ]οῦ πρυτανείου· / [––––––––] δραχμὰς λ′ / [–– δραχμὰς] λ′ καὶ τεχνίτας λ′

"In the archonship of [?] of Isarchos the following contributed to the repair of the prytaneion: [?] thirty drachmai; [?] thirty drachmai and thirty craftsmen; . . ."

Kallatis

334 *SEG* XXIV, 1023, 10–13 III–II B.C.

καλέσαι δὲ αὐτὸν καὶ εἰς πρυτανεῖο[ν / τὸν Βασιλέα]· ἀποστεῖλαι δὲ αὐτῶι καὶ ξένια τοὺς μ[ε/ριστάς, τὸ δὲ] ἀνάλωμα ὑποτελέσαι τὸν ταμίαν.

Resolved . . . "that the king is to invite him into the prytaneion; the distributors are to send Xenia to him, and the treasurer is to pay the cost."

335 *SGDI* 3089, 35 II B.C.
[καλέ/σ]αι δὲ αὐτὸν καὶ τὸν βασιλέα ε[ἰς τὸ πρυ/τ]ανεῖον
Resolved . . . "that the king is to invite him (an ambassador from Apollonia) into the prytaneion."

Karthea

336 *IG* XII^5, 1060, 2 V B.C.
καὶ σίτησιν ἐμ π[ρυτανείωι]
Resolved . . . "that [?] shall have Sitesis in the prytaneion."

Kaunos

337 *Hellenica* 7 (1949) 175, 93–95 II B.C.
πέμψαι δὲ αὐτῶ[ι] / καὶ ξένιον παρὰ τοῦ δήμου τὸ ἐν τῶι νόμωι γεγραμμένον· καλέσαι δὲ αὐτὸν καὶ ἐπὶ ξένια εἰς τὸ / πρυτανεῖον.
Resolved . . . "to send to him (an ambassador from Smyrna) from the Demos the Xenion prescribed in the law; to invite him to Xenia in the prytaneion."

Kimolos

338 *Hesperia* 37 (1968) 188–189, 49–51 250–221 B.C.
καλέσαι δὲ ἐπὶ ξένια τὸν / δικαστὰν Χαρίανθον τὸς ἄρχοντας ἐς τὸ πρυτανεῖον τὸς περὶ Ἀρχί/δαμον.
Resolved . . . "that Archidamos and those archonizing with him should invite Charianthos the judge (now a proxenos) to Xenia in the prytaneion."

Knossos

339 See (A 307) above.

Korcyra

340 *IVM* 44, 40–42 *ca.* 207/6 B.C.
καλέσαι δὲ κα[ὶ αὐτοὺς] ἐν τὸ πρυτανεῖον . . . . . τὸ δὲ ψάφισμ[α . . . 17 . . .] ἀναθέμεν πρὸ τοῦ πρυτανεῖου.
Resolved . . . "to invite them (ambassadors from Magnesia) into the prytaneion . . . and to set up the decree in front of the prytaneion."

Koressos

341 *Michel* 401, 24–25 mid-IV B.C.
καλέσαι δὲ / [κ]αὶ ἐπὶ ξένια εἰς τὸ πρυτανεῖον τοὺς Ἀθηναίους εἰς αὔριον
Resolved . . . "to invite the Athenians to Xenia in the prytaneion on the next day."

Kos

342 *Michel* 426, 35–36 II B.C.
[τ]ὸν δὲ πρεσβευτὰν καλέσαι ἐπὶ ξένια εἰς / [τὸ] πρυτανεῖον

Resolved . . . "to invite the ambassador (from Halikarnassos) to Xenia in the prytaneion."

Lampsakos

343 *CIG* 3641b, 21 II B.C.

ὁ δὲ ἱεροκῆρυξ προσκηρυσσέτω καὶ δ[ιὰ τοῦ πρυ/τα]νείου

"The sacred herald is to proclaim even through the prytaneion."

Laodikaia

344 *IVP* 59, 25 *ca.* 200 B.C.

ὑπάρχειν δὲ τοῖς δικασταῖς καὶ ἐμ πρυτανείωι σίτησιν.

Resolved . . . "that the judges (from Priene) shall have Sitesis in the prytaneion."

Lato

345 See (A 321) above.

346 *ICr* I, xvi, 5, 30–32 III B.C.

καί κα κοσμίων [ἔλ]θηι Λάτιο[ς ἐς 'Ολόντα ἢ 'Ολόντιος] ἐς Λατῶν, τ[ό/τε ἡμά]τιον ἀφφάνω ἐχέτω καὶ ἑρπέτω ἐς π[ρυτανήϊον.]

"If the chief magistrate of Lato comes to Olos, or the one from Olos to Lato, let him have a personal cloak and go into the prytaneion."

Lipara

347 Diodorus Siculus XX, 101, 2 304 B.C.

ἀξιούντων γὰρ τῶν Λιπαραίων εἰς τὰ προσελλείποντα τῶν χρημάτων δοῦναι χρόνον καὶ λεγόντων μηδέποτε τοῖς ἱεροῖς ἀναθήμασι κατακεχρῆσθαι, ὁ Ἀγαθοκλῆς βιασάμενος αὐτοῖς δοῦναι τὰ κατὰ τὸ πρυτανεῖον, ὧν εἶχον ἐπιγραφὴν τὰ μὲν Αἰόλου, τὰ δ' Ἡφαίστου, λαβὼν παραχρῆμα ἐξέπλευσεν.

Agathokles demanded fifty talents of silver and "when the Liparaeans were begging that he give them time for that which was lacking of the money and said that they had never abused the sacred offerings, Agathokles forced them to give him the valuables in the prytaneion of which some were inscribed to Aiolos, some to Hephaistos; taking these he immediately sailed away."

Magnesia

348 *IVM* 15b, 23–24 221/0 B.C.

[καλείτω δὲ] α[ὐ]τοὺς καὶ ὁ στεφανηφόρος εἰς τὸ πρυτανε[ῖον ἐπὶ / τὴν τῆς πόλεως ὑπ]οδο[χ]ήν.

Resolved . . . "that the stephanephoros shall invite them (ambassadors from Knidos) to entertainment by the city in the prytaneion."

349 *IVM* 11, 17 III B.C.
ἔστω / [αὐτῶι ἐμ πρυτανεί]ωι σίτησις
Resolved . . . "that he (a proxenos from Abdera) shall have Sitesis in the prytaneion."

350 *IVM* 89, 87 III–II B.C.
καλεσάτω [δὲ τοὺς / πρ]εσβευτὰς ὁ στεφανηφόρος εἰς τὸ πρυτανεῖον
Resolved . . . "that the stephanephoros shall invite the ambassadors (from Teos) into the prytaneion."

351 *IVM* 97, 88–91 second half II B.C.
ἀποσταλῆναι δὲ αὐ/[τοῖ]ς καὶ ξένια τὰ κατὰ [τ]ὸ ψ[ή]φισμα· [καλεί/τω δ']/ αὐτοὺς καὶ ὁ στεφανηφόρος εἰς [τὸ πρυτα/νεῖ]ον
Resolved . . . "to send Xenia to them (ambassadors from Teos) according to the decree; the stephanephoros shall invite them into the prytaneion."

352 *IVM* 101, 82–84 second half II B.C.
κληθῆναι δὲ αὐτὸν καὶ / [ὑ]πὸ τοῦ στεφανηφόρου εἰς τὸ πρυτανεῖον ἐπὶ τὴν κοινὴν τῆς πό/λεως ὑποδοχήν
Resolved . . . "that he (an ambassador from Larba) be invited by the stephanephoros to common entertainment by the city in the prytaneion."

Mallia

353 *Michel* 448, 36–38 late II B.C.
ἐπεί κά τις [αὐτῶν πα]/ραγένηται ἐς τὰν ἁμὰν πόλιν ἦμεν [αὐτῶι καὶ] / σίτη[σ]ιν ἐν πρυταν[ε]ίοι μετὰ τῶν κόσ[μων]
'When one of them (new citizens) is in our town, we will provide Sitesis for him in the prytaneion in company with the chief magistrates."

Megara

354 *IG* VII, 16a, 3 II B.C.
[καλέσαι τοὺς πρεσβευτὰς εἰς τὸ πρυ]τανεῖον ἐπὶ τ[ὰν κοινὰν ἑστίαν τοῦ δήμου]
Resolved . . . "to invite the ambassadors to the prytaneion at the common hearth of the Demos."

355 Pausanias I, 42, 7 mid-II A.D.
κατὰ δὲ τὴν ἐς τὸ πρυτανεῖον ὁδὸν Ἰνοῦς ἐστιν ἡρῷον.
"Down the road to the prytaneion is the shrine of Ino."

356 Pausanias I, 43, 2 mid-II A.D.
ἐν δὲ τῷ πρυτανείῳ τεθάφθαι μὲν Εὔιππον Μεγαρέως παῖδα, τεθάφθαι δὲ τὸν Ἀλκάθου λέγουσιν Ἰσχέπολιν. ἔστι δὲ τοῦ πρυτανείου πέτρα πλησίον· ἀνακληθρίδα τὴν πέτραν ὀνομάζουσιν.
"They say that in the prytaneion are buried Euippos the son of Megareus and Ischepolis the son of Alkathos. There is a rock near the prytaneion; they call it the 'restoration' rock."

Methymna

357 *IG* XII, Suppl. 114, 25–26 III? B.C.
ὁ πρύτανις καὶ [οἱ βα]σί[λεις / καλέσ]ειαν αὐτοῖς ἐπὶ δεῖπνον εἰς τὸ πρυ[τανεῖον]
"The prytanis and the kings are to make an invitation to them (agoranomoi) for Deipnon in the prytaneion."

358 *IG* XII, Suppl. 139, 100–104 early II? B.C.
ὁ δε πρύτανις καὶ οἱ βασίλεις καλεσσάτωσαν τοὶς δικάσταις καὶ τὸν δικαστάγω/γον εἰς τὸ προτανήιον ἐπὶ τὰν κοινὰν ἑστίαν τᾶς πόλιος.
"The prytanis and the kings are to invite the judges and the guide of the judges into the prytaneion to the common hearth of the city."

359 *IG* XII², 507, 13 II B.C.
[ἡ πομ/π]ὴ τῶν Σαμοθρακιαστῶν παραπ[έμπηται ἐκ / το]ῦ πρυτανείου εἰς τὸ ἱερό[ν]
"The procession of the celebrators of the Samothracian mysteries passes from the prytaneion to the temple."

Miletus

360 *OGIS* 213, 39 306–293 B.C.
δεδόσθ[αι δὲ αὐτῷ καὶ σίτησιν] ἐν πρυτανείωι
Resolved . . . "to grant to him (Prince Antiochus, son of Seleukos I) Sitesis in the prytaneion."

Mytilene

361 Athenaeus X, 425a early VI B.C.
Σαπφώ τε ἡ καλὴ πολλαχοῦ Λάριχον τὸν ἀδελφὸν ἐπαινεῖ ὡς οἰνοχοοῦντα ἐν τῷ πρυτανείῳ τοῖς Μυτιληναίοις.
"The lovely Sappho often praises her brother Larichos as a wine-pourer in the prytaneion at Mytilene."

362 *SGDI* 215 mid-II B.C.
7: *ὥστε ξενίσθειεν ἐν τῶι πρυτ[α]/νείωι*
13: *καὶ ξενισθείη ἐν τῶι πρυτανήωι*
15: *εἰς τὸ πρυτανήιον κληθείη μετὰ τῶν δικάσταν*

47–49: *καλέσαι δὲ ἔπ[ειτα] / τοῖς δικάσταις καὶ τὸγ γραμμάτεα ἐπὶ τὸ πρυτανήιον / ἐπὶ τὰγ κοινὰν ἑστί/αν. καλέσαι δὲ μετ' αὔτων εἰς τὸ πρυτανήιον καὶ τὸν δικαστάγωγον.*
7, 13, 15: Resolved by the Boule . . . "(two judges from Erythrae) are to have Xenia in the prytaneion . . . (the secretary of the judges) is to have Xenia in the prytaneion . . . (the guide of the judges) is to be called into the prytaneion in company with the judges."
47–49: Resolved by the Demos . . . "to invite the judges and the secretary of the judges to the common hearth in the prytaneion; also to invite in their company the guide of the judges into the prytaneion."

363 *OGIS* 335, 85 mid-II B.C.
[καλ]εσσάτωσα[ν δὲ αὐτοὺς ἐπὶ ξέ]νια εἰς τὸ π[ρυτανήιον] ἐπὶ τὰν [κοινὰν ἑστίαν]
Resolved . . . "to invite them (judges from Pergamon) to Xenia at the common hearth in the prytaneion."

364 *IG* XII², 60, 33 Augustan
-- ἐν τῶι π]ροτανηίωι κ[αὶ --
". . . in the prytaneion . . ."

365 *IG* XII², 68, 14 (cf. *Suppl.*, p. 13) mid-II A.D.
δὲ καὶ ἐ[ν τ]ῶ πρυτ[ανε]ίω τούς τε [β]ο[λ]λά[ο]υς
". . . and the council members in the prytaneion . . ."

Nakrasa
366 *Michel* 509, 15–16 241 B.C.
εἶναι δὲ αὐ/τῶι καὶ σίτησιν ἐμ πρυτανή[ωι
Resolved . . . "that he (Apollonios) shall have Sitesis in the prytaneion."

Naukratis
367 Athenaeus IV, 149d III B.C.
Παρὰ δὲ Ναυκρατίταις, ὥς φησιν Ἑρμείας ἐν τῷ δευτέρῳ τῶν περὶ τοῦ Γρυνείου Ἀπόλλωνος, ἐν τῷ πρυτανείῳ δειπνοῦσι γενεθλίοις Ἑστίας Πρυτανίτιδος καὶ Διονυσίοις, ἔτι δὲ τῇ τοῦ Κωμαίου Ἀπόλλωνος πανηγύρει, εἰσιόντες πάντες ἐν στολαῖς λευκαῖς, ἃς μέχρι καὶ νῦν καλοῦσι πρυτανικὰς ἐσθῆτας. καὶ κατακλιθέντες ἐπανίστανται εἰς γόνατα τοῦ ἱεροκήρυκος τὰς πατρίους εὐχὰς καταλέγοντος συσπένδοντες. μετὰ δὲ ταῦτα κατακλιθέντες λαμβάνουσιν ἕκαστος οἴνου κοτύλας δύο πλὴν τῶν ἱερέων τοῦ τε Πυθίου Ἀπόλλωνος καὶ τοῦ Διονύσου· τούτων γὰρ ἑκατέρῳ διπλοῦς ὁ οἶνος μετὰ καὶ τῶν ἄλλων μερίδων δίδοται. ἔπειτα ἑκάστῳ παρατίθεται ἄρτος καθαρὸς εἰς πλάτος

πεποιημένος, ἐφ' ᾧ ἐπίκειται ἄρτος ἕτερος, ὃν κριβανίτην καλοῦσι, καὶ κρέας ὕειον καὶ λεκάριον πτισάνης ἢ λαχάνου τοῦ κατὰ καιρὸν γινομένου ᾠά τε δύο καὶ τυροῦ τροφαλὶς σῦκά τε ξηρὰ καὶ πλακοῦς καὶ στέφανος. καὶ ὃς ἂν ἔξω τι τούτων ἱεροποιὸς παρασκευάσῃ ὑπὸ τῶν τιμούχων ζημιοῦται, ἀλλὰ μὴν οὐδὲ τοῖς σιτουμένοις ἐν πρυτανείῳ ἔξωθεν προσεισφέρειν τι βρώσιμον ἔξεστι, μόνα δὲ ταῦτα καταναλίσκουσι, τὰ ὑπολειπόμενα τοῖς οἰκέταις μεταδίδοντες. ταῖς δ' ἄλλαις ἡμέραις πάσαις τοῦ ἐνιαυτοῦ ἔξεστι τῶν σιτουμένων τῷ βουλομένῳ ἀνελθόντι εἰς τὸ πρυτανεῖον δειπνεῖν, οἴκοθεν παρασκευάσαντα αὑτῷ λάχανόν τι ἢ τῶν ὀσπρίων καὶ τάριχος ἢ ἰχθύν, κρέως δὲ χοιρείου βραχύτατον, καὶ τούτων μεταλαμβάνων -- lacuna -- κοτύλην οἴνου. γυναικὶ δὲ οὐκ ἔξεστιν εἰσιέναι εἰς τὸ πρυτανεῖον ἢ μόνῃ τῇ αὐλητρίδι. οὐκ εἰσφέρεται δὲ οὐδὲ ἀμὶς εἰς τὸ πρυτανεῖον.

"'In Naukratis,' as Hermeias says in the second book of *On the Gryneian Apollo*, 'they dine in the prytaneion on the birthday of Hestia Prytanis and the festival of Dionysos. Also at the celebration of the Komean Apollo, all entering in white robes which even now they call prytanic robes. Having reclined they rise and kneel for the customary prayers of the sacred herald and join in pouring libations, then again reclining each gets two cups of wine except for the priests of Pythian Apollo and Dionysos; to each of them is given a double portion of wine along with a double portion of the other things. Then to each is given wheat made into a flat loaf of bread, upon which lies another wheat loaf which they call oven bread, also pork flesh and a small dish of barley gruel, or of the vegetable in season, and two eggs and a piece of cheese and dried figs and flat cakes and a garland. If any festival supervisor provides something more than these things, he is fined by the timouchos, nor is it permissible for those eating in the prytaneion to bring in something more to eat, but to consume only these, giving the leftovers to the servants. On all other days of the year, it is permissible for one who wishes, of those having Sitesis, to go into the prytaneion and eat, having prepared at home for himself some vegetable or beans and some dried or fresh fish, and a very small piece of pork, and sharing these . . . (? he receives) a cup of wine. It is not permitted for a woman to enter the prytaneion, except for the flute-player, nor to bring a chamber-pot into the prytaneion."

Naxos

368 Theophrastus *apud* Parthenios of Nicaea XVIII, 3 *ca.* 300 B.C.
(*Ἱστορεῖ Θεόφραστος ἐν α' τῶν Πρὸς τοὺς καιτοὺς*) *ἔνθα καὶ ἡ Νέαιρα, δείσασα τὸν Ὑψικρέοντα διέπλευσεν εἰς τὴν Νάξον·*

καὶ ἐπειδὴ αὐτὴν ἐξήτει ὁ Ὑψικρέων, ἱκέτις προσκαθίζετο ἐπὶ τῆς ἑστίας ἐν τῷ πρυτανείῳ. οἱ δὲ Νάξιοι λιπαροῦντι τῷ Ὑψικρέοντι ἐκδώσειν μὲν οὐκ ἔφασεν.
"From the first book of Theophrastus' Political History: 'Then Neaira, fearing Hypsikreon (her husband), sailed to Naxos, and when Hypsikreon sought her out she sat as a suppliant at the hearth in the prytaneion. The Naxians said they would not surrender her to Hypsikreon who was demanding this.'"

Plutarch, *De mulierum virtutibus* 17, relates this same story but without mention of the prytaneion.

369 *IG* XII[5], 35, 11–12 III B.C.
ἀναγράψαι δὲ τόδε ψήφισμα ἐν τῷ πρυ[τανείωι ἐν στή]/λην λιθίνηι
Resolved . . . "to write this law up on a stone stele in the prytaneion."

Nesos
370 *Michel* 363, 32 *ca.* 300 B.C.
δεδόσθαι δὲ καὶ σίτησιν ἐμ προταν[η]ίωι
Resolved . . . "to grant Sitesis in the prytaneion (to a benefactor of the city)."

Olos
371 See (A 346) above.

Olympia
372 Xenophon, *Hellenica* VII, 4, 31 364 B.C.
ἐπεὶ μέντοι κατεδίωξαν εἰς τὸ μεταξὺ τοῦ βουλευτηρίου καὶ τοῦ τῆς Ἑστίας ἱεροῦ καὶ τοῦ πρὸς ταῦτα προσήκοντος θεάτρου.
"When they (the Eleans) had pursued (the Arcadians and Argives) into the area between the Bouleuterion and the Shrine of Hestia and the theater which adjoins them . . ."

See also Appendix D.

373 Pausanias V, 13, 11 mid-II A.D.
κατ' ἔτος δὲ ἕκαστον φυλάξαντες οἱ μάντεις τὴν ἐνάτην ἐπὶ δέκα τοῦ Ἐλαφίου μηνὸς κομίζουσιν ἐκ τοῦ πρυτανείου τὴν τέφραν, φυράσαντες δὲ τῷ ὕδατι τοῦ Ἀλφειοῦ κονιῶσιν οὕτω τὸν βωμόν.
"Every year the manteis, having watched out for the nineteenth of the month Elaphios, carry off the ash from the prytaneion and having mixed it with the water of the Alpheios, they thus plaster the altar of Zeus)."

374 Pausanias V, 15, 8–9 mid-II A.D.
τὸ πρυτανεῖον δὲ Ἠλείοις ἐστι μὲν τῆς Ἄλτεως ἐντός, πεποίηται δὲ παρὰ τὴν ἔξοδον ἥ ἐστι τοῦ γυμνασίου πέραν· ἐν τούτῳ δὲ οἵ τε δρόμοι τῷ γυμνασίῳ καὶ τοῖς ἀθληταῖς εἰσὶν αἱ παλαῖστραι. τοῦ πρυτανείου δὲ πρὸ μὲν τῶν θυρῶν βωμός ἐστιν Ἀρτέμιδος Ἀγροτέρας· ἐν δὲ αὐτῷ τῷ πρυτανείῳ παριόντων ἐς τὸ οἴκημα, ἔνθα σφίσιν ἡ ἑστία, Πανός ἐστιν ἐν δεξιᾷ τῆς ἐσόδου βωμός. ἔστι δὲ ἡ ἑστία τέφρας καὶ αὕτη πεποιημένη, καὶ ἐπ' αὐτῆς πῦρ ἀνὰ πᾶσάν τε ἡμέραν καὶ ἐν πάσῃ νυκτὶ ὡσαύτως καίεται· ἀπὸ ταύτης τῆς ἑστίας τὴν τέφραν κατὰ τὰ εἰρημένα ἤδη μοι κομίζουσιν ἐπὶ τὸν τοῦ Ὀλυμπίου βωμόν, καὶ οὐχ ἥκιστα ἐς μέγεθος συντελεῖ τῷ βωμῷ τὸ ἀπὸ τῆς ἑστίας ἐπιφορούμενον.
"The Eleans have their prytaneion inside the Altis; it is built by the exit which is beyond the gymnasion. In this gymnasion are the tracks and wrestling areas for the athletes. In front of the doors of the prytaneion is the altar of Artemis Agrotera. In the prytaneion itself entering the room where is their hearth, on the right of the entrance is the altar of Pan. The hearth itself was also made of ashes and on it a fire burns every day and every night just so. From this hearth, as I have already said, they carry off the ash to the altar of Olympian Zeus, and that brought from the hearth to the altar contributes not a little to its size."

375 Pausanias V, 15, 11 mid-II A.D.
ὁπόσα δὲ ἐπὶ ταῖς σπονδαῖς λέγειν σφίσιν ἐν τῷ πρυτανείῳ καθέστηκεν, ἢ καὶ ὕμνους ὁποίους ᾄδουσιν, οὔ με ἦν εἰκὸς ἐπεισαγαγέσθαι καὶ ταῦτα ἐς τὸν λόγον.
"How much is established for them (a priest, manteis, libation-bearers, exegete, fluteplayer, woodman) to say at the libations in the prytaneion, or what sort of hymns they sing, it were not seemly to introduce into my story."

376 Pausanias V, 15, 12 mid-II A.D.
Ἠλεῖοι δὲ καὶ ἥρωσι καὶ γυναιξὶ σπένδουσιν ἡρώων, ὅσοι τε ἐν τῇ χώρᾳ τῇ Ἠλείᾳ καὶ ὅσοι παρὰ Αἰτωλοῖς τιμὰς ἔχουσιν. ὁπόσα δὲ ᾄδουσιν ἐν τῷ πρυτανείῳ, φωνὴ μέν ἐστιν αὐτῶν ἡ Δώριος, ὅστις δὲ ὁ ποιήσας ἦν τὰ ᾄσματα, οὐ λέγουσιν. ἔστι δὲ καὶ ἑστιατόριον Ἠλείοις· καὶ τοῦτο ἔστι μὲν ἐντος τοῦ πρυτανείου, τοῦ οἰκήματος τοῦ τῆς ἑστίας ἀπαντικρύ. τοὺς δὲ τὰ Ὀλύμπια νικῶντας ἑστιῶσιν ἐν τούτῳ τῷ οἰκήματι.
"The Eleans also pour libations to all the heroes and wives of heroes who have honors in the Elean land and those among the Aetolians. As many as they sing in the prytaneion are in the Doric dialect, but who was the composer of the songs they do not say. The

Eleans also have a hestiatorion. This is in the prytaneion opposite the room with the hearth. They feast the Olympic winners in this room."

377 Pausanias V, 20, 10 mid-II A.D.

τοῦτο τὸ οἴκημά ἐστι μὲν κατὰ τὴν ἔξοδον τὴν κατὰ τὸ πρυτανεῖον ἐν ἀριστερᾷ.

"This building (the Philippeion) is on the left of the exit by the prytaneion."

Boeotian Orchomenos

378 *IG* VII, 4138, 26–28 mid-II B.C.

[καλέσαι δὲ] αὐτοὺς καὶ ἐπὶ ξένια εἰς / [τὸ πρυτα]νεῖον ἐπὶ τὴν κοινὴν ἑστίαν τ[ῆς / πό]λεως.

Resolved . . . "to invite them (ambassadors of Akraiphiai) to Xenia in the prytaneion at the common hearth of the city."

Paros

379 *IVM* 50, 67–68 207/6 B.C.

καλέσαι [δὲ καὶ]/τοὺς θεωροὺς ἐ[πὶ ξέ]νια τοὺς ἄρχοντα[ς / εἰς τὸ πρυταν]εῖον

Resolved . . . "that the magistrates are to invite the ambassadors (from Magnesia) to Xenia in the prytaneion."

380 *SEG* XXIII, 489b, 4–7 mid-II B.C.

καλ[έσαι δὲ καὶ τοὺς ἄρχον/τας] ἐπὶ τὰ ἱερὰ εἰς τὸ πρυτ[ανεῖον τοὺς πρεσβευ/τὰ]ς καὶ τὸν γραμματὴ καὶ [τοὺς ἥκοντας μετ' αὐ/τ]ῶν ἄνδρας πάντας·

Resolved . . . "that the archons are to invite the ambassadors (from Pharos) and the secretary and all the men having come with them to the sacrifices in the prytaneion."

381 Dio Cassius LV, 9 6 B.C.

καὶ τήν τε ὁδὸν ἰδιωτικῶς ἐποιήσατο, πλὴν καθ' ὅσον τοὺς Παριοὺς τὸ τῆς Ἑστίας ἄγαλμα πωλῆσαι οἱ ἠνάγκασεν, ὅπως ἐν τῷ Ὁμονοείῳ ἱδρυθῇ.

"He (Tiberius) made the journey as a private citizen, except to the extent that he forced the Parians to sell him the statue of Hestia so that it might be set up in the Temple of Concord."

Although an explicit reference to the prytaneion is lacking here, it is known that the Parians possessed such a building, and it can be assumed that the prytaneion was the most likely place for a statue of Hestia to have been. For an inscription recording Hellenistic repairs to the statue see G. Despinis, "*Τιμητικονψήφισμα ἐκ Πάρου,*" *ΔΕΛΤΙΟΝ* 20 (1965) 119–133.

382 *IG* XII^5, 274 mid-I A.D.
ἡ βουλὴ καὶ ὁ δῆμος Πραξικλῆν ἐτίμησεν .... καὶ σιτήσει ἐν πρυτανείωι
"The Boule and the Demos honor Praxikles ... and with Sitesis in the prytaneion."

383 *IG* XII^5, 281, 1–3 mid-I A.D.
ἡ βουλὴ καὶ ὁ δῆμος ἐτίμησεν Θράσωνα .... καὶ σιτήσ[ει] ἐν πρυτανείωι
"The Boule and the Demos honor Thrason ... and with Sitesis in the prytaneion."

Peparethos

384 Thucydides III, 89, 4 426 B.C.
ἐγένετο δὲ καὶ ἐν Πεπαρήθῳ κύματος ἐπαναχώρησίς τις, οὐ μέντοι ἐπέκλυσέ γε· καὶ σεισμὸς τοῦ τείχους τι κατέβαλε καὶ τὸ πρυτανεῖον καὶ ἄλλας οἰκίας ὀλίγας.
"Also at Peparethos there was a certain recession of the water, but there was no flood; and an earthquake threw down part of the wall and the prytaneion and a few other houses."

385 *IG* XII^8, 640, 35–37 *ca.* 196 B.C.
καλεσάτωσαν δὲ αὐτὸν / οἱ ἄρχοντες ἐπὶ ξένια εἰς τὸ πρυτανεῖον ἐπὶ τὴγ / [κ]οινὴν ἑστίαν
"The magistrates are to invite him (Philoxenos of Athens) to Xenia in the prytaneion at the common hearth."

386 *IG* XII^8, 641, 3–5 II B.C.
ἄρξαντες ἐν πρυτανεί[ωι] / ἀνέθηκαν Ἑρμεῖ
"(Kleon and Kleodikos) having been magistrates dedicated (it) to Hermes in the prytaneion."

Pergamon

387 *IGRom* IV, 292, 42 *post* 133 B.C.
σ[ταλῆ]ναι πομπὴν ἐκ τοῦ πρυτανείου εἰς τὸ τέμενος αὐτοῦ
"The procession is to set out from the prytaneion to his (Apollo's) temenos."

388 *IGRom* IV, 293, II *post* 133 B.C.
26–28: *προσφέρεσθαι δὲ αὐτῶι καὶ ἐν τῷ πρυτανείωι τὸν λιβανωτὸν καθό/πι καὶ τῶι πρυτάνει, ἵνα καθάπερ παρὰ τῶν ἡγουμένων οὕτως καὶ παρὰ τῶν θεῶν αἰ/τῆται τῷ δήμωι τἀγαθά.*
34–35: *ποιεῖσθαι δὲ διὰ παντὸς τὴν ἐπιμέλειαν τούτων ἐμ μὲν τῷ πρυτανείῳ / τὸν πρύτανιν.*
26–28: Resolved ... "that frankincense be offered to him (Diodoros Pasparos) in the prytaneion as if to the prytanis in order that, just as

from the governors so also from the gods, good things be asked for the city."
34–35: Resolved . . . "that the prytanis is to take complete care of these (honors for Diodoros) in the prytaneion."

389 *IVPerg* II, 252, 34 I B.C.
[ὑπάρχει]ν δὲ αὐτῶι καὶ σίτησιν ἐμ πρυ/τανείωι
Resolved . . . "that he (Metrodoros, a gymnasiarch) shall have Sitesis in the prytaneion."

Phaistos
390 *ICr* I, xxiii, 1, 65–66 III–II B.C.
ἀναγράψαι δὲ τὰς συνθήκας ἐμ Φαιστῶι μὲν εἰς τὸ πρυτανεῖον, ἐμ Μιλήτωι ‹δὲ› εἰς τὸ ἱερὸν τοῦ Ἀπόλλωνος.
Resolved . . . "to write up the treaty in Phaistos in the prytaneion, and in Miletus in the temple of Apollo."

Philippi
391 *SEG* XII, 373, 49–51 243/2 B.C.
δοῦναι δὲ τὸν ταμίαν τοῖς θεωροῖς ὑπὲρ τῆς πόλεως εἰς ξένια / ὅσον καὶ τοῖς τὰ Πύθια ἐπαγγέλλουσιν δίδοται ἐν τῶι νόμωι γεγράπται· καλέσαι δὲ / τοὺς θεωροὺς καὶ ἐπὶ τὰ ἱερὰ ὑπὲρ τῆς πόλεως τὸν ἄρχοντα εἰς τὸ πρυτανεῖον.
"The treasurer on behalf of the city is to give to the ambassadors (of Kos) Xenia, as much as is given to those announcing the Pythian oracles according to written custom; the archon is to invite the ambassadors to the sacrifices on behalf of the city in the prytaneion."

Priene
392 *IVP* 3, 16 *ca.* 334 B.C.
εἶν[αι δὲ / α]ὐτῶι καὶ ἐμ πρυτανείωι σίτησ[ιν]
Resolved . . . "that he (Megabyzos of Ephesos) shall have Sitesis in the prytaneion."

393 *IVP* 4, 35–36 332–326 B.C.
δεδόσ[θαι δ]ὲ αὐτῶι . . . . . καὶ ἐμ πρυτα/[νείωι] καὶ ἐμ Π[α]ν[ιωνί]ωι σίτησιν
Resolved . . . "to grant him (Apellis, a phrourarch) . . . and Sitesis in the prytaneion and the Panionion."

394 *IVP* 7, 19–20 *ca.* 330 B.C.
καὶ [ἐμ πρυτανείωι σίτη]/σιν. ταῦτα δὲ ὑπάρ[χειν καὶ αὐτῶι καὶ] / ἐκγόνοις.
Resolved . . . "that he (Theodoros of Miletus) and his descendants shall have Sitesis in the prytaneion."

395 *IVP* 8, 39–41 *ca.* 328/7 B.C.
δεδόσθαι δὲ αὐτοῖς ..... καὶ ἐμ πρυτανε[ίωι / κ]αὶ ἐμ Πανιωνίω[ι] σίτ[η]σιν
Resolved ... "to grant them (judges from Phokaia, Astypalaia, and [?]) Sitesis in the prytaneion and the Panionion."

396 *IVP* 12, 28 *ca.* 300 B.C.
καὶ σίτησι[ν ἐμ] πρυ[τανεί]ωι
Resolved ... "that (Euandros of Larissa, a proxenos) is to have Sitesis in the prytaneion."

397 *IVP* 18, 4 270–262 B.C.
δεδόσθαι δὲ αὐτῶι .... καὶ σίτησιν ἐμ πρυτανείωι καὶ ἐμ Πανιωνίωνι
Resolved ... "to grant him (a priest of Dionysos) ... and Sitesis in the prytaneion and the Panionion."

398 *IVP* 13, 5 III B.C.
Πριηνεῖς ἔδωκαν Καλλιστράτωι .... καὶ ἐμ πρυτανείωι σίτησιν
"The people of Priene granted to Kallistratos ... and Sitesis in the prytaneion."

399 *IVP* 26, 13–14 III B.C.
εἶναι αὐτῶι .... καὶ / σίτησιν ἐμ πρυτανείωι
Resolved ... "that he (Menares, a citizen) is to have ... and Sitesis in the prytaneion."

400 *IVP* 34, 3–4 III B.C.
[εἶναι δὲ καὶ / ἐμ] Πανιωνίωι σίτησιν κ[αὶ ἐμ πρυτανείωι]
Resolved ... "that [?] shall have Sitesis in the Panionion and the prytaneion."

401 *IVP* 82, 3–4 *ca.* 200 B.C.
[σιτήσει ἐμ πρυτανείωι καὶ / ἐμ Π]ανιωνίω[ι
"(The Boule and the Demos honor Diokles) with Sitesis in the prytaneion and the Panionion."

402 *IVP* 201, 10–11 *ca.* 200 B.C.
ἐξ]εῖν[αι δὲ αὐ]τῶι καὶ ἐμ πρυταν[είωι καὶ ἐμ Πανιωνίωι / σίτησιν, ὅταμ πόλις ἱε]ρὰ ποιῆι
"Sitesis in the prytaneion and the Panionion shall be permissible for him (the purchaser of the priesthood of Poseidon Helikonios) when the city makes sacrifices."

403 *IVP* 202, 6–7 *ca.* 200 B.C.
ἐξεῖναι δὲ αὐτῶι καὶ ἐμ πρυτανείωι [καὶ ἐμ Πανιωνί]ωι σίτησιν, [ὅτ]αμ πόλις ἱερὰ ποιῆι

"Sitesis in the prytaneion and the Panionion shall be permissible for him (the purchaser of the priesthood of Poseidon Helikonios) when the city makes sacrifices."

404 *IVP* 203, 6–7 *ca.* 200 B.C.
εἶναι δὲ αὐτῶι ἐμ [πρυτανείωι καὶ ἐμ Πανιωνίω]ι σίτησιν, ὅταμ πόλι[ς ἱερὰ ποιῆι]
"He (the purchaser of the priesthood of Poseidon Helikonios) shall have Sitesis in the prytaneion and the Panionion when the city makes sacrifices."

405 *IVP* 108, 321–323 *ca.* 129 B.C.
ὑπάρχειν δὲ Μοσχίωνι .... καὶ σίτησιν ἐμ πρυτανείωι καὶ ἐμ Πανιωνίωι
Resolved ... "that Moschion shall have ... and Sitesis in the prytaneion and the Panionion."

406 *IVP* 109 *ca.* 120 B.C.
7: *καὶ ἐμ πρυ/τανείωι καὶ ἐμ Πανιωνίωι καὶ ὅταν ἡ / βουλὴ συνῆι σιτήσει*
248: *δεδό[σ]θαι δὲ [καὶ σίτησιν ἐμ πρυτανείωι καὶ ἐμ Πανιων]ίωι*
7: "(The Boule and the Demos honor Herodes) ... and with Sitesis in the prytaneion and the Panionion when the Boule convenes."
248: "Grant (to Herodes) Sitesis in the prytaneion and the Panionion."

407 *IVP* 133, 7 II B.C.
καὶ ἐμ Πα[νι]ων[ίωι καὶ ἐμ πρυτανείωι] σ[ιτή]σ[ει]
"(The Boule and the Demos honor Isodoros) ... and with Sitesis in the Panionion and the prytaneion."

408 *IVP* 174, 6–8 II B.C.
εἶναι / δὲ αὐτῶι καὶ ἐμ πρυτανείωι καὶ ἐμ Πανιωνί/ωι σίτησιν πάσας τὰς ἡμέρας
"He (the purchaser of the priesthood of Dionysos) shall have Sitesis in the prytaneion and the Panionion for all his days."

409 *IVP* 103, 11–12 *ca.* 100 B.C.
δεδόσθαι δὲ αὐτῶι καὶ ἐμ πρυτανείωι καὶ ἐμ Πανιωνίωι / σίτησιν
Resolved ... "to grant him (Thrasyboulos) Sitesis in the prytaneion and the Panionion."

410 *IVP* 110, 4 early I B.C.
καὶ σ[ιτήσ]ει ἐν πρυτανείωι καὶ ἐν Πανιωνίωι
"(The Boule and the Demos honor Menedemos) ... and with Sitesis in the prytaneion and the Panionion."

411 *IVP* 111, 314 early I B.C.
[εἶναι δὲ / αὐ]τῶ[ι σίτηνσι]ν μὲν [ἐν πρυτανεί]ωι [καὶ ἐν Πανιωνίωι]
Resolved . . . "that he (Krates) shall have Sitesis in the prytaneion and in the Panionion."

412 *IVP* 113 *ca.* 84 B.C.
6–7: *κ]αὶ σειτήσει ἐν πρυτανεί/ωι καὶ ἐμ Πανιωνίωι*
108: *ὑπάρχηι δὲ αὐτῶι καὶ σίτησις ἐν πρυτανείωι καὶ ἐν Πανιωνίωι*
6–7: "(The Boule and the Demos honor Aulus Aemilius Zosimos) . . . and with Sitesis in the prytaneion and the Panionion."
108: "He shall have Sitesis in the prytaneion and the Panionion."

413 *IVP* 117 I B.C.
4–5: *[καὶ ἐμ πρ]υτανείωι καὶ /[ἐμ Πανιωνίωι καὶ ὅταν ἡ βουλὴ συνῆι σιτήσει]*
69: *ὑπάρχειν δὲ αὐτῶι καὶ σί[τησιν καὶ ἐμ πρυτανείωι καὶ] ἐμ Πανιωνίωι*
4–5: "(The Boule and the Demos honor Herakleitos) . . . and with Sitesis in the prytaneion and the Panionion when the Boule convenes."
69: "He shall have Sitesis in the prytaneion and the Panionion."

Ptolemais

414 *OGIS* 49, 12–13 275–250 B.C.
δ]εδόσθαι δ' αὐτῶι καὶ ἐγγόνοις σίτησιν / [ἐ]μ πρυτανείωι διὰ βίου
Resolved . . . "to grant to him (Antiphilos, a new citizen) and to his descendants Sitesis in the prytaneion for life."

415 *Michel* 1017, 23–24 *ca.* 239 B.C.
ἀναθεῖναι δ' αὐτ[οῦ] / καὶ εἰκόνα γραπτὴν ἐν τῶι προστάδι τοῦ πρυτανείου
Resolved . . . "to dedicate a painted statue of him (Lysimachos) in the prostas of the prytaneion."

Rhegium

416 *Dessau* 5471 I B.C.–I A.D.
T. Bervenus T. F. Sabinus / Triumvir Aed Pot II Testamento Legavit Municipi/bus Reginis Iul. in Prytaneo Statuam / Aeream Mercuri, Trullam Argenteam / Anaglyptam P. $\overline{II}$ S$^{==-}$, Lares Argenteos / Septem P. $\overline{II}$ S$^{=}$, Pelvim Aeream Corintheam.
"Titus Bervenus Sabinus, son of Titus, a triumvir and aedile twice, left in his will to the citizens of Rhegium in the prytaneion: a bronze statue of Mercury; a silver bowl with relief work of two pounds,

eleven ounces; seven silver Lares of two pounds, eight ounces; and a bronze Corinthian basin."

Rhodes

417 *Lindos* II, 117, 17 *ca.* 227 B.C.

καὶ σιτήσει ἐν πρυτανείωι

Resolved to grant to Archyllos . . . "and also Sitesis in the prytaneion."

418 *Michel* 431, 27–28 202 B.C.

[τοὺς δὲ παρα/γενομένους πα]ρὰ Ἰασέων καλέσαι ἐπὶ [ξένια εἰς τὸ πρυτανεῖον]

Resolved . . . "to invite those from Iasos to Xenia in the prytaneion."

419 Polybios XV, 23, 3 *ca.* 202 B.C.

παρῆν τις ἐκ κατάπλου πρὸς τὸ πρυτανεῖον ἀναγγέλλων τὸν ἐξανδραποδισμὸν τῶν Κιανῶν

"Someone from a returning ship came by the prytaneion announcing the enslavement of the Keans."

420 Polybios XVI, 15, 8 201 B.C.

τῆς ἐπιστολῆς ἔτι μενούσης ἐν τῷ πρυτανείῳ

"The letter (which the admiral sent to the Boule and the prytaneis after the Battle of Lade) is still extant in the prytaneion."

421 *IG* XII[1], 85, 2 *ca.* 200 B.C.

[σειτήσει ἐν πρυτα]νείωι

Resolved . . . "that [?] is to have Sitesis in the prytaneion."

422 *Nuova Silloge di Rodi e Cos* 2, 7 II A.D.

σειτήσ[ει ἐν πρυτανείῳ]

Marcus Claudius Caneinicus Severus is to have "Sitesis in the prytaneion."

423 *Nuova Silloge di Rodi e Cos* 3, 2 II A.D.

σειτήσει ἐν πρυτανείῳ

The same Severus (?) as in (A 422) is to have "Sitesis in the prytaneion."

Same

424 *IVM* 35, 22 II B.C.

καλέσαι δὲ αὐτοὺς καὶ ἐπὶ ξένια ἐμ πρυτανεῖον ἐπὶ τὰν κοινὰν ἑστίαν

Resolved . . . "to invite them (ambassadors from Magnesia) to Xenia in the prytaneion at the common hearth."

Samos

425 *IVM* 103, 64 second half II B.C.

[*καλέσαι*] *εἰς τὸ πρυτανεῖον ἐπὶ* [*ξένια*]

Resolved . . . "to invite (the ambassadors from Magnesia) to Xenia in the prytaneion."

426 *Ath. Mitt.* 72 (1957) 176, 5–6 II B.C.

[*καλέσαι δὲ* . . . .]*ίστρατον ἐπὶ* / [*δεῖπνον εἰς τὸ πρυτα*]*νεῖον αὔριον*

Resolved . . . "to invite . . . istratos to Deipnon in the prytaneion next day."

Sigeion

427 *Michel* 1313 550–540 B.C.

A: *Φανοδίκο* / *ἐμὶ τὀρμοκ/ράτερος τõ Προκοννη/σίο· κρατῆρ/α δὲ καὶ ὑποκ/ρητήριον κ/αὶ ἠθμὸν ἐς π/ρυτανήιον* / *ἔδωκαν Σιγε/εῦσι.*

B: *Φανοδίκο εἰμὶ τõ h/Ερμοκράτος τõ* / *Προκο/ν(ν)εσίο κἀγό· κρατε̃ρα* / *κἀπίστατον καὶ hεθμ/ὸν ἐς πρυτανεῖον ἔ/δοκα μνε̃να Σιγευ/εῦσι.*

A: "I belong to Phanodikos, son of Hermokrates, of Prokonnesos. He gave a krater and a krater stand and a wine strainer in the prytaneion to the people of Sigeion."

B: "I belong to Phanodikos, son of Hermokrates, of Prokonnesos. I gave a krater and a krater stand and a wine strainer in the prytaneion as a memorial to the people of Sigeion."

See M. Guarducci in G. Richter's *The Archaic Gravestones of Attica* (London 1961) 165–168, for a discussion of this bilingual (Ionic and Attic) inscription and its date.

Sikyon

428 Herodotus V, 67 early VI B.C.

ἐπαγαγόμενος δὲ ὁ Κλεισθένης τὸν Μελάνιππον τέμενός οἱ ἀπέδεξε ἐν αὐτῷ τῷ πρυτανηίῳ καί μιν ἵδρυσε ἐνθαῦτα ἐν τῷ ἰσχυροτάτῳ.

"Kleisthenes introduced Melanippos (a dead hero) and assigned a temenos to him in the very prytaneion and in the strongest part therein."

Siphnos

429 Herodotus III, 57 *ca.* 525 B.C.

Ἀλλ' ὅταν ἐν Σίφνῳ πρυτανήια λευκὰ γένηται λεύκοφρύς τ' ἀγορή, τότε . . . . . . τοῖσι δὲ Σιφνίοισι ἦν τότε ἡ ἀγορη καὶ τὸ πρυτανήιον Παρίῳ λίθῳ ἠσκημένα.

"(Oracle:) 'but when the prytaneion at Siphnos is white and the agora white-browed, then . . .' At this time the agora and the prytaneion at Siphnos were adorned with Parian marble."

Smyrna

430 *Michel* 19, 30–31 mid-III B.C.

καλεσάτωσαν δὲ οἱ ἐπιμήνοι τῆς βουλῆς καὶ τοὺς πρεσβευτὰς τοὺς παραγεν[ομένους] / ἐγ Μαγνεσίας ἐπὶ ξενισμὸν εἰς τὸ πρυτανεῖον.

Resolved . . . "that the monthly officials of the Boule are to invite the ambassadors who are present from Magnesia to Xenismos in the prytaneion."

Syracuse

431 Cicero, *In Verrem* IV, 53, 119 70 B.C.

Altera autem est urbs Syracusis, cui nomen Achradina est; in qua forum maximum, pulcherrimae porticus, ornatissimum prytanium, amplissima est curia templumque egregium Iovis Olympii.

"There is another part of the city of Syracuse the name of which is Achradina; in it are the great forum, very lovely stoas, a very ornate prytaneion, a most ample bouleuterion, and the excellent temple of Zeus Olympios."

432 Cicero, *In Verrem* IV, 57, 125 70 B.C.

Nam Sappho, quae sublata de prytanio est, dat tibi iustam excusationem.

"Now Sappho, who was stolen from the prytaneion, gives you a proper defense."

Tanagra

433 *IG* VII, 20, 24–25 I B.C.

δοῦναι δ[ὲ] αὐτοῖς καὶ ξέν[ια] τὰ [μέγιστα] ἐκ τῶν νόμ[ων, καὶ καλέσαι αὐτοὺς ἐ]/πὶ ξένια εἰς [τ]ὸ [π]ρ[υ]τανεῖον ἐ[π]ὶ [τὴ]ν [ἑσ]τ[ίαν τ]ο[ῦ δήμου]

Resolved . . . "to grant them (ambassadors from Megara) the greatest Xenia allowed by custom, and to invite them to Xenia in the prytaneion at the hearth of the Demos."

Tarentum

434 Athenaeus XV, 700d *ca.* 360 B.C.

Εὐφορίων δ' ἐν Ἱστορικοῖς Ὑπομνήμασιν Διονύσιόν φησι τὸν νεώτερον Σικελίας τύραννον Ταραντίνοις εἰς τὸ πρυτανεῖον ἀναθεῖναι λυχνεῖον δυνάμενον καίειν τοσούτους λύχνους. ὅσος ὁ τῶν ἡμερῶν ἐστιν ἀριθμὸς εἰς τὸν ἐνιαυτόν.

"Euphorion, in his *Historical Notes*, says that Dionysios the Younger, tyrant of Sicily, dedicated in the prytaneion at Tarentum a lamp stand which was able to burn as many lamps as the number of days in the year."

Teos

435 *SEG* II, 580, 4 II B.C.

. . . .]οις καὶ [τὸν / πρ]ύτανιν ἐν τῶι πρυ[τανείωι·]

". . . and the prytanis in the prytaneion . . ."

Tenedos

436 Pindar, *Nemean* XI, 1–9 446? B.C.

Παῖ Ῥέας, ἅ τε πρυτανεῖα λέλογχας, Ἑστία,
Ζηνὸς ὑψίστου κασιγνήτα καὶ ὁμοθρόνου Ἥρας,
εὖ μὲν Ἀρισταγόραν δέξαι τεὸν ἐς θάλαμον,
εὖ δ' ἑταίρους ἀγλαῷ σκάπτῳ πέλας,
οἵ σε γεραίροντες ὀρθὰν φυλάσσοισιν Τένεδον,
πολλὰ μὲν λοιβαῖσιν ἀγαζόμενοι πρώταν θεῶν,
πολλὰ δὲ κνίσσᾳ· λύρα δέ σφι βρέμεται καὶ ἀοιδά·
καὶ ξενίου Διὸς ἀσκεῖται Θέμις αἰενάοις
ἐν τραπέζαις.

"Child of Rhea, who has for her share the prytaneia, Hestia, sister of Zeus most high and of Hera, partner of his throne, graciously receive Aristagoras into your hall, also graciously receive his companions near by the gleaming scepter, those who honor you properly and guard Tenedos. Often they admire you as the first of the gods with libations, often with the savour of a victim. The lyre and the song are sounded by them and Themis is honored at the eternal tables of Zeus Xenios."

437 *Scholion*, Pindar, *Nemean* XI

πρυτανεῖά φησι λαχεῖν τὴν Ἑστίαν, παρόσον αἱ τῶν πόλεων Ἑστίαι ἐν τοῖς πρυτανείοις ἀφίδρυνται καὶ τὸ ἱερὸν λεγόμενον πῦρ ἐπὶ τούτων ἀπόκειται. τοῦ δὲ ἱεροῦ πυρὸς ἐν τοῖς πρυτανείοις φυλαττομένου εἴη ἂν τὸ ἔτυμον πυροταμεῖον, κατὰ συγγένειαν τοῦ μ εἰς τὸ ν, ὡς τὸ μίν καὶ τὸ νίν· ἢ κατὰ κοινωνίαν τοῦ β πρὸς τὸ π, βρυτανεῖον παρὰ τὸ βρύειν, ὅ ἐστι θάλλειν καὶ αὔξεσθαι, ἀφ' οὗ καὶ τὸ ἔμβρυον τὸ ἐν τῇ γαστρὶ αὐξανόμενον. 'καί τε βρύει ἄνθεϊ λευκῷ': Ὅμηρος P 56.

"They say that Hestia got the prytaneia as her share inasmuch as the hearths of the cities are established in the prytaneia and the fire called sacred is kindled on them. From the sacred fire guarded in the prytaneia should be the true etymology pyrotameion, according to the relationship of the *mu* to the *nu*, as is the case with μιν and νιν. Or, according to the association of *beta* to *pi*, brytaneion would come from the word 'to swell', that is, to thrive and grow, from which the embryo grows in the stomach. 'and it (an olive tree) swells with white flowers': Homer, *Iliad* XVII, 56."

438 *Scholion* B, Pindar, *Nemean* XI
ὁ δὲ νοῦς· ὦ Ἑστία, τῆς Ῥέας παῖ, ἥτις ἔλαχες τὰ πρυτανεῖα, τοῦ ὑψίστου Διὸς ἀδελφὴ τυγχάνουσα καὶ τῆς Ἥρας τῆς ὁμοθρόνου καὶ συμβασιλευούσης τῷ Διΐ, καλῶς μὲν τὸν Ἀρισταγόραν ὑπόδεξαι εἰς τὸ πρυτανεῖον, καλῶς δὲ καὶ τοὺς ἑταιροὺς τοὺς συμπρυτανεύοντας αὐτῷ, τοῦ σοῦ σκήπτρου πέλας· ἐκ τούτου οὖν πρόδηλον, ὡς εἰς τὴν πρυτανείαν γράφεται ἵδρυται δὲ ἐν τοῖς πρυτανείοις ἡ Ἑστία.
"The meaning is: 'O Hestia, child of Rhea, you who have the prytaneia as your share, sister of Zeus most high and of Hera the partner of the throne and fellow ruler with Zeus, graciously welcome Aristagoras into the prytaneion, graciously welcome the companions who are fellow leaders with him near your scepter.' It is therefore clear from this that when Hestia is described with the word prytaneia, she is established in (the buildings known as) prytaneia."

Thasos

439 *IG* XII[8], 262, 1 412/1 B.C.
. . . . ἐς τὸ πρυτα]νεῖον παρα[. . . .
". . . in the prytaneion . . ."

440 Theophrastos, *De odoribus* 51 *ca.* 300 B.C.
καὶ γὰρ ὁ ἐν Θάσῳ ὁ ἐν τῷ πρυτανείῳ διδόμενος, θαυμαστός τις ὡς ἔοικε τὴν ἡδονὴν, ἠρτυμένος ἐστίν.
"And that (wine) given in the prytaneion in Thasos, apparently something wonderfully pleasureful, is so prepared (by storing it with honeyed dough)."

This passage is also quoted by Athenaeus I, 32a.

Thebes

441 *SEG* XII, 372, 11–12 242 B.C.
[καλέσαι δὲ κ]αὶ ἐπὶ ξένια τοὺς θεωροὺς / [εἰς τὸ πρυτανεῖον]
Resolved . . . "to invite the ambassadors (from Kos) to Xenia in the prytaneion."

Themisonion

442 *Michel* 544, 55–56 114 B.C.
εἶναι δὲ αὐτῶι καὶ ἔφοδον [κα/ὶ] σίτησιν ἐν πρυτανείωι
Resolved . . . "that he (a gymnasiarch) shall have the right of access and Sitesis in the prytaneion."

Thespiae

443 *BCH* 60 (1936) 179, 32 IV–III? B.C.

τὼς δὲ εἱρ[ε]/θέντας ἐγδόμεν τὰν ἐνκόλαψιν τῶν γραμμάτων ἐν τὰν στάλαν τὰν ἐν τῦ προυτανίυ ὅπ[ως ἀνγ]ράψει

Resolved... "that those who have been elected turn over the inscribing of the records on the stele in the prytaneion as set down."

Thisbe

444 *IG* VII, 4139, 28–29 late II B.C.

καλέσαι δὲ αὐτοὺς καὶ ἐπὶ ξένια εἰς τὸ / πρυτανεῖον ἐπὶ τὴν κοινὴν ἑστίαν τῆς πόλεως.

Resolved... "to invite them (ambassadors from Akraiphiai) to Xenia in the prytaneion at the common hearth of the city."

Tlos

445 *CIG* 4239, 1–2 IV B.C.

ἐν πρυτανείωι, ἄνδρα ἀγαθὸν γε/γονότα καὶ διὰ προγόνων εὐεργέ/την τοῦ δήμου.

"... in the prytaneion, having been a good man and by means of his ancestors a benefactor of the Demos."

Unknown Sites and General References

446 Aristophanes, *Ranae* 761–765 405 B.C.

νόμος τις ἐνθάδ' ἐστὶ κείμενος
ἀπὸ τῶν τεχνῶν, ὅσαι μεγάλαι καὶ δεξιαί,
τὸν ἄριστον ὄντα τῶν ἑαυτοῦ συντέχνων
σίτησιν αὐτὸν ἐν πρυτανείῳ λαμβάνειν,
θρόνον τε τοῦ Πλούτωνος ἑξῆς.

"There is a custom here (in Hades) laid down by the crafts, as many as are great and proper ones, that whoever is the best of his fellow workers should get Sitesis in the prytaneion and a chair next to that of Pluto."

447 Aeneas Tacticus X, 4 *ca.* 360–355 B.C.

τάς τε ἑορτὰς κατὰ πόλιν ἄγειν, συλλόγους τε ἰδίους μηδαμοῦ μήτε ἡμέρας μήτε νυκτὸς γίγνεσθαι, τοὺς δὲ ἀναγκαίους ἢ ἐν πρυτανείῳ[1] *ἢ ἐν βουλῇ ἢ ἐν ἄλλῳ φανερῷ τόπῳ.*

1 Casaubon; *πυρσανείω* mss.

Included among proclamations which should be made to frighten and deter conspirators within the city are: "The festivals are to be celebrated in the city, but private gatherings are not to occur either by day or by night, but those which are necessary (are to take place) either in the prytaneion or in the boule or in another visible place."

If the prytaneion was really intended in the text, it is surprising that it should have been set off against the boule rather than the bouleuterion. We can suspect a fair amount of corruption.

448 Theocritus XXI, 34–37 *ca.* 265 B.C.

τι γὰρ ποιεῖν ἂν ἔχοι τις
κείμενος ἐν φύλλοις ποτὶ κύματι μηδὲ καθεύδων;
ἀλλ' ὄνος ἐν ῥάμνωι τό τε λύχνιον ἐν πρυτανείῳ·
φαντὶ γὰρ ἀγρυπνίαν τάδ' ἔχειν.

"What has one who lies awake in the leaves by the shore to do? It is the ass in the thorns and the lamp in the prytaneion; for these are the proverbs for sleeplessness."

449 Callimachus, *Demeter* 128–130 *ca.* 260 B.C.

μέσφα τὰ τᾶς πόλιος πρυτανήια τὰς ἀτελέστως,
τὰς δὲ τελεσφορέας ποτὶ τὰν θεὸν ἄχρις ὁμαρτεῖν
αἵτινες ἑξήκοντα κατώτεραι·

"Let the uninitiated follow as far as the prytaneia, but the initiated even into the very shrine of the goddess—as many (women) as are under sixty years of age."

450 *IVM* 26, 19 *ca.* 207 B.C.

ξένια ἐν [τ]ὸ [π]ρ[υτα]νε[ῖον]

"... Xenia in the prytaneion ..."

This appears to be a decree from a Thessalian town honoring ambassadors from Magnesia, but it can be connected to no particular city.

451 *IVM* 49, 9–10 *ca.* 207 B.C.

[καλέ]σαι δὲ [αὐ]τοὺς καὶ ἐπὶ ξέ[νια ...]θ[...15... εἰς τ]ὸ πρυτ[α]νεῖον

Resolved ... "to invite them to Xenia ... in the prytaneion."

452 *IVM* 57, 38–39 *ca.* 207 B.C.

[τοὺς δὲ παραγενο]μένους παρὰ / Μαγνήτω[ν] κ[αλέσαι] ἐπὶ [ξέν]ια [ε]ἰς τὸ πρ[υ]τανεῖο[ν]

Resolved ... "to invite those present from Magnesia to Xenia in the prytaneion."

The language of this decree allows the author state to be identified as Doric. The editor suggested Kos, but the attribution is not certain.

453 *IVM* 60, 26 *ca.* 207 B.C.

[τοὺς θεωροὺς καλέσαι εἰς τὸ π]ρυτανεῖ[ον]

Resolved . . . "to invite the ambassadors (of Magnesia) to the prytaneion."

454 *IVM* 78, 26 *ca.* 207 B.C.
ἐπὶ ξένια εἰς τὸ πρυτανεῖον καλέσ[αι δὲ καὶ ---- τοὺς θεωρ]οὺς Ζώϊλον καὶ Λέοντιν
Resolved . . . "to invite the ambassadors Zoilos and Leontis to Xenia in the prytaneion."

455 *SGDI* 5016, 4–7 mid-II B.C.
πὰρ τὰνς τῶ Φρασινίκω τῶ Καράνω σ[τοὰν/ς] κἄνδον καὶ ἐπὶ τὰν ἀγορὰν, εὐώνυμο[ν / ἔ]χοντας τὸ βρυτανήϊον ἐνς ὀρθὸν ἀν' [ἁ/μ]αξιτὸν ἐπὶ τὰν λίμναν
". . . (a line running) beside the stoas of Phrasinikos of Karanos and in and across the agora, keeping the prytaneion on the left side, in a straight line down the wagon road to the lake."

> The boundary line established by this inscription runs through an unknown Cretan town and fixes the border between Knossos and Gortyn, which are to have the north and south sides respectively. M. Guarducci has suggested that the town was Rhaukos (*ICr* I, p. 291; cf. *ICr* IV, p. 261).

456 *ID* 1515, 5 *post* 166 B.C.
[καλεσάντω]ν δὲ αὐτόν τε καὶ τὸν ἀδ[ελφὸν οἱ ἄρχ]οντες ἐπὶ τὰ ἱερὰ εἰς τὸ πρυτ[ανεῖον]
"The archons are to invite him and his brother to the sacrifices in the prytaneion."

> This may be a decree of Delos itself, but lacking specific information from the text, it must be considered as from an unknown city.

457 *IG* VII, 4140, 6–7 *ca.* 146 B.C.
[καλέσαι δ']αὐτοὺς καὶ ἐπὶ ξένια / [εἰς τὸ πρυτανεῖον ἐπὶ τὴν κοινὴν τῆς πόλε]ως ἑστίαν
Resolved . . . "to invite them to Xenia in the prytaneion at the common hearth of the city."

458 *IVP* 71 II B.C.
ὑπάρχειν δὲ αὐτοῖς καὶ σί/τησιν ἐμ πρυτανείωι
Resolved . . . "that they (judges from Priene to [?]) shall have Sitesis in the prytaneion."

459 Dionysius of Halicarnassus, *Ant. Rom.* II, 23 *ca.* 20 B.C.
καθωσίωτό τις, ὥσπερ ἐν τοῖς Ἑλληνικοῖς πρυτανείοις, ἑστία κοινὴ τῶν φρατριῶν

"(Romulus built a hestiatorion for each curia and in each) was dedicated, as in Greek prytaneia, a common hearth of the phratries."

460 Dionysius of Halicarnassus, *Ant. Rom.* II, 65 *ca.* 20 B.C.
ἔθη μιμησάμενος, ἅπερ ἐν ταῖς ἀρχαιοτάταις τῶν πόλεων ἔτι γίγεται. τὰ καλούμενα πρυτανεῖα παρ' αὐτοῖς ἐστὶν ἱερὰ καὶ θεραπεύεται πρὸς τῶν ἐχόντων τὸ μέγιστον ἐν τῇ πόλει κράτος.
"(Romulus) imitated the customs (of the Greeks) which are still in existence in the most ancient cities. What are called prytaneia among them are sacred and are attended by those who have the most power in the city."

461 Philo Alexandrinus, *De Mundi opificio* I, 17 *ca.* A.D. 40
διαγράψαι πρῶτον ἐν ἑαυτῷ τὰ τῆς μελλούσης πόλεως, ἀποτελεῖσθαι μέρη σχεδὸν ἅπαντα, ἱερά, γυμνάσια, πρυτανεῖα, ἀγοράς, λιμένας, νεωσοίκους, στενωπούς, τειχῶν κατασκευάς, ἱδρύσεις οἰκιῶν καὶ δημοσίων ἄλλων οἰκοδομημάτων.
"First he (an architect) diagrams in his mind the things of the city that is to be, dividing off nearly all the parts, temples, gymnasia, prytaneia, agoras, harbors, docks, alleys, the constructions of walls and the erection of houses and other public buildings."

462 [Plutarch], *Quaestiones Convivales* 667D I A.D.
τὸν Κελεόν, ὃν πρῶτον ἱστοροῦσιν εὐδοκίμων καὶ ἀγαθῶν ἀνδρῶν κατασκευάσαντα σύνοδον καθημερινὴν ὀνομάσι πρυτανεῖον.
"Keleos, whom they say was the first of famous and good men to construct a daily assembly to be called a prytaneion . . ."

463 [Aristotle], *De mundo* 400b I A.D.
καὶ ὁ μέν τις εἰς τὸ πρυτανεῖον βαδίζει σιτησόμενος
"(According to the law of the state) one man goes to the prytaneion to have Sitesis (while another goes to jail)."

464 Lucian, *Prometheus* 4 second half II A.D.
ὃς τὰ τοιαῦτά μοι προφέρεις, ἐφ' οἷς ἔγωγε τῆς ἐν πρυτανείῳ σιτήσεως, εἰ τὰ δίκαια ἐγίγνετο, ἐτιμησάμην ἂν ἐμαυτῷ.
"You (Hermes) reproach me (Prometheus) for such things as for which, if there were justice, I would have sentenced myself to Sitesis in the prytaneion."

465 Pollux I, 7 second half II A.D.
ἐφ' ὧν δὲ θύομεν ἢ πῦρ ἀνακαίομεν, βωμός, θυμιατήριον, ἑστία· ἔνιοι γὰρ οὕτως ὠνομάκασιν. οὕτω δ' ἂν κυριώτατα καλοίης τὴν ἐν πρυτανείῳ, ἐφ' ἧς τὸ πῦρ τὸ ἄσβεστο ἀνάπτεται.
"Those things upon which we sacrifice or kindle a fire are the altar, the censer, the hearth; for thus some are called. Thus one would

most correctly call that in the prytaneion on which the eternal fire burns."

466 Pollux IX, 40 second half II A.D.

εἰσὶ δ' ἐν αὐτῇ πρυτανεῖον καὶ ἑστία τῆς πόλεως, παρ' ᾗ ἐσιτοῦντο οἵ τε κατὰ δημοσίαν πρεσβείαν ἥκοντες καὶ οἱ διὰ πρᾶξειν τινα σιτήσεως ἀξιωθέντες, καὶ εἴ τις ἐκ τιμῆς ἀείσιτος ἦν.

"There are on this (an acropolis) the prytaneion and the hearth of the city, at which dine those coming on a public embassy and those thought worthy of Sitesis because of some deed, and he who might have been honored as aeisitos."

APPENDIX B

Dining Rooms and Couches

Although not unique to prytaneia, dining rooms invariably appear in this type of building, as has been seen in the *testimonia* and in the remains. It is, therefore, desirable (see chapter two) to be able to determine whether or not some room in a suggested prytaneion was, in fact, a dining room. In certain buildings discussed in chapters three, four, and five, dining couches have been restored. These restorations demand a definition of the method by which one may identify a room as once having contained dining couches. Indeed, several studies have appeared in recent years which have included restorations of dining couches in rooms of certain ancient buildings. Perhaps the two scholars most responsible for this type of restoration are J. Travlos[1] and R. A. Tomlinson[2] but nowhere do they state the basic principles behind these restorations.[3] There are, of course, the obvious indicators of raised borders or physical remains of the couches themselves. But even when these are lacking, there are other ways of identifying some dining rooms.

1 J. Travlos, *Pictorial Dictionary of Ancient Athens* (London 1971) fig. 602 (Pompeion), figs. 618–619 (Propylaia), figs. 692–693 (Tholos).

2 R. A. Tomlinson, "Ancient Macedonian Symposia," *Ancient Macedonia* (Thessalonike 1970) 308–315; cf. notes 4 and 6 to Table 2.

3 Tomlinson, *op. cit.* 309, comes the closest to defining the requirements for a dining room, but he does not provide a discussion of the underlying mathematical principle and its force in the restoration of dining couches in a room.

There are, in a constructional sense, two types of dining rooms. One is a room which has been built with the standard dimensions of a couch as a module of construction. This type uses space more economically and by the early Hellenistic period this planning approach was very frequently, although perhaps not universally, used.[4] The other type of dining room is that which has been constructed without forethought regarding couches. In such a room one will find leftover space after couches have been arranged, or couches of varying dimensions.[5] If the physical remains of the couches are not preserved in such a room, there will be no way to identify the use of that room for dining.

The first type of room can, however, be identified with relative security even if it lacks a raised border or couches. This is so because all the couches in such a room will have been of precisely the same size and will have fitted around the room, filling the length and width, and the wall length on either side of the door. This means that there will be recoverable a standard unit of measurement, feasible for a dining couch, which must fit in some multiple the four dimensions of a room as outlined above. Such a fourfold coincidence, when it occurs, is not be to ignored. Furthermore, it is quite clear that the dining couch was used as a means of noting the size of a room in antiquity. Thus one hears of "*τρίκλινοι οἶκοι καὶ τετράκλινοι καὶ ἑπτάκλινοι καὶ ἐννεάκλινοι*" and from such mentions one can form an idea of the size of the rooms involved.[6] One can

4 See the list of buildings and their dates provided below.

5 This is the case, for example, with the dining caves at Isthmia (see O. Broneer, *Hesperia* 31 (1962) 4–6) and with the many dining rooms in the sanctuary of Demeter and Kore at Corinth; see R. S. Stroud, *Hesperia* 37 (1968) 315–317; N. Bookidis, *Hesperia* 38 (1969) 306; N. Bookidis and J. E. Fisher, *Hesperia* 41 (1972) 288–307. In the latter case, the couches are constructed of a continuous bench of built rubble with the subdivisions of moulded plaster applied to the top of the bench. This is a case of couches made to fit a room, not of a room made to fit a preconceived couch unit. If the physical remains of couches had not been recovered in these rooms, one could not have been certain that they had, in fact, been dining rooms.

6 Athenaeus II, 47; see E. S. McCartney, "The Couch as a Unit of Measurement," *CP* 29 (1934) 30–35. Although McCartney uses the couch as an indicator of the area of a dining room, the excavated examples make it quite clear that the sources refer to the perimeter of the room as shown by the couches lining the walls.

TABLE 2. Dining Couch Dimensions at Seven Sites

Site	*Structure*	*Date*	*Size (meters)*
Argive Heraion[1]	West Building	late V B.C.	0.75 × 1.70
Brauron[2]	Stoa	late V B.C.	0.80 × 1.77
Corinth[3]	Asklepieion	late IV B.C.	0.80 × 1.89
Epidauros[4]	"Gymnasion"	late IV B.C.	0.85 × 1.79
Megara[5]	Zeus Aphesios	late Classical?	0.80 × 1.85
Perachora[6]	"Hestiatorion"	late IV B.C.	0.89 × 1.90
Troizen[7]	Asklepieion	early Hellenistic	0.80 × 1.78

NOTE: There is little variation within the dimensions of the couches at each site, and those dimensions given above are the average of the remains within each building. Those dimensions, taken together, yield an average width and length of 0.82 × 1.80 meters, which can be taken as a normal dining couch size.

1 A. Frickenhaus, *JdI* 32 (1917) 121–131. The original publication is by Tilton in C. Waldstein, *The Argive Heraeum* I (Cambridge, Mass. 1902) 131–134. For the date cited above see S. G. Miller, "The Date of the West Building at the Argive Heraion," *AJA* 77 (1973) 9–18.

2 Ch. Bouras, *Η ΑΝΑΣΤΗΛΩΣΙΣ ΤΗΣ ΣΤΟΑΣ ΤΗΣ ΒΡΑΥΡΩΝΟΣ* (Athens 1967) 74–78. Although Bouras feels that the couch size indicated at Brauron is rather small and may therefore have been used by children, the size fits well within the range indicated in the list above. Bouras, following Tilton (see note 1 above), used a much smaller couch size than that listed above for the Argive Heraion couches. Both failed to acknowledge that the length of couches at the Heraion is the distance between the supports, *plus* the width of one support (i.e., half the width of two supports).

3 C. Roebuck, *Corinth* XIV (Princeton 1951) 52–53.

4 R. A. Tomlinson, "Two Buildings in Sanctuaries of Asklepios," *JHS* 89 (1969) 106–117.

5 D. Philios, "*Ἀνασκαφαὶ παρὰ τὰ Μέγαρα, Ἐφημερὶς Ἀρχαιολογική*," 1890, 35 ff.

6 R. A. Tomlinson, "Perachora: The Remains outside the Two Sanctuaries," *BSA* 64 (1969) 164–172, and plates 49a, 49b, and 49d.

7 G. Welter, *Troizen und Kalaureia* (Berlin 1941) 31 ff., and plates 14 and 16. Both this building and the one at Epidauros (note 4 above) have, rather than a single line of couches around a relatively small room, a larger room with the interior space broken up into smaller rectangular groupings of couches, several clusters of which would then line the room. A similar arrangement was probably used for the couches in the Skene of Ptolemy II as described by Kallixeinos *apud* Athenaeus V, 196–197c, and reconstructed by F. Studniczka, *Das Symposion Ptolemaios II* (Abh. d. sächs. *Ges. d. Wiss.* XXX[2], 1914), plate II.

go even further and ascertain with a fair degree of accuracy just how large a room is indicated in absolute terms since there is good evidence for determining the size of dining couches used in such rooms. Some such couches are in table 2.[7]

Using the average from table 2—0.82 × 1.80 meters—one can tell with some precision the size of a room which is described in the sources as having a certain number of couches. One can, in fact, prescribe a formula to determine the size of any room with five or more couches. Where P equals the perimeter of the room, and x the number of couches, the formula will be: $P = 1.8x + 3.3 + 2$. The precision to be gained from this formula is not so great as it would appear, but then neither is exact precision implied in terming a room large enough for five, or seven, or nine couches. The reason for this lack of precision is that the constants used in the formula are only approximations. The standard length of a couch, 1.80 meters, is only an average true to $\pm$ 0.10 meters of the real length of a couch, while the width of a couch is likewise an average which yields the constant 3.3 meters when multiplied by the number of walls—and hence couch widths—in a room ($4 \times 0.82 = 3.28$): along the length of each wall of a room there will be a certain number of couches, plus the width of one couch which overlaps in the corner. This overlapping technique can be observed in the buildings cited in table 2, and it was occasioned by the desire to conserve space in the room and yet allow each diner easy access to his table. This constant, and thus the formula, will change when the number of corners in which couches overlap is less than four, as when the number of couches is less than five. For example, in the case of a *triclinium*, there will be only two overlapping corners and the constant will be reduced to 1.64 meters (i.e., 2 × 0.82). The constant of 2.00 meters is only the estimated size for the door into the couch-lined room.[8]

7 The average size given by Richter, *The Furniture of the Greeks, Etruscans and Romans* (London 1966) 54, is based on funerary couches which differ from couches used for dining. The position of the diner (slightly elevated on his left elbow with his knees somewhat bent and legs drawn up) is different from that of the deceased, and indicates a shorter couch. In deriving the average size of dining couches, it is better to rely only on those couches known to have been used for dining.

8 The limits of the accuracy of the formula can be checked by the application of it to excavated rooms with couches. For example, in the central room of

The purpose of this mathematical discussion has been two-fold. First, it will be observed that the rooms in the various buildings listed in table 2 share a peculiarity which is forced upon them by the couches which they contain; all have their doorways off-center with relation to their axes. It will be noted that, because of the nature of the couch overlapping in the corners of the rooms, the removal of a couch for the entrance space will always yield an off-center door. Thus, if one finds a building with a room which has its doorway off-center, one may think it a possible dining room. Second, the formula can be reversed when one has an excavated room which one suspects was a dining room. Then the formula becomes:

$$x = \frac{P - 3.3 - 2}{1.8}$$

This formula can be applied to a room to find the number of couches (x) the room could have contained. In every case, it will always be more accurate to measure each wall and fit the couches to the particular dimensions of each room, working within the limits which have been indicated for the size of couches. The formula simply provides an easily derived indication of the number of couches to be fitted into the room.[9]

To summarize, any room originally designed for dining with

---

the West Building at the Argive Heraion, the remaining couch supports indicate that there were originally eleven couches. In this case the perimeter of the room, according to the formula, should be 25.10 meters ($1.8 \times 11 + 3.3 + 2$). The actual perimeter is measureable to 25.80 meters. Part of the difference is due to the fact that the width of the doorway in this room is 2.40 meters rather than the assumed 2.00 meters; and more precision than this would be fortuitous.

9 For example, in the rooms of South Stoa I in the Athenian agora, the perimeter is 19.20 meters. The formula would indicate a total of 7.7 couches to be restored in these rooms. In a drawing of one of these rooms seven couches have been neatly restored; see H. A. Thompson, *Hesperia* 23 (1954) 43–45. The literary sources tend to mention rooms with an odd number of couches in them. This is because any room built to accommodate couches would hold an even number of couches only if they were lined around the walls without a break for the door. To provide the door area, one couch would be removed, with an odd number of couches remaining. Thus, when the formula indicates a fraction between two whole numbers (as 7.7 couches above), one should always choose the odd whole number (7 in the cited example) to attempt the more precise fit into the room.

a couch module in mind must have a size and shape which would precisely accommodate a determinable number of couches all of the same size. Such rooms are not easily found, for they must correspond to multiples of the lengths and widths of a given couch size along four different dimensions. The inability to fit the same couch module into all these dimensions for any room will argue against that room having been originally designed as a dining room, but obviously does not preclude the use of the room as a dining area.[10]

10 The rooms in the stoa at Brauron were equipped with moveable couches, and hence could contain less than their maximum number. An inscription found nearby appears to be an inventory of the tables and couches in each room (*ΤΟ ΕΡΓΟΝ* 1961, 20–24). There are listed ten couches in one room, eleven (the full capacity) in the next, nine in the next, and ten in the last room mentioned in the preserved text of the inscription. The number of tables in each room as recorded in the inscription is always less than the number of couches since corner tables would be shared by the occupants of two couches.

Probably a similar room which contained less than its full capacity of couches is to be understood in the description by Plutarch of Kleomenes' dining habits (*Kleomenes* XII, 3): "His daily dinners in a *triclinium* were exceedingly simple and laconic, but if he would receive ambassadors or foreign friends, two other couches were added alongside" (*τῶν δὲ δείπνων αὐτοῦ τὸ μὲν καθημερινὸν ἦν ἐν τρικλίνῳ σφόδρα συνεσταλμένον καὶ Λακωνικόν, εἰ δὲ πρέσβεις ἢ ξένους δέχοιτο, δύο μὲν ἄλλαι προσπαρεβάλλοντο κλίναι*).

APPENDIX C

Prytaneia: Suggested but Unproven

In the following discussion there will be listed, in alphabetical order, the sites at which some building has been suggested to be a prytaneion. None of these buildings can, in my opinion, be identified as prytaneia. The reasons vary from an insufficiency of evidence to definite evidence making the identification impossible.

Aigai

In the last century, an expedition to Aigai in Asia Minor recovered the remains of a large building with which was associated a number of fragments of a Doric façade.[1] The epistyle of this building carried the following inscription: *Ἀντιφάνης Ἀπολλωνίδα Δίι Βολλαίω καὶ Ἱστία Βολλαία καὶ τῶ Δάμω.* Although the plan of the building was obscure, R. Bohn was tempted to identify the remains as those of a prytaneion or a combination prytaneion-bouleuterion. Finally, however, he concluded that the structure was most probably only a bouleuterion. This was surely the proper conclusion, and can be compared with the association of Zeus Boulaios and

1 R. Bohn and C. Schuchhardt, "Altertümer von Ägä," *JdI* Ergänzungsheft II (1889) 33–35.

Athena Boulaia[2] with Hestia Boulaia[3] in the Athenian bouleuterion.

The Argive Heraion

The West Building at the Argive Heraion has been brought into the ranks of prytaneia by R. E. Wycherley.[4] The building consists of a large peristyle court with three rooms on the northern side which were all used for dining.[5] With three such rooms, rather than one, and without an area for the hearth of Hestia, it seems highly unlikely that the West Building was a prytaneion. It ought rather to belong to a building type like that at the Asklepieion at Corinth, a type erected at shrines for the comfort of visitors. Furthermore, a politically oriented building like the prytaneion ought not to appear at a shrine such as the Argive Heraion.

Argos

On the southwest slope of the Aspis hill at Argos are several ancient remains. Among these is a nearly square building, with a circular structure in the center, which has been called a prytaneion. The identification was based on the erroneous tholos-prytaneion equation (see chapter two) and has nothing to recommend it.[6] More complete study of the area has shown that the rectilinear remains are to be understood as a terrace supporting a peripteral tholos, and that these are a part of the sanctuary of Apollo.[7]

2 Antiphon IV, 45.

3 Diodorus Siculus XIV, 4, 7; cf. *Hesperia* 12 (1943) 63–66.

4 R. E. Wycherley, *How the Greeks Built Cities*[2] 99, 218 with note 31; cf. Appendix B, table 2, note 1.

5 Cf. Frickenhaus, *JdI* 32 (1917) 129.

6 See *testimonia* (A 9). As far as I can discover, this building was first called a prytaneion in the third edition of E. Kirsten and W. Kraiker, *Griechenlandkunde* (Heidelberg 1955) 234–235. In the fourth and fifth editions (1962 and 1967, p. 345) the structure has been called "*wohl ein Heiligtum der 'klarblickenden' Athena.*" Unfortunately, the prytaneion label was picked up in the meantime by N. Papahatzes, *ΠΑΥΣΑΝΙΟΥ ΕΛΛΑΔΟΣ ΠΕΡΙΗΓΗΣΙΣ I* (Thessalonike 1963) 149, fig. 81, and 150, note 2.

7 W. Vollgraff, *Le Sanctuaire d'Apollon Pythéen à Argos* (Paris 1956) 74 ff.; cf. G. Roux, "Le Sanctuaire Argien d'Apollon Pythéen," *REG* 70 (1957) 477–478.

Recently another building has been identified as the prytaneion mentioned by Diodorus Siculus (A 9).[8] This building is the large square hall located on the west side of the agora.[9] Although the position and construction suggest that the structure was public and may even have been a bouleuterion, there is no basis for identifying it as a prytaneion, nor for suggesting that Diodorus confused the bouleuterion with a prytaneion. The bouleuterion-prytaneion confusion is modern, not ancient.

Cyrene

Epigraphical mention of a prytaneion at Cyrene makes it quite clear that such a building ought to be found at the site. There is a structure at Cyrene which has been called the prytaneion, but it has never been properly presented.[10] Until it is excavated and studied together with the surrounding area and with the artifacts found therein, one cannot pass judgement on its identification as a prytaneion.

Delphi

Two-thirds of the way down the eastern side of the sanctuary of Apollo there is the treasury-like Building XIV which has, for two reasons, been called the prytaneion of Delphi (pl. 16b).[11] The first reason is that Plutarch (A 304), in mentioning

8 R. A. Tomlinson, *Argos and the Argolid* (Ithaca 1972) Chapter 2, note 12 and p. 195.

9 *BCH* 77 (1953) 244–248, pls. XXXV–XXXVI.

10 See G. Pesce, "Cirene," *EAA* II (1959) 676–677; and R. G. Goodchild, *Kyrene und Apollonia* (Zürich 1971) 91–92. For relevant *testimonia*, see (A 270–274).

11 This is the structure designated as Building XIV on the French plans of the sanctuary; see J. Pouilloux and G. Roux, *Énigmes à Delphes* (Paris 1963) fig. 34. The same structure, but differently restored, is no. 99 on the plan of Delphi which is presented by H. Pomtow, "Delphoi," *RE*, suppl. IV (1924) 1199–1202. We will not treat the identification of the prytaneion with the tholos in the Marmaria at Delphi as suggested by H. Pomtow, "Die grosse Tholos zu Delphi," *Klio* 12 (1912) 289–307. That suggestion has been effectively discarded by J. Charbonneaux, *Fouilles de Delphes* II[4] (Paris 1925) 28–30. Furthermore, the inscription which will be discussed below shows conclusively that the prytaneion was near the peribolos wall of the sanctuary of Apollo (A 289) and thus cannot have been in the Marmaria.

R. Martin, *Recherches sur l'Agora Grecque* (Paris 1951) 240, note 2, says that

a monthly procession of the Pythia from the Temple of Apollo to the prytaneion, uses the verb καταγωγεῖν. Second, an inscription which records the repairs of Agathon to the peribolos wall (A 289) defines the area of his work as παρὰ τὸ πρυτανεῖον.[12] Part of the wall which Agathon repaired forms the east wall of Building XIV. The structure is not bonded into the wall, however, but is built up against it (pl. 16c). Building XIV must, therefore, be later than the peribolos wall which Agathon repaired, but the inscription shows that the prytaneion must have been in existence when Agathon started work. It follows that Building XIV cannot have been the prytaneion of Delphi.[13]

Eleusis

The building called a prytaneion at Eleusis is a fourth century B.C. structure with a central courtyard surrounded on three sides by smaller subsidiary rooms, and on the fourth by two larger dining rooms.[14] The building lacks, however, the all-important hearth room which militates against a prytaneion identification. More conclusively, the identification of any building at Eleusis as a prytaneion directly contradicts the evidence of Thucydides (A 11; see also A 12) who explicitly states that, from the "time of Theseus," there was only one prytaneion for all Attica and it was in Athens.

Kassope

The large, nearly square building north of the agora of Kassope has been identified as a prytaneion, or a "prytaneion-kata-

---

the disposition of the foundations of Building XIV does not admit of a treasury plan. The reason why this is so is neither explained by Martin nor obvious to me. Of course, a treasury plan, as Martin realizes, is not to be associated with a prytaneion, the name by which Martin calls Building XIV. For relevant *testimonia*, see (A 288–305).

12 J. Bousquet, *Le Trésor de Cyrène* (Paris 1952) 26–27, has been able to localize the repairs of Agathon to the east peribolos wall between the Stoa of Attalos I and Gate B in the wall just below the Treasury of Cyrene.

13 Bousquet, *ibid.* 28–29, succinctly pointed this out, but the prytaneion label for Building XIV has shown great staying powers as, for example, in Pouilloux and Roux, *op. cit.* (note 11) 70 and 74.

14 J. Travlos, *ΠΡΑΚΤΙΚΑ* 1955, 62–66; *ΠΡΑΚΤΙΚΑ* 1956, 55–56; cf. E. Vanderpool, *AJA* 60 (1956) 268; and Wycherley, *How the Greeks Built Cities*[2] 137.

gogeion".[15] This structure has a large central courtyard which is surrounded by small rooms, one of which served as the entrance to the building. Although many of these rooms contain small hearths, they all seem to be for cooking purposes and there is no single dominant hearth with its own dominant room in the plan. Furthermore, none of the rooms has the proper dimensions to accommodate standard-size couches. The building is certainly a public one, but it does not have the attributes of a prytaneion. The discovery of stone liquid measures and of dedications by strategoi in the building[16] indicates a function more like a strategeion or thesmotheteion, where office space was provided for officials concerned with both the civic and commercial activities of the agora at Kassope.[17]

Kourion

A structure at the Cypriote city of Kourion, once discussed as a possible prytaneion,[18] has been recently studied in depth.[19] It is a long colonnaded building with five large rooms of equal size (perhaps for dining) behind the colonnade. Lacking courtyard and hearth room, it ought to be considered an adjunct to the sanctuary of Apollo for the accommodation of visitors.

Megara Hyblaea

Outside the southeast corner of the agora of Megara Hyblaea is a substantial building which has been labeled a prytaneion.[20] The structure has three rectangular rooms which open onto a

15 S. Dakaris, *ΠΡΑΚΤΙΚΑ* 1952, 331–362; *ΠΡΑΚΤΙΚΑ* 1953, 164–174; *ΠΡΑΚΤΙΚΑ* 1954, 201–209.

16 See Dakaris, *ΠΡΑΚΤΙΚΑ* 1952, 357–358; *ΠΡΑΚΤΙΚΑ* 1954, 206.

17 The nearest parallel in function, although not in form, to this building at Kassope is perhaps South Stoa I in the Athenian agora where there is a series of rooms, clearly used for dining, with traces of burning from portable braziers (cf. the more permanent hearths in Kassope), on the edge of the commercial and civic center of Athens; see *Agora* XIV, 78 ff.

18 W. A. McDonald, *AJA* 52 (1948) 375.

19 R. Scranton, "The Architecture of the Sanctuary of Apollo Hylates at Kourion," *TAPhS* 57 (1967) 27–38.

20 G. Vallet and F. Villard, "Megara Hyblaea: I Problemi dell'Agorà Arcaica," *Bolletino d'Arte* 1967, 36–37. For earlier reports on the building see "Chronique" in *MélRome* 75 (1963) 249–250 and 78 (1966) 285–286; and A. W. Van Buren, *AJA* 66 (1962) 400 and 70 (1966) 360.

court (pl. 16d). Although the excavators claim that the easternmost of the three rooms has cuttings for couch supports, these cuttings do not form the typically regular pattern seen at other sites. Furthermore, the dimensions of these rooms (3.80 × 3.20 meters) do not accommodate standard-size couches. This does not prove that couches were not used in these rooms, but it shows that the building was not planned for couches of a regular size. Moreover, there is no provision for a hearth room and, rather than two principal rooms for dining and the hearth of Hestia along with two or more subsidiary rooms, there are three rooms of equal size. If any of the artifacts from the building help document its identification as a prytaneion, they have not been made public.[21] That the building at Megara Hyblaea is an important public structure is certainly indicated by its location and its handsome construction; that it is the prytaneion is unproven and improbable.

Messene

In the middle of the southern side of the so-called agora of Messene lies Building E, which, it has been suggested, was a prytaneion.[22] The scanty remains indicate a structure with a small peristyle courtyard on one side and small rooms opening off this court on the other side. The basis for identification of this building as the prytaneion was essentially the proximity of the "agora." More recent excavations, however, have shown that this area may be the Asklepieion mentioned by Pausanias

21 The excavators may have been led to their identification by the similarity in plan between the buildings at Megara Hyblaea and the Argive Heraion. This similarity may indicate a common building type, but that type is not necessarily the prytaneion.

22 A. Orlandos, *ΠΡΑΚΤΙΚΑ* 1958, 183; *ΤΟ ΕΡΓΟΝ* 1958, 147. The best overall picture of the structure is in *ΤΟ ΕΡΓΟΝ* 1958, 146, fig. 153, but in that photograph there is a substantial layer of vegetation. Does this mean that no photograph exists from the time of excavation when the area would have been clear from such weeds and greenery? It is curious that Orlandos never mentions any objects found in the building. Was Building E excavated or lying open before Orlandos began his work at Messene? It might well be so. G. Oikonomos, *ΠΡΑΚΤΙΚΑ* 1925, 65, fig. 6, although he does not mention Building E, does talk of its eastern neighbor, Building *Δ*, and publishes a photograph of the latter which was taken from the east. Behind Building *Δ* in the photograph are several dim white spots which look suspiciously like the blocks of Building E.

(IV, 31, 10).[23] If so, then there is very little reason to think of Building E as the prytaneion of Messene.

Miletus

Since the building at Miletus which is called a prytaneion is relatively well known and frequently reproduced in handbooks,[24] I include that plan for ease of reference (fig. 15).[25] The building is located on the western side of the North Agora of Miletus about 25 meters northwest of the bouleuterion. The basic problem with the identification of the building as a prytaneion is that only about half of the presumed area of the structure was ever excavated. The plan is restored solely on the two assumptions of a splendidly symmetrical original ground plan, and of the Roman reproduction of the parts of the original plan which were not found by the excavators.[26] Therefore, the only argument for the building's identification as a prytaneion is its proximity to the agora and the bouleuterion. The objects discovered in the building might have been helpful in this context, but they are not included in the published materials. Thus we must reserve judgement in the hope that an area so favorable for the location of a prytaneion will one day be completely explored and the actual ground plan revealed.

Olynthos

In the northeast area of the south hill of Olynthos is a building which was once identified as a prytaneion.[27] A more recent

23 The identification of the "agora" as the Asklepieion was first suggested by E. Kirsten and W. Kraiker, *Griechenlandkunde*[4] (Heidelberg 1962) 426–428. More recent excavations have uncovered a temple in the center of the area; see *ΠΡΑΚΤΙΚΑ* 1969, 98 ff.; *AJA* 75 (1971) 308–310. We might note, among other indications of the Asklepieion in this area, two inscriptions found among the remains: *IG* V[1], 1462, which mentions repairs to the four stoas of the Asklepieion done by a certain Marcus Kaisios Gallos; and *ΤΟ ΕΡΓΟΝ* 1958, 142, which is a dedication by a victor in the games of Asklepios and Rome.

24 E.g., by Wycherley, *How the Greeks Built Cities*[2] 69, 137, fig. 16.

25 The original publication is by A. von Gerkan, *Der Nordmarkt und der Hafen an der Löwenbucht* (Berlin 1922) 88–89; cf. 30. Among the *testimonia*, (A 360) applies to Miletus.

26 E.g., the case of the inner court of the building about which von Gerkan, *ibid.* 30, says: "*Da die letzte römische Umgestaltung einen Innenhof hatte, muss das gleiche auch für die früheren Zeiten gelten.*"

27 D. M. Robinson, *Excavations at Olynthus* II (Baltimore 1930) 24–28.

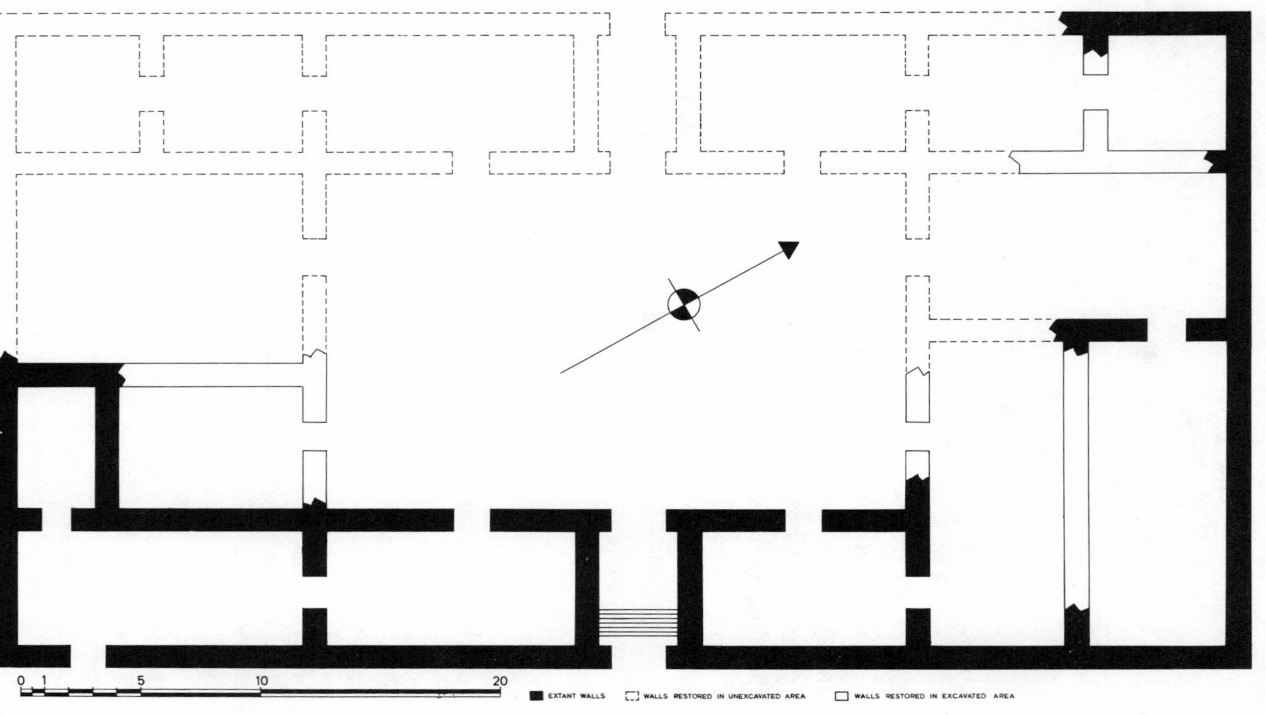

FIGURE 15. Plan of the building at Miletus.

study of the structure has tentatively proposed a reconstructed ground plan suitable for a bouleuterion or ekklesiasterion.[28] Although even that suggestion cannot be regarded as secure, it seems most likely the correct interpretation of the scanty remains of this building.

Palatitza

The building at Palatitza with a circular chamber as one of its elements was once identified as a prytaneion.[29] This identification was based on the now-defunct theory of the round prytaneion, and further study and excavations have shown that the structure is more probably to be recognized as a royal(?) eating and drinking establishment.[30]

Pergamon

Located on a terrace on the southern slopes of Pergamon's acropolis between the Sanctuary of Demeter on the west and the Temple of Hera on the east are the remains of Building Z, which has been identified as the prytaneion of Pergamon.[31] Because the whole structure was never excavated, a complete plan cannot be discerned. Dörpfeld sought to identify a building in this area of Pergamon as the prytaneion because several inscriptions recording dedications by prytaneis and honors to

28 *McDonald* 231–236.

29 W. J. Anderson, R. P. Spiers, and W. B. Dinsmoor, *The Architecture of Ancient Greece*[2] (London 1927) 186. The prytaneion appellation does not recur, however, in the third edition of 1950, p. 326.

30 See S. G. Miller, *AJA* 76 (1972) 78–79, and references to earlier bibliography therein.

31 W. Dörpfeld, *Ath. Mitt.* 37 (1912) 270. Dörpfeld earlier, *Ath. Mitt.* 35 (1910) 352–353, had sought to call the next building to the south (Building H) the prytaneion, but O. Kern, *Hermes* 46 (1911) 436, showed the impossibility of that identification. I refer to the building labeled Z by Dörpfeld in *Ath. Mitt.* 37 (1912) plate XVIII. Another building, not to be confused with the one under discussion, had been called Z by Dörpfeld in *Ath. Mitt.* 35 (1910) plate XV.

A century earlier Choiseul-Gouffier, *Voyage Pittoresque de la Grèce* II (Paris 1809) 33, had identified the prytaneion with what is now known to be the Asklepieion located in the plain of Pergamon some distance to the southwest of the citadel. He had seen there a block with the letters *ΠΡΥΤ* preserved on it. The impossibility of such an identification was pointed out by A. Conze, *Pergamon* I[1] (Berlin 1912) 6. For relevant *testimonia*, see (A 387–389).

prytaneis were found in the Demeter Sanctuary just to the west.[32] This is hardly adequate justification for the identification of any building in the area as a prytaneion, and the remains of Building Z are too slight for the application of our criteria.

Thasos

Excavating in an area earlier explored by E. Miller,[33] Ch. Picard discovered ancient remains on Thasos which he put together to reconstruct a building measuring 32.50 × 32.50 meters and dated to the period 490–470 B.C.[34] Based on the similarity of the restored dimensions for this building with those restored (incorrectly, see chapter four) for the prytaneion at Olympia, and on the discovery in a nearby church of an inscription which has the letters *NEION* preserved in its first line (A 439), Picard did not hesitate to call his structure the prytaneion of Thasos. Because of Picard's dogmatic assertions that he had found the prytaneion of Thasos, a body of literature has appeared which deals with the cults of the various gods in the prytaneion.[35] These discussions were based on dedications discovered in Picard's "prytaneion."

More recent excavations have shown that the remains in question are actually parts of three or four different structures at the northeast corner of the Thasian agora.[36] For example, the entrance to Picard's prytaneion is now known as the Passage of the Theoroi and is actually the paved area between two different buildings. Although there certainly was a prytaneion at Thasos (A 440) and although this should be near the agora, there is no likely candidate for such an identification available at present.

32 E.g., see H. Hepding, *Ath. Mitt.* 35 (1910) nos. 25, 27, 38; and A. Ippel, *Ath. Mitt.* 37 (1912) nos. 24, 25.

33 E. Miller, *Le mont Athos, Vatopéta, l'île de Thasos* (Paris 1889) 188 ff. See *testimonia* (A 439–440).

34 Ch. Picard, *Monuments et Mémoires, Fondation Piot* 20 (1913) 58–59; cf. *CRAI* 1914, 290–305; *BCH* 45 (1921) 93–94.

35 Most notable among these is M. Launey, *Le sanctuaire et le culte d'Héraklès à Thasos* (Paris 1944) 126, 137–138, 188, 211.

36 E. Will and R. Martin, *BCH* 68–69 (1944–1945) 129–137; G. Roux, *BCH* 79 (1955) 353–364; and R. Martin, *L'Agora de Thasos* (Paris 1959) 6, plans A and B.

APPENDIX D

The Ἱερὸν τῆς Ἑστίας and the Prytaneion at Olympia

In his account of the battle of 364 B.C. between the Eleans and the Arcadians at Olympia, Xenophon (*Hell.* VII, 4; see A 372) mentions *τὸ ἱερὸν τῆς Ἑστίας*. This shrine of Hestia has usually been identified with the prytaneion where Pausanias located *τὸ οἴκημα τῆς Ἑστίας* (A 376). J. Kondis, however, questioned this identification and argued that the shrine of Hestia was to be identified with the Southeast Building which is located diagonally across the Altis from the prytaneion.[1] At the time when I presented the results of my re-examination of the remains of the prytaneion, I did not think it worthwhile to refute this theory.[2] In the meantime, however, the theory has been advanced once again by Mallwitz.[3] Inasmuch as Mallwitz's book will undoubtedly and deservedly gain wide circulation, the theory of a shrine of Hestia separate from the prytaneion ought to be examined closely.[4]

1 J. Kondis, *ΤΟ ΙΕΡΟΝ ΤΗΣ ΟΛΥΜΠΙΑΣ ΚΑΤΑ ΤΟΝ Δ′ π.Χ. ΑΙΩΝΑ* (Athens 1958) 19–27.

2 *Miller* 81–82 and note 7.

3 A. Mallwitz, *Olympia und seine Bauten* (Munich 1972) 202–205.

4 A situation analogous to that at Olympia seems to have pertained at Paros where we hear of a prytaneion (A 379–383) and of a shrine of Hestia; see G. Despinis, "*Τιμητικονψήφισμα ἐκ Πάρου*," *ΔΕΛΤΙΟΝ* 20 (1965) 120. Despinis has argued (p. 131) that the shrine of Hestia and the prytaneion of Paros were the same, or parts of the same, structure.

I will summarize the evidence which has been adduced in favor of the separate shrine theory, and attempt to refute each point individually. Then other problems which have not been solved by the advocates of a shrine of Hestia separate from the prytaneion will be presented. The objections and difficulties are, in my opinion, fatal to the suggestion.

1) The objects found in the Southeast Building (pottery, ashes, etc.) are similar to those found in the prytaneion. Since the prytaneion was sacred to Hestia, the Southeast Building must also be sacred to Hestia.[5]

> The conclusion drawn is obviously not necessarily true, since such artifacts indicate only an area of dining, not necessarily an area sacred to any god, much less sacred specifically to Hestia. Furthermore, the facts regarding the relevance of the objects to the Southeast Building are suspect. Those objects were part of a leveling fill put down before the construction of the building and could have come from some other area of the Olympia sanctuary.[6]

2) Some of the pottery was marked *Δαμόσιον* and was similar to objects discovered in the tholos in the Athenian Agora. Since the tholos in Athens was sacred to Hestia, the Southeast Building must also be sacred to Hestia.[7]

> The questionable relevance of these artifacts to the Southeast Building has already been noted, as has the lack of evidence that the tholos in the Athenian Agora was sacred to Hestia (chapter three, p. 60).

3) A courtyard and a round structure exist in the Southeast Building. That the Southeast Building was the shrine of Hestia is, therefore, very probable.[8]

> The exclusive relevance of a courtyard to Hestia eludes me, and the circular structure is not necessarily pertinent. If the reference is to the tholos at Athens, we have already seen that there is no connection with Hestia. The allusion may be to the circular common hearth at Mantinea,[9] but a *ἑστία* was not

5 Kondis, *op. cit.* 20.
6 Mallwitz, *op. cit.* 204.
7 Kondis, *op. cit.* 24.
8 Mallwitz, *op. cit.* 202.
9 Pausanias VIII, 9, 5.

necessarily round,[10] nor was the circular form unique to Hestia.[11]

4) Xenophon would have used the word *πρυτανεῖον*, not *τὸ ἱερὸν τῆς Ἑστίας*, if he had been referring to the building at the northwest corner of the Altis (i.e., the prytaneion).[12]

This is an argument from silence which is particularly dangerous, for Xenophon's vocabulary nowhere contains the word *πρυτανεῖον*.

5) The description of the course of the battle between the Eleans and the Arcadians in 364 B.C. makes better sense topographically if the shrine of Hestia is at the southeast rather than the northwest corner of the Altis.

This point has been debated elsewhere.[13] The reader will have to decide, having read the arguments, which situation is the more likely. Neither can be proven conclusively.

6) Pausanias actually mentions the shrine of Hestia as an entity separate from the prytaneion. Starting at V, 14, 4, Pausanias lists the altars at Olympia in the order in which the Eleans sacrificed upon them. He starts with the altar of Hestia, but does not mention its location. He ends in the prytaneion at the hearth of Hestia (V, 15, 8). The mention of the hearth of Hestia in the prytaneion is the introduction of a new and different item not previously referred to (except for the incidental mention of the hearth in the prytaneion with regard to the Great Altar of Zeus; V, 13, 11). Therefore the hearth in the prytaneion is not the place where the first sacrifice in the series took place. Where did the first sacrifice take place? It is logical that it took place in the shrine of Hestia (the Southeast Building) since the Temple of Zeus, where the second sacrifice in the series took place, is adjacent to the Southeast Building.[14]

The argument from proximity is completely invalid here. Pausanias (V, 14, 8) reminds us that he lists the altars not as they

10 For example, note the square *hestia* dedicated at Magnesia; *IVM* 220.

11 Note the variety of buildings, monuments, and hearths of circular form which were dedicated to divinities and heroes other than Hestia; F. Robert, *Thymélè* (Paris 1939) 6 ff., and *passim*.

12 Kondis, *op. cit.* 20.

13 Mallwitz, *op. cit.* 203-204; *Miller* 82-83 and fig. 1.

14 Kondis, *op. cit.* 25.

> stand, but in the order which the Eleans observed when they sacrificed upon them. With regard to the suggestion that the first sacrifice to Hestia did not take place in the prytaneion, I can only ask that the reader turn to Pausanias V, 14, 5–V, 15, 12. The above argument will seem, I believe, not only specious but also unnecessary. Pausanias begins with the sacrifice to Hestia in the prytaneion, enumerates the other altars in his series, and then returns to the prytaneion to describe the building, the cults in it, and the monuments surrounding it in more detail. It is a well known trait of Pausanias to use a particular monument or building as a fixed point to which he returns after one exegesis, in order to begin another.[15]

In addition to the above refutation of the various points adduced by Kondis and Mallwitz as evidence for a shrine of Hestia separate from the prytaneion at Olympia, there are more serious difficulties with this theory. I refer, in particular, to the archaeological evidence concerning the Southeast Building. Two fragments of columns from the Temple of Zeus, as well as Doric capitals of Classical date, are built into the foundations of this structure.[16] Inasmuch as these architectural fragments most likely could not have been built into the foundations until after the earthquake of 374 B.C. (see above, chapter four, note 47), the Southeast Building can have been constructed only shortly before the battle of 364, if it had been constructed by then at all. Furthermore, no earlier architectural remains are known on this spot, which means that the hypothetical cult of Hestia in this area must have been very new in the second quarter of the fourth century B.C.[17] Moreover, the cult of Hestia in this area was short-lived since the Southeast Building underwent serious remodeling later in the fourth century.[18] It is, of course, possible to hypothesize that the cult continued in this new and different building, but since the existence of the cult is hypothetical in the first place, and the location of this cult in

15 This is Pausanias' method, for example, in the Athenian agora where he uses the Royal Stoa for his fixed point; see I, 3, 1 and 14, 6. Even more pertinent is Pausanias' use of the Athenian prytaneion as another fixed point; see I, 18, 4 and 20, 1 (A 221, 222), and chapter three, pp. 46–48.

16 Mallwitz, *op. cit.* 204 and fig. 162.

17 *Ibid.* No evidence is presented for the suggestion by Mallwitz that the "shrine of Hestia" belonged to the late fifth century B.C. The known building can have been built, at the earliest, in the second quarter of the fourth century.

18 *Ibid.*

the Southeast Building is a second hypothesis, a third hypothesis is surely too many.

Of the arguments for a separate shrine outlined above, the first three are irrelevant, while the last three can actually be held to argue that the shrine of Hestia was in the prytaneion. The archaeological evidence, moreover, weighs the case heavily against the Southeast Building having been the shrine of Hestia. In the absence of facts which prove the location of the *ἱερὸν τῆς Ἑστίας* mentioned by Xenophon, it is surely easier to identify this shrine with the prytaneion which we know was sacred to Hestia than to hypothesize a new cult in a different location.

SITE BIBLIOGRAPHY

Chapters IV and V

Delos

Roussel, P., "Fragments d'une Liste d'Archontes Déliens," *BCH* 35 (1911) 432.

Dürrbach, F., *Inscriptiones Graecae* XI[2] (Berlin 1912) 1.

Roussel, P., *Délos colonie Athénienne* (Paris 1916) 47, note 6; 221–222.

Vallois, R., *L'Architecture Hellénique et Hellénistique à Délos* I (Paris 1944) 64, note 6; 171–178.

———, *Les Constructions Antiques de Délos: Documents* (Paris 1953) pl. IV.

Gallet de Santerre, H., *Délos Primitive et Archaïque* (Paris 1958) 272–273, 298.

Orlandos, A., *ΤΑ ΥΛΙΚΑ ΔΟΜΗΣ ΤΩΝ ΑΡΧΑΙΩΝ ΕΛΛΗΝΩΝ* II (Athens 1960) 9, note 2.

Bruneau, P, and Ducat, J., *Guide de Délos* (Paris 1965) 88–89.

Vallois, R., *L'Architecture Hellénique et Hellénistique à Délos* II (Paris 1966) 18, 40, 48–49, 103–105, 133.

Dreros

Xanthoudides, S., "Dreros," *ΔΕΛΤΙΟΝ* 4 (1918) 23–30.

Marinatos, S., "Le Temple Geometrique de Dreros," *BCH* 60 (1936) 232–233, 254, note 4.

Demargne, P., and van Effenterre, H., "Recherches à Dreros," *BCH* 61 (1937) 5–32.

Kirsten, E., "Dreros," *RE, Suppl. VII* (1940) 131–132.

Ephesos

Wood, J. T., *Discoveries at Ephesus* (London 1877) 102, figure on 101.

Keil, J., "Kulte im Prytaneion von Ephesos," *Anatolian Studies Presented to W. H. Buckler* (Manchester 1939) 119–128.

Miltner, F., "Vorläufiger Bericht über die Ausgrabungen in Ephesos," *Jahreshefte* 43 (1956) Beiblatt 27–39.

———, "Ergebnisse der österreichischen Ausgrabungen in Ephesos im Jahre 1956," *AAW* (1957) 23–25.

———, "Bericht über die Ausgrabungen in Ephesos," *Türk Arkeoloji Dergisi* 8 (1958) 19–25.

———, *Ephesos* (Vienna 1958).

———, "Vorläufiger Bericht über die Ausgrabungen in Ephesos," *Jahreshefte* 46 (1959) Beiblatt 289 ff.

Eichler, F., "Die österreichischen Ausgrabungen in Ephesos im Jahre 1960," *AAW* (1961) 68.

Alzinger, W., *Die Stadt des siebenten Weltwunders* (Vienna 1962) 226–232.

Eichler, F., "Die österreichischen Ausgrabungen in Ephesos im Jahre 1961," *AAW* (1962) 38–41.

———, "Die österreichischen Ausgrabungen in Ephesos im Jahre 1962," *AAW* (1963) 46.

———, "Die österreichischen Ausgrabungen in Ephesos im Jahre 1963," *AAW* (1964) 40.

Kolophon

Holland, L. B., "Colophon," *Hesperia* 13 (1944) 103–107.

Lato

Demargne, J., "Fouilles à Lato en Crète," *BCH* 27 (1903) 216–221.

Pomtow, H., "Die grosse Tholos zu Delphi," *Klio* 12 (1912) 302–303.

Frickenhaus, A., "Griechische Banketthäuser," *JdI* 32 (1917) 131, note 2.

Weickert, C., *Typen der archaischen Architektur in Griechenland und Kleinasien* (Augsburg 1929) 174, 177.

Karo, G., "Archäologische Funde von Mai 1932 bis Juli 1933: Griechenland und Dodekanes," *Archäologischer Anzeiger* (1933) 222–223.

Kirsten, E., "Lato," *RE, Suppl. VII* (1940) 352–355.

Ducrey, P., and Picard, O., "Recherches à Latô V, Le Prytanée," *BCH* 96 (1972) 567–592.

Magnesia on the Maeander

Kern, O., *Die Inschriften von Magnesia am Maeander* (Berlin 1900) 143.

Humann, K., *Magnesia am Maeander* (Berlin 1904) 137–138.

Morgantina

Sjöqvist, E., "Excavations at Serra Orlando (Morgantina), Preliminary Report II," *AJA* 62 (1958) 161.

Stillwell, R., "Excavations at Serra Orlando 1958, Preliminary Report III," *AJA* 63 (1959) 167–168.

Miller, S. G., "A Public House at Morgantina," forthcoming.

Olympia

Baumeister, A., *Denkmäler des klassischen Altertums* (Munich 1887) 1074.

Furtwängler, A., *Die Bronzen von Olympia* IV (Berlin 1890) 5–6, and *passim.*

Dörpfeld, W., *Die Baudenkmäler von Olympia* II (Berlin 1892) 58–61, 140, 180.

Dittenberger, W., and Purgold, K., *Die Inschriften von Olympia* V (Berlin 1896) *passim.*

Treu, G., *Die Bildwerke von Olympia* III (Berlin 1897) *passim.*

Frazer, J., *Pausanias's Description of Greece* III (London 1898) 580–583.

Weniger, L., "Olympische Forschungen: Die Frühlingseinigung," *Klio* 4 (1906) 1–33.

Weege, F., "Einzelfunde von Olympia 1907–1909," *Ath. Mitt.* 36 (1911) 187–188.

Gardiner, E. N., *Olympia and Its Remains* (Oxford 1925) 267–269.

Dörpfeld, W., *Alt-Olympia* (Berlin 1935) 16, 263–266.

Kondis, J., *ΤΟ ΙΕΡΟΝ ΤΗΣ ΟΛΥΜΠΙΑΣ ΚΑΤΑ ΤΟΝ Δ'π. Χ. ΑΙΩΝΑ* (Athens 1958) 19–27.

Herrmann, H., "Zur ältesten Geschichte von Olympia," *Ath. Mitt.* 77 (1962) 17–18.

Miller, S. G., "The Prytaneion at Olympia," *Ath. Mitt.* 86 (1971) 79–107.

Mallwitz, A., *Olympia und seine Bauten* (Munich 1972) 125–128, 200–206.

Priene

Wiegand, T., and Schrader, H., *Priene* (Berlin 1904) 231–234.

Kleiner, G., "Priene," *RE, Suppl. IX* (1962) 1202–1205.

Schede, M., *Die Ruinen von Priene*[2] (Berlin 1964) 63–67.

SELECTED BIBLIOGRAPHY

(See also the Site Bibliography above)

Boersma, J. S., *Athenian Building Policy from 561/0 to 405/4 B.C.* (Groningen 1970).

Bötticher, K., "Untersuchungen auf der Akropolis von Athen," *Philologus, Suppl.* III (1863) 345–360.

Charbonneaux, J., "Tholos et Prytanée," *BCH* 49 (1925) 158–178.

———, "La Tholos," *Fouilles de Delphes* II⁴ (Paris 1925) 28–30.

Curtius, E., *Attische Studien* II (Göttingen 1865).

———, *Die Stadtgeschichte von Athen* (Berlin 1891).

Dörpfeld, W., *Alt-Athen und seine Agora* (Berlin 1937).

Dow, S., "Prytaneis," *Hesperia, Suppl.* I (1937).

Dyer, T., *Ancient Athens* (London 1873).

Eliot, C. W. J., "Aristotle Ath. Pol. 44.1 and the Meaning of Trittys," *Phoenix* 21 (1967) 79–84.

Frazer, J., "The Prytaneum, the Temple of Vesta, the Vestals, Perpetual Fires," *JPh* 14 (1885) 145–172.

Frickenhaus, A., "Griechische Banketthäuser," *JdI* 32 (1917) 114–133.

Fuchs, W., "Hestia," *EAA* IV (Rome 1961) 18–22.

Gschnitzer, F., "Prytanis," *RE, Suppl.* XIII (1973) 801–809.

Hagemann, G., *De Prytaneo* (Breslau 1880).

Hill, I. T., *The Ancient City of Athens* (London 1953).

Holland, L. B., "The Hall of the Athenian Kings," *AJA* 43 (1939) 289–298.

Judeich, W., *Topographie von Athen*² (Munich 1931).

Keil, J., "Kulte im Prytaneion von Ephesos," *Anatolian Studies Presented to W. H. Buckler* (Manchester 1939) 119–128.

Kirsten, E., "Lato," *RE, Suppl.* VII (1940) 352–355.

Lange, K., *Haus und Halle* (Leipzig 1885).

Leake, W. M., *The Topography of Athens*[2] (London 1841).

Leroux, G., *Les Origines de l'Édifice Hypostyle* (Paris 1913).

Levi, D., "Il Pritaneo e la Tholos di Atene," *Annuario* 6 (1923) 1–6.

Marindin, G., "Prytaneion," in Smith's *Dictionary of Greek and Roman Antiquities* II (London 1891) 514–515.

Martin, R., *Recherches sur l'Agora Grecque* (Paris 1951).

McCartney, E., "The Couch as a Unit of Measurement," *CP* 29 (1934) 30–35.

McDonald, W. A., *The Political Meeting Places of the Greeks* (Baltimore 1943).

———, "Types of Greek Civic Architecture—The Prytaneion" (Summary of paper presented at annual meeting of the Archaeological Institute of America), *AJA* 52 (1948) 374–375.

———, "A Linguistic Examination of an Epigraphical Formula," *AJA* 59 (1955) 151–155.

———, "Villa or Pandokeion?," *Studies Presented to David M. Robinson* (St. Louis 1951) 365–367.

Meritt, B. D., and Traill, J. S., *Agora* XV: *Inscriptions, the Athenian Councillors* (Princeton 1974).

Michel, C., "Prytaneum," in *Dar Sag* (1887) 742–743.

Milchhöfer, A., "Athen (nördlicher Teil)," in Baumeister's *Denkmäler des klassischen Altertums* I (Munich 1885) 172–173.

Oikonomides, A. N., *The Two Agoras in Ancient Athens* (Chicago 1964).

Picard, C., "Le complexe Métrôon-Bouleutérion-Prytanikon à l'Agora d'Athènes," *RA* 12 (1938) 97–101.

Pittakes, K. S., *L'ancienne Athènes* (Athens 1835).

Preuner, A., *Hestia-Vesta* (Tübingen 1864).

———, "Hestia," in Roscher's *Lexicon der griechischen und römischen Mythologie* I (Leipzig 1890) 2605–2653.

Preuner, E., "Zum attischen Gesetz über die Speisung im Prytaneion," *Hermes* 61 (1926) 470 ff,

Robert, F., *Thymélè* (Paris 1939).

Robertson, D. S., *A Handbook of Greek and Roman Architecture*[2] (Cambridge 1945).

Schöll, R., "Die Speisung im Prytaneion zu Athen," *Hermes* 6 (1872) 14–54.

———, "Polykrite," *Hermes* 22 (1887) 559–565.

Segre, M., "L' 'agora degli dei' Camirese," *Athenaeum* 12 (1934) 147–150.

Süss, W., "Hestia," *RE* VIII (1913) 1257–1304.

Thompson, H. A., "Buildings on the West Side of the Athenian Agora," *Hesperia* 6 (1937) 115–127.

———, "The Tholos of Athens and its Predecessors," *Hesperia, Suppl.* IV (1940).

———, and Wycherley, R. E., *Athenian Agora XIV: The Agora of Athens* (Princeton 1972).

Tomlinson, R. A., "Two Buildings in Sanctuaries of Asklepios," *JHS* 89 (1969) 106–117.

———, "Perachora: The Remains outside the Two Sanctuaries," *BSA* 64 (1969) 164–172.

———, "Ancient Macedonian Symposia," *Ancient Macedonia* ed. B. Laourdas and Ch. Makaronas (Thessalonike 1970) 308–315.

Tosi, G., "Contributo allo studio dei pritanei," *Arte Antica e Moderna* 33 (1966) 10–20, 151–172.

Travlos, J., *ΠΟΛΕΟΔΟΜΙΚΗ ΕΞΕΛΙΞΙΣ ΤΩΝ ΑΘΗΝΩΝ* (Athens 1960).

———, *Pictorial Dictionary of Ancient Athens* (London 1971).

Vanderpool, E., "Tholos and Prytanikon," *Hesperia* 4 (1935) 470–475.

Wachsmuth, C., *Die Stadt Athen im Altertum* I (Leipzig 1874).

Weickert, C., *Typen der archaischen Architektur in Griechenland und Kleinasien* (Augsburg 1929).

Wycherley, R. E., *How the Greeks Built Cities*^{2} (London 1962).

———, "Pausanias at Athens II," *Greek, Roman, and Byzantine Studies* 4 (1963) 161–162.

———, "Archaia Agora," *Phoenix* 20 (1966) 288–293.

INDEX OF ANCIENT SOURCES

Epigraphic

Literary

INDEX OF NAMES AND SUBJECTS